☆ ☆ ☆ ☆ ☆ ☆ ☆ ☆

Commemorative Edition

☆ ☆ ☆ ☆ ☆ ☆ ☆ ☆

The PRESIDENTS
of the
UNITED STATES

by

John and Alice Durant

VOLUME TWO

Benjamin Harrison to Lyndon B. Johnson

*Concluding Volume of a History of the Presidents of the United States with
an Encyclopedic Supplement on the Office and Powers of the Presidency,
Chronologies, and Records of Presidential Elections*

GACHÉ PUBLISHING CO., INC., NEW YORK, N. Y.

★

CONTENTS

BENJAMIN HARRISON 1833–1901
PRESIDENT 1889–1893

Benjamin Harrison, grandson of our ninth President, William Henry Harrison, drifts through the four-year interlude between the two Cleveland administrations as a cautious, frigid, unimaginative little man (five feet, six inches) who was content to sit in the White House and let Congress run the country. The men who put Harrison in office—the rich manufacturers seeking high-tariff benefits—contributed the largest campaign fund in history up to that time and did not expect their man to shape the policies of the Government, as Cleveland had done. He did not disappoint them. His administration was more responsive to the "special interests" than any since Grant's. Unlike Grant, however, he was free from scandal and his regime was an honest one.

Harrison's career is as uninspiring as the man himself. He was born at North Bend, Ohio, graduated from Miami College and studied law for two years in Cincinnati. In 1853 he married Caroline Scott (above), a preacher's daughter. The couple moved to Indianapolis where he took his first job as court crier for $2.50 a day. Later he became city attorney,

court reporter, and when the Civil War came he was commissioned colonel of an Indiana regiment and rode with Sherman. Returning to Indianapolis after the war, he was nominated as the Republican candidate for governor, but met defeat. In 1881 the Indiana legislature elected him to the United States Senate where he served one term without distinction. Defeated for re-election, he left Washington in 1887, convinced that his political career was behind him. In two years he was president.

Life in the White House with the Harrisons was, like his administration, plain and uneventful. There was little entertaining, no glamorous dinners. The systematic President never varied his daily habits; breakfast at eight followed by a half hour of prayer by the entire family closeted in one room, a one o'clock lunch, early dinner and early to bed. The new electric lights, installed in 1891, baffled the Harrisons. They let the lights burn all night in the halls and parlors, fearing that if they turned them off they would get a shock. They were extinguished by the White House electrician when he came on duty in the morning. For a long time the Harrisons did not use the lights in their bedrooms, and were even fearful of pushing the electric bell buttons.

He went to the war at the first call for men.

Whilst Cleveland was a bar-room lounger.

His bravery in the field was noted and conspicuous.

Whilst Cleveland paid a substitute to fight for him.

He stands between the workman and Free Trade.

Whilst Cleveland attempts to smash our Industries.

During the Harrison-Cleveland campaign of 1888 the above cartoons appeared in *Judge*, a humorous weekly devoted to the Republican cause. Political cartoonists pulled no punches in those days, were often unfair and vicious. In the top four cartoons Harrison (left column) is shown as a war hero, Cleveland, a saloon loafer and slacker. (Cleveland was a moderate drinker, occasionally frequented saloons in his early Buffalo days, but was attracted by food rather than liquor. His war record is noted on page 184.) Harrison was a high-tariff man (bottom two cartoons) while Cleveland stood for lowering duties on manufactured goods, but he was not a free trader. Cleveland's stand on the tariff was instrumental in his defeat for re-election—although he received more popular votes than his opponent.

The strongly Democratic weekly, *Puck*, delighted in showing the diminutive Harrison almost lost under the big hat of his grandfather, William Henry Harrison. In this cartoon, below, published in 1890, the President appears to be of such small stature that Uncle Sam has to peer through a microscope in order to see him. Though small in many ways, Harrison was an honest middle-of-the-roader. His administration enacted the highest protective tariff thus far reached (the McKinley Tariff Act), a pension act for Union war veterans which soon depleted the Treasury's enormous surplus, a silver bill (increasing the Government's purchase of silver), and the Sherman Anti-Trust Act which was ineffective and practically became a dead letter. None of these measures originated with the President himself.

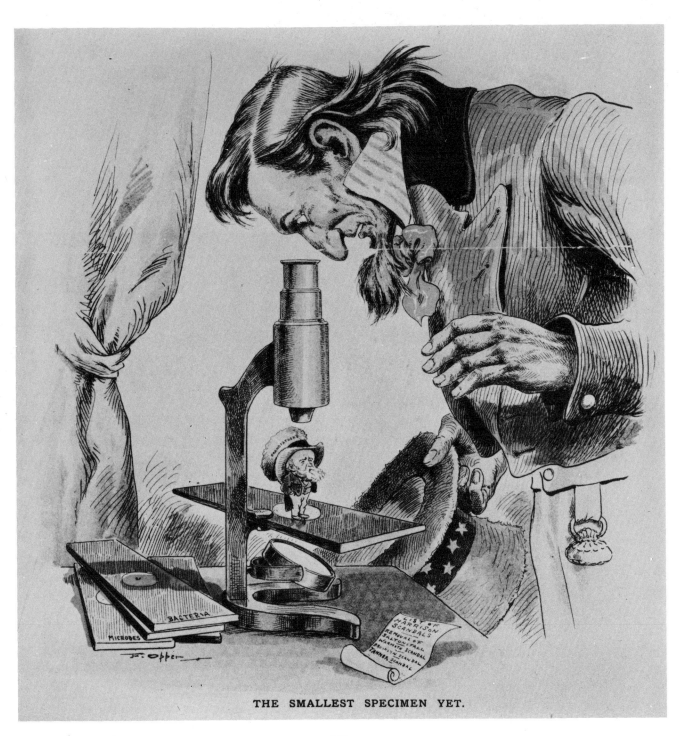

THE SMALLEST SPECIMEN YET.

WHEN BENJAMIN HARRISON WAS PRESIDENT: The country suffered its worst peacetime disaster when Conemaugh Dam, twelve miles above Johnstown, Pennsylvania, broke on May 31, 1889, and a runaway lake swept down the valley submerging the city and outlying towns. About 2,205 lives were lost and the damage was estimated at ten million dollars. In a deep irregular valley, Johnstown got the full force of Lake Conemaugh which, before the dam broke, was two and a half miles long and one hundred feet deep in places.

America's fistic hero in the eighties and nineties was John L. Sullivan (below) who fought the last bareknuckle bout at Richburg, Mississippi, on July 8, 1889, defeating Jake Kilrain in seventy-five rounds (two hours and sixteen minutes).

The last pitched battle between Indians and white men (above) took place at Wounded Knee Creek, South Dakota, on December 29, 1890, when the Seventh Cavalry rushed a Sioux encampment and slaughtered over two hundred men, women and children in a few minutes. The massacre was the army's terrible revenge for Custer's defeat in 1876. The Battle of Wounded Knee completed the conquest of the Indian and marked the end of an epoch.

WORKMEN CANNONADING THE BARGES.

WORKMEN ATTACKING THE BARGES.

COPYRIGHT 1892 BY EDWIN ROWE, HOMESTEAD, PA.
SURRENDER OF THE PINKERTON MEN

KURZ & ALLISON-ART STUDIO, CHICAGO.
PINKERTON'S CAPTIVES ON THEIR WAY TO PRISON.

The first great industrial strike, the Homestead (Pennsylvania) strike of 1892, was a result of wage cutting by the Carnegie Steel Company. Some three hundred armed Pinkerton men surrendered to the strikers after a battle on July 6 in which ten people were killed (above). The strike was broken in six months.

Joseph Jefferson III (above) delighted American audiences from 1859 to 1904 by playing the role of Rip Van Winkle.

One of the first automobiles was this one-cylinder, 4-h.p. Duryea which was made in Springfield, Massachusetts, in 1893.

THE GREATEST CURIOSITY OF THE NINETEENTH CENTURY.

GROVER CLEVELAND 1837–1908
PRESIDENT 1893–1897 (SECOND TERM)

When Mrs. Cleveland departed from the White House on March 4, 1889, an hour or so before the Harrisons moved in, she said to the staff, "Take good care of all the furniture and ornaments in the house . . . for I want to find everything just as it is now when we come back again. We are coming back just four years from today."

Four years later to the day (March 4, 1893) in a sleet storm, Cleveland drove up Pennsylvania Avenue by the side of the man who had taken the Presidency from him (above) and was now returning it to him. Never before had a once-defeated president been able to enjoy such a triumph. With 277 electoral votes against Harrison's 145, his victory was the most decisive since the re-election of Lincoln. In a complete Democratic sweep the party controlled both houses of Congress as well as the Presidency for the first time since the Civil War.

"Grover! Grover! four more years of Grover! Out they go, in we go; then we'll be in clover."

So went the victors' song, but there was little clover in the fields for Grover, or for the country. A depression was already under way due to a number of causes, among them the depletion of the nation's gold reserve during Harrison's administration. A world-wide business depression further darkened the clouds.

Hard times were probably inevitable, but as usual the party in power was held responsible—as the cartoon from *Judge* on the opposite page illustrates. How could anyone but a moron be glad that he voted for Cleveland, asked *Judge* in 1894, when the greatest number of men in United States history (up to that time) were unemployed, hundreds of banks had failed, railroad construction had almost ceased, agricultural prices were at the bottom, mercantile failures amounted to $347,000,000 and ruin had visited many thousands of honest, toiling people.

The Hoffman House Bouquet Cigar
Foster-Hilson Company, Makers

SPARKS' PERFECT HEALTH

Compliments of the Sparks Medicine Co.

FOR KIDNEY AND LIVER DISEASES

Advertisers in the last century made free use of national celebrities, and even the President and First Lady, to promote their products. In the above picture, for example, Cleveland and other well-known figures of the time stand in the lobby of New York's Hoffman House, unwitting endorsers of a brand of cigar. Far left is United States Senator David B. Hill; in the foreground Cleveland chats with Chauncey M. Depew, president of the New York Central Railroad. Others distributed about the lobby are: "Buffalo Bill" Cody, Tony Pastor (creator of American vaudeville), and at the counter (far right), Professor Herrman, the magician, and actor Nat Goodwin.

The Spark's Medicine Company offered with their compliments this porcelain tray (left) bearing a picture of the First Lady.

WHEN CLEVELAND WAS PRESIDENT: The Chicago World's Fair (Columbian Exposition) ran from May through October, 1893, and attracted more than 21,000,000 people. Almost every country in the world was represented. Among the innovations: the Ferris Wheel and the 250,000 electric lamps lighting the grounds.

In 1894 J. S. "General" Coxey led an "army" of about three hundred unemployed men from Ohio to Washington seeking work and federal aid.

The first movie studio (below), called the Kinetographic Theater, was built for Edison in 1893 at West Orange, New Jersey. Here the inventor made movies, synchronized the action with his phonograph and thus produced what was later known as the "talkies."

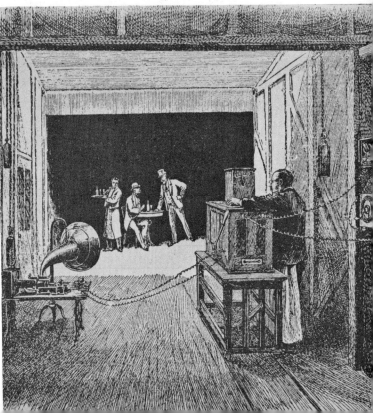

A wage cut by the Pullman Company in 1894 resulted in a strike called by socialist Eugene Debs, who ordered a boycott of all trains entering Chicago with Pullman cars. Federal troops were used to quell riots.

198

WILLIAM McKINLEY 1843–1901
PRESIDENT 1897–1901

William McKinley, the third martyred President within a space of thirty-six years, was the last Civil War veteran to become president. A gentle, dignified man of great kindness and sincerity, he was one of the few who frankly sought the Presidency (in 1888 and 1892) and finally achieved his goal.

The great issue of 1896—on the surface, at least—was gold versus silver: the Democratic stand for unlimited coinage of silver to expand the currency, against the Republican pledge to maintain the gold standard. Inflation against sound money. Underlying it all was a deeper conflict—the agrarian West and South opposed to the industrial East; the "toiling masses" against the "special interests," as the Democrats put it.

In an exciting campaign that at times reached the fanaticism of the Crusades, William Jennings Bryan, the Democratic candidate, toured the country four times and made more than six hundred speeches. McKinley, whose campaign was ably handled by multimillionaire Mark Hanna of Ohio, stayed at home in Canton and spoke from his front porch.

The candidates characterized the issues—the conservative, calm McKinley stressing prosperity and "the full dinner pail;" the thirty-six-year-old Bryan, "The Boy Orator of the Platte," attacking the trusts and Wall Street as he whirled eighteen thousand miles around the country. He failed to convince the country of the virtue of his panacea, however. McKinley was elected by a landslide, receiving 271 electoral votes to Bryan's 176.

No more devoted nor more pathetic couple than the McKinleys (above) ever dwelt in the White House. When Ida Saxton, the pretty and well-educated daughter of a Canton banker, married McKinley in 1871 she had every reason to look forward to a life of normal happiness. But within three years she lost her mother and two baby daughters. The calamities so shattered her nervous system that she developed epilepsy. For the rest of her life she could not tell from minute to minute when she would fall unconscious. With a patience and kindness rarely seen, McKinley shielded her, insisted that she go everywhere with him and responded to her every summons. When he was not working he took no recreation but remained at her side, trying to make her existence more liveable.

"If Willie is a good boy, and minds Papa and Nursie, they will try to let him keep the pretty house until he is eight years old."

GRANT HAM

BACK TO THE FARM.

Little boy McKinley taking orders from the trusts and Mark Hanna, was the view taken by the Hearst papers in 1896 (above, left). While McKinley did represent the business interests, he was in no sense the puppet of Mark Hanna who twice successfully managed his campaigns. The President was re-elected in 1900 by a greater majority than before, defeating Bryan by 292 electoral votes to 155.

Bryan as seen by *Judge* in 1900 (above), skulks off to his Nebraska farm carrying the full dinner pail of Republican prosperity. At this time a greater abundance of gold in the country had all but killed the silver issue and Bryan's campaign, following our war with Spain, was based on anti-imperialism. He predicted that America's acquisition of islands and rise to a world power would lead to national decay, similar to that of ancient Rome. In 1908 Bryan made his last hopeless fight for the Presidency.

Left, McKinley's second inaugural, March 4, 1901. The President was then at the apex of his popularity.

WHEN McKINLEY WAS PRESIDENT: The Boxer Rebellion in China (1900), aimed against foreign nations, resulted in the murder of many missionaries and other foreigners. To relieve the besieged Americans and Europeans in danger of massacre at Peking, the United States and five other nations sent relief troops, and the uprising was suppressed. Over a $300,000,000 indemnity was levied upon China, and many Boxers were executed. Right, Li Hung Chang, Chinese executioner, with a collection of Boxer heads.

Finley Peter Dunne (above), Chicago humorist and creator of the Irish saloon-keeper-philosopher "Mr. Dooley" and his friend "Mr. Hennessy," was at his prime in the late nineties and early 1900's. His books, written in Irish brogue, were widely quoted.

Carry Nation (below), Kansas temperance agitator, became a country-wide, notorious figure from 1900 on as a saloon wrecker. Wielding a hatchet, Carry took joy in destroying liquor, furniture and fixtures in establishments that sold intoxicants.

LOOK OUT, BOYS!
THE WEATHER MAN PROGNOSTICATES A CYCLONE FROM KANSAS.

The first action of the Spanish-American War took place on May 1, 1898, when Commodore George Dewey (above, directing maneuvers from the flagship *Olympia*) steamed into Manila Harbor with four cruisers and two gunboats to engage the Spanish fleet. Within a few hours the accurate and devastating fire of the Americans silenced all shore batteries and annihilated the Spanish fleet. The Americans did not lose a ship or a man and had only eight men slightly wounded. The Spanish lost eight ships, 167 men killed, 214 wounded.

McKinley did not want the war, but the blowing up of the United States battleship *Maine* in Havana Harbor, causing the death of 260 of her officers and crew, brought forth the vengeful cry "Remember the Maine!" and the war was on. In the shortest, most unique and one-sided war America ever fought, not a single reverse was suffered and not a soldier, gun, color, nor an inch of ground was captured by the enemy.

The cartoon (right) shows Uncle Sam making the final extraction—the surrender of Santiago, following the destruction of the remnants of the Spanish fleet. On July 26, Spain asked for peace terms.

The signing of the peace protocol (below) took place in the White House on August 12, 1898. In this picture the President observes the signing by (left to right) William R. Day, Secretary of State, and Jules Cambon, the French ambassador. Spain gave up Cuba and ceded Guam, Puerto Rico and the Philippines to the United States.

Ha! ha! "It didn't hurt a bit," Spain says.—*Los Angeles Times.*

On September 6, 1901, at Buffalo's Pan-American Exposition, a young anarchist named Leon Czolgosz, who had a revolver concealed in a handkerchief, took his place in the reception line filing past the President. As he came face to face with McKinley he fired twice through the handkerchief. One bullet struck McKinley in the breastbone; the other ripped through his abdomen. As the wounded President was caught and supported by his aides, he whispered to his secretary, "My wife—be careful, Cortelyou, how you tell her—oh, be careful."

BUFFALO ~ MORNING EXPRESS.

Price ONE CENT a Copy

ESTABLISHED 1846. Vol. LVI. No. 209.   BUFFALO, N. Y., SATURDAY, SEPTEMBER 14, 1901.   TWELVE PAGES.

RESIDENT M'KINLEY IS DEAD-- HIS SOUL FREED AT 2.15 O'CLOCK

THE WEATHER.

gton, D. C., Sept. 13.—For Western
Fair on Saturday, Sunday partly
probably showers in western portion
winds becoming south.

McKinley died eight days after the shooting. "I thought it would be a good thing for the country to kill the President," said Czolgosz in his cell. He was electrocuted forty-five days after McKinley's death. Mixed with the sorrow of the people was a wave of humiliation that such a terrible record of assassination could exist in America.

Below, a soldier boy stands guard over the departed President—a typical bit of sentiment of the times.

Above, the ambulance that took the President from the Exposition to the Buffalo home where he and his wife were staying.

Below, the .32-calibre Iver Johnson revolver used by the assassin, and the handkerchief that covered it.

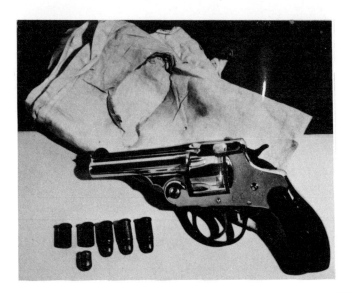

THEODORE ROOSEVELT 1858–1919
PRESIDENT 1901–1909

Theodore Roosevelt was the youngest man to become president, the wealthiest (up to his time), the most popular since Andrew Jackson, and by far the most athletic, dynamic, colorful and adventurous. No shrinking violet was our twenty-sixth President. "I took the Canal Zone and let Congress debate," he said. "I and my people thank you," read his cable to the President of Peru. A true extrovert, yet of great intellectual power, he wrote some 150,000 letters while he was in the White House and over thirty books during his lifetime. The wide range of subjects in his books reveals the man's many-sided character; a history of the War of 1812, *The Deer Family*, *Through the Brazilian Wilderness*, *Life of Oliver Cromwell*, *The Winning of the West*, *History as Literature*, *African Game Trails*, and so on. No other president ever led such a strenuous or diversified life.

The line from Browning, "I was ever a fighter" should stand as Roosevelt's epitaph, for that was the keynote of his career. His first fight began in the house where he was born on East Twentieth Street,

New York (above), when he was nine years old. Frail of body and asthmatic, he fought for physical power in a gymnasium his father had constructed on the third floor of the house. He fought at Harvard in boxing tournaments (as a lightweight) and as a young assemblyman he fought the corrupt legislature of New York. His battles continued, both physical and political, as a Dakota rancher, New York police commissioner, colonel in the Spanish-American War, governor of New York, and president.

Perhaps the most important battle he ever fought was one with himself, which he lost but which proved to be the turning point of his career. It concerned the Vice-Presidency. When it was offered him in 1900 by "Tom" Platt, Republican boss of New York, Roosevelt replied, "I would a great deal rather be anything . . . than Vice-President." Nine days before the convention he wrote, "I will not accept under any circumstances and that is all there is about it." But when Roosevelt was convinced that his refusal might mean the election of Bryan, he reluctantly accepted the nomination. Having lost the battle with himself, he said, "I do not expect to go any further in politics."

Roosevelt in the eighties (when these photographs were taken) was, according to one newspaper reporter, ". . . short and slight and with an ordinary appearance, although his frame is wiry and his flashing eyes and rapid nervous gestures betoken a hidden strength. . . . Although of the old Knickerbocker stock, his manner and carriage is awkward, and not at all impressive." The Old Guard in the New York Assembly saw him as a Harvard dude and a "goo-goo"—a derisive term applied to one devoted to "good government."

A few months after his graduation from Harvard in 1880, Roosevelt married Alice Lee, shown on the left in the above picture. They went to Europe, where young Teddy climbed the Matterhorn to equal the feat of two boastful Englishmen who had recently made the climb. (Above, left: Roosevelt in his mountain-climbing outfit.) After his wife's death in 1884 Roosevelt (left) went west and spent two years working his ranch on the banks of the Little Missouri River in Dakota. Working on the round-up and riding for days, he won the strength of body he had set out to gain.

When the war with Spain came, Roosevelt quit his job as assistant secretary of the Navy and helped organize the Rough Riders, a picturesque cavalry regiment composed of cowboys, Indians and eastern college football players. The famed charge of the Rough Riders up San Juan Hill, Cuba, where Roosevelt led his men in the face of heavy fire, is shown in the above illustration. It was drawn by Frederick Remington, who was in the engagement. At a barbed wire fence at the crest of the hill Roosevelt sprang off his horse and plunged on, his men following. The Spaniards were put to rout, thus placing the American army on high ground overlooking Santiago.

The colorful Rough Riders captured the imagination of the country, and when Roosevelt returned from Cuba he found himself a popular hero. So great was his fame that this letter (left) bearing only a crude likeness was delivered to him at his home in Oyster Bay, Long Island.

Twenty-eight Pages.

PART 2—PAGES 9 TO 28—Vol. LVIII. No. 50.

THE ILLUSTRATED

BUFFALO EXPRESS.

Printed by Electric Power
from Niagara Falls.
D

BUFFALO, N. Y., SUNDAY, SEPTEMBER 15, 1901.

PRICE FIVE CENTS

ROOSEVELT QUICKLY SWORN IN AS PRESIDENT-- M'KINLEY'S BODY TO LIE IN THE CITY HALL

THE WEATHER.

Washington, D. C., Sept. 14.—For Western
New York: Showers on Sunday and probably
on Monday; fresh west to south winds.

On September 13, 1901, Roosevelt was in the heart of the Adirondacks when a guide brought him a telegram to the effect that McKinley was dying. He hastened to Buffalo, arriving there thirteen hours after the President's death, and took the oath of office. On the McKinley funeral train leaving Buffalo, Mark Hanna said, "Now look, that damned cowboy is President of the United States."

"ISN'T IT JUST POSSIBLE THAT I'M OVERDOING THIS BUSINESS?"

At the turn of the century the American people were greatly concerned over the growing power of the trusts, or monopolies, which were threatening the economic life of the country. Trust magnates believed that they were a privileged class beyond the reach of restraint. But they were destined to a rude awakening, for Roosevelt, under the banner of a "square deal," fought the monopolistic combinations which were suppressing free competition.

Roosevelt's many-sidedness appealed to all manner of men. He was, as Secretary of State John Hay wrote: "Of gentle birth and breeding, yet a man of the people . . . with the training of a scholar and the breezy accessibility of a ranchman; a man of the library and a man of the world; an athlete and a thinker; a soldier and a statesman . . . with the sensibility of a poet and the steel nerve of a rough rider." The mass of Americans agreed. Roosevelt was elected in 1904 by an unprecedented majority.

His greatest service to the cause of peace was performed in 1905 when, through his initiative, Russian and Japanese delegates met at Portsmouth, New Hampshire (above), and agreed upon a peace that ended the war between those two nations. Roosevelt received the Nobel Peace Prize for this achievement.

Right: Teddy in Panama, 1906. He was the first president to leave the shores of the United States.

The above picture was taken at "Sagamore Hill," Roosevelt's Oyster Bay home, which was the summer capital of the United States for seven seasons. Left to right: Kermit, Archie, the President, Ethel, Mrs. Roosevelt (Edith Kermit Carow), Quentin and (standing) Theodore, Jr. Not shown is Alice, Roosevelt's daughter by his first wife.

On the opposite page the President is depicted by cartoonist John McCutcheon of the Chicago *Tribune* pursuing his creed, "The Strenuous Life."

First he chops down a few trees.

Then takes a cross-country canter.

And a twenty-minute brisk walk.

After which he gives the children a wheel-barrow ride.

He then rests for a moment

By which time he is ready for breakfast.

WHEN ROOSEVELT WAS PRESIDENT: The Wright brothers of Dayton, Ohio, made the first successful airplane flight on December 17, 1903, at Kitty Hawk, North Carolina. This picture (left) shows Orville at the controls at the moment of launching (the flight lasted twelve seconds) with his brother, Wilbur, at the right. A newspaper reporting the event next day headlined the story: "NO BALLOON ATTACHED TO AID IT." Roosevelt paid $25,000 to the Wrights in 1909 for a plane, thus beginning the United States Air Force.

After many unsuccessful attempts to reach the North Pole, Admiral Robert E. Peary (below) sailed north on the 184-ton *Roosevelt* in 1908 for a final try. Then fifty-three, his life's ambition was realized on April 6, 1909, when he reached the Pole.

Anxious Boatman: NOW, MARY, WHATEVER HAPPENS, DON'T MOVE YOUR HEAD, OR WE'LL CAPSIZE!

This cartoon from *Life* (1909) pokes fun at the enormous wide-brimmed hat then in vogue. With it came the flaring, gored skirt that swept the street on all sides.

214

HIS FAVORITE REMEDY.

A man called six times to give Mr. Rockefeller a cure for dyspepsia. But John D. knows what he needs.

Jolted by severe earthquakes on April 18, 1906, the city of San Francisco suffered greater devastation when a fire broke out and burned for three days (above). In the quake and fire 452 people were killed; property damage was over $350,000,000.

When the above cartoon appeared in 1903, showing the saintly John D. Rockefeller about to swallow the globe, the Standard Oil king had amassed some $300,000,000 and his fortune was increasing daily.

The Great Train Robbery (right) was the first moving picture to tell a story. Produced by the Edison Company in the fall of 1903, the epoch-making thriller was filmed in New Jersey and directed by Edwin S. Porter, the first man to use the "cutback." The film was tinted yellow for the dance-hall scene, bluish green for the woods. One of its actors, G. M. Anderson of Brooklyn, later achieved stardom in Western roles as "Broncho Billy."

Roosevelt left the Presidency in March, 1909 (left), and sailed for Africa with his twenty-two-year-old son Kermit, to hunt big game. Teddy carried with him a rabbit's foot given to him by his friend, John L. Sullivan. The charm worked, for the two hunters killed over five hundred animals and birds, including seventeen lions and an assortment of rhinos, elephants, hippopotami, and giraffes. Upon emerging from the jungle in April, 1910, he visited Rome, where he sought an audience with the Pope. The Pope agreed to see him, provided that Roosevelt would not call on some Methodist missionaries in Rome. Roosevelt had no intention of doing this, but he declined to submit to the Pope's conditions and the interview did not take place. "An elegant row," said Teddy of this episode. He went on to Paris, Berlin (where he reviewed the Kaiser's troops), Christiania (for the Nobel Prize), Oxford and London, returning home in June, 1910.

GOOD BOY!

Upon his return Roosevelt found the Republican party disrupted by factional strife and headed for disaster. "My hat's in the ring," he said to his followers, who bolted the Republican convention in 1912 to form the Progressive party. "I feel as fit as a Bull Moose." The phrase gave the new party the unofficial name of the Bull Moose Party. On October 14, 1912, while speaking in Milwaukee, he was shot in the breast by a crazed assailant. "I have just been shot," he said calmly. "But it takes more than that to kill a Bull Moose . . . The bullet is in me now, so that I cannot make a very long speech . . . I want you to understand that I am ahead of the game anyway. No man has had a happier life than I have led; a happier life in every way."

In a three-cornered election in 1912, Roosevelt polled over four million votes, but was defeated by Woodrow Wilson, the Democratic candidate. A year later he led an expedition into the jungles of Brazil where he explored nine hundred miles of an unknown river, since named the Río Teodoro by the Brazilian government. When the war with Germany came Roosevelt offered again to raise a division of troops, but Wilson refused his consent.

Above, "The Long Long Trail," J. N. (Ding) Darling's famous drawing which appeared shortly after Roosevelt's death on January 6, 1919. This is the reverse of the original drawing which showed T. R. with his right hand holding the reins, his left waving his hat.

"And in his time a man plays many parts."
Shakespeare.

Cowboy   Historian   Police Commissioner   Naval Secretary   Rough Rider   Governor of New York   Vice President   President   Peacemaker   Mighty Hunter all the time

WILLIAM HOWARD TAFT 1857–1930
President 1909–1913

"Big Bill" Taft, our largest President, stood six feet, two inches, weighed over three hundred pounds, and was the only man in American history to hold the two highest offices in the land—the Presidency and the Chief Justiceship of the Supreme Court. The good-natured, jovial Taft had no taste for politics, was lacking in executive force and probably would have been better off if he had never hearkened to the lure of the Presidency. Although he was brilliant (he stood second in a class of 121 at Yale), honest and more successful than many presidents, he was at heart a judge. He spent the first twenty years of his career, save two, in courts as a law officer and judge, and his ambition was to attain the Supreme Bench.

"I do not want my son to be president," said his mother. "His is a judicial mind and he loves the law." His wife (Helen Herron), however, opposed a judicial career as being a "fixed groove." The picture above of Taft and his wife driving from the 1909 inauguration shows who won the contest between the two ladies.

Taft left his chosen career at the urging of Presi-dent McKinley in 1900 to head the newly formed Philippine Commission. In his new role at Manila the big, genial fat man treated the Filipinos with an openness and sincerity they had never before experienced from foreign rulers. He spoke warmly of them as "my little brown brothers." Twice while he was governor of the Philippines, President Roosevelt offered him a berth on the Supreme Court and twice Taft refused because he felt that his first duty was toward the Filipinos.

A disturbing report that Taft's health was failing caused Secretary of War Elihu Root, to send a cabled inquiry. Taft replied that his health was fine, that he had just ridden twenty-five miles on horseback. "How is the horse?" cabled Root. Taft's great tonnage inspired many jokes and no one enjoyed them more than he did. Arthur Brisbane said that Taft looked "like an American bison, a gentle, kind one."

When Root resigned his Cabinet post, Roosevelt offered Taft the vacant office. The War portfolio appealed to him because it would permit him to administer to the Filipinos. On February 1, 1904, he took the oath of office as secretary of war.

!brawroForward!

These two cartoons illustrate the shattering of the Taft-Roosevelt friendship which shocked the country and brought defeat and humiliation to both men.

Above (from *Puck*, 1909), Teddy joyfully presents his good friend Taft, the "Crown Prince," to the American public. Above, right (from *Life*, 1912), Taft and Roosevelt, now enemies, strain against each other in a bitter fight for the Republican nomination. What caused this unhappy quarrel?

Toward the end of Roosevelt's administration the President was at the peak of his popularity. He was only forty-nine and would have liked the Presidency for another four years, but he had given his word not to run again. "Under no circumstances will I be a candidate for or accept another nomination," he had publicly stated. As the 1908 convention drew near Roosevelt determined to turn the nomination over to Taft, "the most lovable personality I have ever come in contact with." Having made the decision, Roosevelt dedicated himself to his loyal friend. He engineered his nomination, campaigned vigorously for his election and saw him through to a

smashing victory over William Jennings Bryan (321 electoral votes to 162). "Taft will carry on the work substantially as I have. His policies, principles, purposes and ideals are the same as mine," said Teddy.

But the genial Taft was no Roosevelt. The minute Teddy was gone the standpatters took the tiller from Taft's uncertain hands and steered a reactionary course. Roosevelt returned to find his party disrupted, many of his reforms cast aside and the Taft administration steadily losing prestige.

Thus ended the long friendship. At first there was a coolness between the two. Then came the open break when Roosevelt sought the Republican nomination in 1912. Teddy's anger carried him to extremes. Taft, he bellowed, was "useless to the American people" . . . "disloyal to every canon of decency and fair play." Taft did not reply in kind but his supporters did. A pamphlet distributed in Chicago when the egotistical Teddy was there read: "At three o'clock Thursday afternoon Theodore Roosevelt will walk on the waters of Lake Michigan."

The Taft administration was one of strife between the standpatters and the insurgents, or progressives, and little was accomplished. Taft, however, created several presidential "firsts" during his regime. He became the first president to set foot on foreign soil when he visited President Diaz of Mexico in 1909. He was the first golfing president (right), the first to open the baseball season by tossing out a ball, the first to have a government car (an electric runabout, a gasoline-powered sedan, and a White steamer). He was the first president to draw a salary of $75,000. (Prior to Grant, who received $50,000, the salary was $25,000.)

Taft left the White House in 1913 with no regrets. As he departed he said to President Wilson, "I'm glad to be going. This is the lonesomest place in the world." He found contentment as professor of law at Yale (below) for nine years and as chief justice of the Supreme Court from 1921 until his death in 1930.

WHEN TAFT WAS PRESIDENT: Glenn H. Curtiss (above) won a prize of ten thousand dollars by flying from Albany to New York City on May 29, 1910. The 143-mile flight took two hours, fifty-one minutes. He made two stops en route for gas and repairs.

On October 1, 1910, the Los Angeles *Times* building was dynamited, killing twenty-one. The McNamara brothers, strike leaders, pled guilty and were sentenced to San Quentin.

In the pre World War I era when Enrico Caruso was at the height of his fame, he drew this caricature of himself as Pagliacci.

AT LAST.

Old Earth—"What a relief to have that spot scratched. It's been itching for fifty thousand years."

The Cook-Peary fight over who discovered the Pole was settled in Peary's favor.

Above, four musical comedy favorites as they appeared in *Hokey Pokey* in 1912. From left to right: Lillian Russell, Joe Weber, William Collier and Lew Fields.

To thousands of farm families in the Taft-Wilson era the most prized possession was the Model-T Ford, shown (right) on the porch of an imperiled farmhouse during a flood at Shaw, Mississippi, in 1913. Henry Ford began to mass-produce the Model-T in 1908 and by 1913 his assembly lines were turning out about one thousand cars a day. In 1914 when a half a million flivvers were on the road, Ford announced that he would pay a minimum wage of five dollars per eight-hour day to his thirteen thousand employees.

WOODROW WILSON 1856–1924
PRESIDENT 1913–1921

Thomas Woodrow Wilson, who dropped his first name while a boy, as did Stephen Grover Cleveland before him, came to the Presidency by an unusual path. He was president of Princeton University, had never held political office, and had never taken more than a theorist's interest in politics when, at fifty-three, he was called off a golf course one afternoon in 1910 to receive the nomination for the governorship of New Jersey. Two years later he was elected president of the United States.

Wilson, like Jefferson and Theodore Roosevelt, was among the most literate of the presidents. He was a historian of recognized authority whose books were used as texts in schools, and had been a professor of jurisprudence and political economy in three colleges. He was cold, aloof and often arrogant, but he was not all intellect. At Wesleyan University in Connecticut he coached the football team for two years. He liked vaudeville better than *Hamlet*. He wrote scores of limericks. He was the most popular lecturer at Princeton where he gained the reputation of being both interesting and weighty.

As president of Princeton, Wilson made headlines by trying to abolish the exclusive eating clubs on the campus, and although he failed he was lauded as a champion of the underdog. New Jersey politicians began to wonder if this fighting professor wouldn't be a good vote-getter, even if he was a Ph.D. Wilson accepted the nomination for governor with the understanding that if he were elected he would govern, and not the machine politicians. The Democratic bosses of New Jersey smiled at such simplicity and laughed aloud when the professor sat down in the governor's chair. But he soon let them know who was the boss and put through a series of reforms such as the state had never before known.

"A presidential campaign may easily degenerate into a more personal contest and so lose its real dignity. There is no indispensable man," said Wilson in his speech accepting the Democratic nomination on August 7, 1912. Thus did Wilson state his political philosophy and his personal platform. He refused to take part in the public brawl between Taft and Roosevelt and the people liked him for it. He was always suavely polite to his two opponents, and even praised Taft for his patriotism and integrity. When Roosevelt was shot, Wilson halted his campaign until his opponent recovered. The country admired this gesture of sportsmanship. By limiting himself to the realm of ideas and avoiding personalities, the dignified and sensible Wilson got results. The conviction spread that this clear-thinking professor knew what he was talking about. The election was no upset. Although he received fewer popular votes than Taft and Roosevelt combined, Wilson carried forty out of the forty-eight states, polling 435 electoral votes to his opponents' 96.

Below, the Wilson family in 1912. From left to right: Eleanor, Mrs. Wilson, the President, Margaret and Jessie. The President's wife died in the White House on August 6, 1914. In December of the following year Wilson married Mrs. Edith Bolling Galt.

Taft was glad to dispose of the "Mexican situation" by handing the troublesome infant to his successor in 1913. Wilson was confronted with a civil war in Mexico which kept the Rio Grande country in a constant state of turmoil. When the bandit chief "Pancho" Villa raided Columbus, New Mexico, in 1916 and killed fifteen Americans, Wilson ordered General John J. Pershing to invade Mexico and get Villa. The expedition, which cost about $150,000,000, was unsuccessful. American troops kept watch along the Rio Grande until 1920.

As a youthful scholar at Johns Hopkins University working on his thesis for a Ph.D., Wilson conceived a philosophy of government which he put into practice when he went into politics. It was, basically, that a governor or president should lead, rather than be led by a political machine or by Congress. A president should act more like a prime minister, less like a "mere department" isolated from Congress. His theory had worked well when he put it to the test as governor of New Jersey, and he intended to continue it as president. The country was electrified when Wilson, at a special session of Congress a month after his inauguration, walked in and delivered his message in person. Not since John Adams had a president addressed Congress. In a brief, pithy address Wilson summarized his policy with pointed recommendations of things to be done. The state-ment was received with a thunderous ovation. Soon Congress was grinding out the greatest number of reform laws that had ever been passed in an equal length of time. Among them were: The Federal Reserve Act which gave the nation the control of its own money for the first time; a lower tariff revision; a more forceful anti-trust law, a child-labor law; and the creation of the Federal Trade Commission, designed to prevent large corporations from using unfair methods of competition. Wilson's first administration was crowded with accomplishments, most of which remain in force today.

The cartoon below illustrates America's attitude toward the quarrelling European powers when war broke out in August, 1914. Like Wilson, the country felt that it was none of our business.

DON'T MIX IN A FAMILY QUARREL, UNCLE

England's scorn for Wilson and the American people because of our reluctance to enter the war is illustrated in this cartoon (left) from *Punch*, October 18, 1916. Entitled "Bringing It Home," Wilson says, "What's that? U-boats blockading New York? Tut! tut! Very inopportune."

Wilson's early attitude toward the war was to turn his back upon it, to snub it. "There is such a thing as a man being too proud to fight," he said in a speech on May 10, 1915. The phrase "too proud to fight" was later hurled back at him with contempt. The campaign for his re-election was waged mainly on the slogan, "He kept us out of war." But the war could not be snubbed.

Germany's proclamation of unrestricted submarine warfare caused Wilson to go before Congress on February 3, 1917 (below), and advise a severance of diplomatic relations. On April 2 he again addressed Congress. This time he called for war. To go into a war in whose origin we had no part was a fearful thing to do, he said, but it was necessary "to make the world safe for democracy."

To many men Wilson was distant and "school-masterly," a thinking machine. Women, especially attractive women, did not find him so, however. He responded to their admiration, was gay and warm in their company and liked to have them about. He was dependent upon them to an extraordinary degree. Before he was president, Wilson's home was a fortress of femininity. His three adoring daughters and his devoted wife continually pampered and petted him, and looked upon him as their lord and master. Less than a year after his first wife's death

Wilson fell in love with Mrs. Galt, the handsome forty-three-year-old widow of a Washington jeweler. The President, then fifty-eight, became an ardent wooer. He sent her flowers daily, had a private wire installed between her home and the White House and put aside all save the most important affairs of state to be with her. They were married on December 18, 1915.

Above, the President and his wife drive back from the Capitol, March 4, 1917. This was the last time a carriage was used at an inauguration.

VIVE WILSON

Early in December, 1918, Wilson sailed for France to attend the Paris Peace Conference. In a triumphant tour of France, England and Italy the President received tremendous ovations. He was hailed as "the people's man," the apostle of a new order. He did not ask for land or money, the usual prizes of war; he sought only a secure peace, a League of Nations to make future wars impossible.

Below, left: Wilson with President Poincaré of France; below, right: with England's King George V.

The Peace Conference was a prelude to the final work—the Treaty of Versailles, which was signed at three o'clock on the afternoon of June 28, 1919, in the great Hall of Mirrors in the Palace of Versailles. At that moment the first World War came to an end.

In this picture of the signing, Wilson sits between United States Secretary of State Robert Lansing (with hand to cheek) and Georges Clemenceau, Premier of France. On Clemenceau's left is Lloyd George, Britain's Prime Minister.

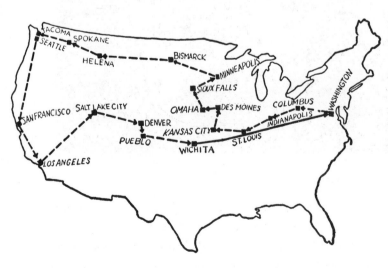

Governor Calvin Coolidge of Massachusetts (far right in the above picture) greeted the Wilsons when they landed in Boston on February 24, 1919. The President came home to consult leaders of both parties about the peace treaty, stayed only two weeks, then returned to France. In July he returned for good. At this time the Treaty of Versailles, which included the League of Nations Covenant, had been signed, but it had yet to be approved by the United States Senate. The League was Wilson's great dream. It was the heart of the treaty and he supposed it unthinkable that it would be rejected. But to his horror he found that there was much objection to it. In an effort to win support Wilson took a "swing around the circle" (left) and appealed directly to the American people.

Against the advice of his physician, Admiral Grayson, Wilson started out on his speech-making tour on September 3, 1919. At sixty-three the President had aged noticeably. One side of his face twitched and he was continually in a state of nervous exhaustion—in turn despondent and irritable. Yet he was determined. "There will come sometime . . . another struggle in which, not a few hundred thousand fine men from America will have to die, but many millions . . . to accomplish the final freedom of the peoples of the world," he warned a St. Louis audience. At Pueblo, Colorado, he suffered a stroke and the rest of the trip was cancelled. With drawn blinds, the train switched around the city of Wichita, Kansas, where he was scheduled to speak, and went directly to Washington. The physical breakdown of the President was hastened by the Senate's rejection of the Treaty in November. Below, one of the last photographs of the President, taken shortly before his death on February 3, 1924.

WHEN WILSON WAS PRESIDENT: The Panama Canal, begun in 1904, was formally opened to commerce on August 15, 1914. The engineer chiefly responsible for the completion of the fifty-mile-long ditch was Colonel George W. Goethals. Without the aid of army surgeon William C. Gorgas, however, the canal might never have been completed. As chief sanitary officer, Gorgas did notable work in suppressing yellow fever, thus making the digging of the canal possible.

Below, the celebration in Wall Street, November 7, 1918, of the false armistice, released prematurely by the United Press. Four days later came the announcement of the real armistice and an even greater nation-wide celebration.

The *Oscar II*, chartered by Henry Ford (below, at left), sailed from Hoboken, December 4, 1915 (without Ford) for Norway with a party of peace lovers determined "to get the boys out of the trenches by Christmas." The "Peace Ship," a squirrel cage of do-gooders and free-loaders, failed in its purpose.

234

"Freed From Demon Rum," the country went dry in 1919 under a wartime prohibition act to continue until the end of mobilization. But the Eighteenth Amendment replaced it in 1920. The United States was constitutionally a Sahara for fourteen long years.

In 1920 Charlie Chaplin made *The Kid* (above), one of his greatest pictures, in which he appeared as the tramp foster father of a small boy played by Jackie Coogan.

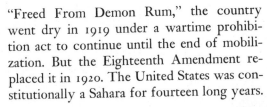

Prior to the first World War a trend called "feminism"—the emancipation of women from old taboos—was taking place in the country. One of its manifestations was the woman's suffrage movement. By 1912 women had the right to vote locally in ten states and had partial suffrage in twenty-one others. Not until the Nineteenth Amendment went into effect in 1920, however, could women everywhere vote in a presidential election. The Amendment added some nine million women voters to the seventeen million who already had the right to vote in local elections.

WARREN G. HARDING 1865–1923
PRESIDENT 1921–1923

Warren Gamaliel Harding, Ohio's seventh President, was a successful small-town businessman, genial and easygoing, who wanted more than anything else to be liked by his fellow men. He was a typical "Main-Streeter" of the 1920's. In Marion, Ohio, where he lived most of his life, he was the owner of the local newspaper, director of a bank, a lumber company and the telephone exchange. He played the cornet in the Marion band. He chewed tobacco. He was a "joiner." Popular with the home-town folks, he was extremely kind and sympathetic. In thirty-six years as publisher of the Marion *Star* he never dismissed a single employee. He was soft-hearted to a fault and could not believe that there was evil in any man. He never learned to say no. "It is a good thing I am not a woman. I would always be pregnant. I cannot say no," he once told some Press Club friends.

In 1891 when he was twenty-six and on his way to becoming Marion's leading citizen, he married Florence De Wolfe Kling (shown above with his father, Dr. George T. Harding). Some six years older than her husband, Florence Kling was the daughter of the town's leading banker. She was the pusher of the family, always ambitious for her husband's success. Harding called her "the Duchess" and often followed her advice, which was sometimes based on her consultations with an astrologer.

Harding looked like a president. He was superbly handsome, big-framed, with large, wide-set eyes, and he had a pleasant resonant voice. Of the many people who were impressed by the Harding personality, one was Harry M. Daugherty, a sharp-eyed Ohio politician. The first time the two met, Daugherty saw in the big genial man the possibilities of a president. He became Harding's mentor and master-minded his political career as he rose from state senator to United States senator. "I found him sunning himself, like a turtle on a log," said Daugherty of his protégé, "and I pushed him into the water."

The 1920 Republican convention shaped up as a fight between General Leonard Wood and Frank O. Lowden, Governor of Illinois. Behind them came the other possible candidates: Senator Hiram Johnson of California and Nicholas Murray Butler, President of Columbia University. Harding's name was far down the list but Daugherty had a plan he had long been working on.

Foreseeing a deadlocked convention, Daugherty told a reporter what he thought would take place. "After the other candidates have failed . . . the leaders, worn out and wishing to do the very best thing, will get together in some smoke-filled hotel room about 2:11 in the morning. Some fifteen men, bleary-eyed from lack of sleep, and perspiring profusely with the excessive heat, will sit down around a big table. I will be with them and present the name of Senator Harding. When that times comes, Harding will be selected." Daugherty proved to be an amazing prophet. The event came off almost exactly as he had predicted, even to the bleary-eyed leaders in the smoke-filled hotel room at 2:11 A.M. Harding was stunned to learn that he had been chosen. He did not want the Presidency. He only wanted to remain in the Senate for the rest of his life.

In an uninteresting campaign conducted from the front porch of his Marion home (above), Harding stressed a return to "normalcy." He defeated the Democratic candidates, James M. Cox and his running mate, Franklin D. Roosevelt.

As president, Harding's small-town habits did not change much. He played poker most every night with his cronies, played golf (mid 90's) and took in baseball games (below, shaking hands with Babe Ruth). His Cabinet contained some able men, and some obviously unfit for public office. Daugherty, his Attorney-General, was soon under fire for irregularities, as this cartoon (right) indicates, and was later brought to trial. The jury was unable to agree after sixty-six hours of deliberation. Harding's corrupt Secretary of the Interior, Albert B. Fall, who accepted a $100,000 bribe for leasing United States oil reserves to private interests, was convicted and sent to prison. There were other scandals. The trusting, unsophisticated President had no part in them. He simply did not know what was going on.

WHEN HARDING WAS PRESIDENT:
The radio became a fact (above). In 1920
there were five thousand receiving sets in
the United States, over two and one-half
million four years later. Harding was the
first president to speak over the air (at
the Minnesota State Fair, September, 1920).

Above, opening night program of *Abie's
Irish Rose*, a play described by reviewers as
"something awful." It stayed on the boards
for five years, five months, playing 2,327
performances—a record up to that time.

In the presence of 100,000 people, Chief
Justice Taft on May 30, 1922, presented the
Lincoln Memorial to President Harding, who
accepted it in behalf of the American people.
One of the most beautiful buildings in
America, its walls are surrounded by thirty-
six Doric columns of white marble, each one
representing a state at the time of Lincoln's
death. In the center space within is a colossal
statue of Lincoln.

In 1923 when this picture was taken of a Ku Klux Klan parade in Youngstown, Ohio, the organization numbered some four million people, most of whom were dedicated to the hatred of Jews, Catholics, Negroes, immigrants, the League of Nations and pacifism. Revived in 1915 by William J. Simmons, a circuit-rider of the Methodist Episcopal Church from Atlanta, Georgia, the Klan became a powerful force in southern and midwestern states in the mid-twenties and at one time had political control of seven states.

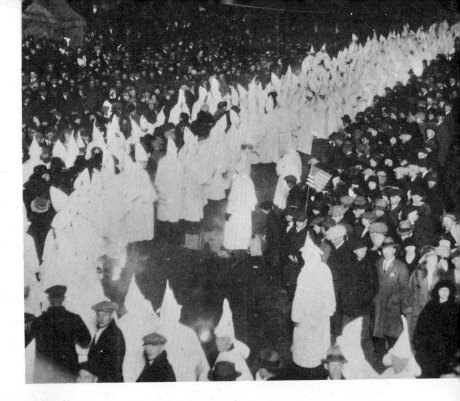

Another phenomenon of the zany twenties was the dance marathon, introduced to America on March 31 in 1923 by Alma Cummings who established a record of twenty-seven hours of continuous dancing. This picture (left) shows Joie Ray, famed miler and long-distance runner, with his partner, Alice King, during a contest at Newark, New Jersey. The craze lasted well into the 1930's.

Emile Coué (right, pointing) came to the United States from France in 1923 with his cure-all autosuggestion system, organized a clinic and treated thousands of gullible patients.

CALVIN COOLIDGE 1872-1933
PRESIDENT 1923-1929

Calvin Coolidge, Vice-President of the United States, went to bed at nine o'clock as usual on the night of August 2, 1923, at his father's home in Plymouth, Vermont, where he was enjoying a short vacation. At half past two in the morning he was awakened and told that President Harding was dead. Coolidge hastily dressed and went downstairs to the parlor which was lighted by a flickering kerosene lamp. There he was addressed for the first time as "Mr. President," the words being spoken by his father. A copy of the Constitution was found and Calvin took the oath of office administered by the elder Coolidge, a notary public (above).

Thus did the famed "Coolidge Luck" persist. Had Harding died twenty-four hours later, Coolidge would have taken the oath in the home of a multimillionaire friend he was planning to visit. But luck gave him a perfect setting—the old family farmhouse in the Vermont hills, his mother's Bible on which he took the oath, the bespectacled farmer-father. The simple ceremony appealed greatly to the American people and was in perfect character with the tight-lipped, industrious Vermont farm boy with the nasal twang. "Calvin," said his father, "could get more sap out of a maple tree than any of the other boys around here." Cal got votes out of the people as he did sap out of the trees from the beginning of his career. On the way up he held more elective offices than any other president (nineteen) and was only once defeated—for a school committee in Northampton, Massachusetts. As governor of the state in 1919, when it was supposed that he would go no higher, the ordinarily taciturn Coolidge made a statement during the Boston police strike that drew the attention of the country: "There is no right to strike against the public safety by anybody, anywhere, any time."

The people welcomed to the White House this solid, determined man who was of a different breed from the pleasure-loving Harding. "The business of America is business," said Coolidge, and rolled up his sleeves. He did not play golf, or cards, ride horseback, swim, hunt, or bowl. His only recreation was walking, and fishing while on vacation. He worked hard and succeeded with his policy of rigid economy in government. Coolidge was the high priest of stability whose main desire was to keep out of trouble.

One reason the Presidency is such a killing job is that in addition to the continual pressure of official business, the Chief Executive is forced to submit to a series of indignities in the form of welcoming groups of a various sort. (Eight presidents have died in office—four from assassins' bullets; several others, broken in health, died soon after leaving the White House.) On these pages are shown some of the ordeals that Coolidge had to endure.

Above: Cal greets Republican leaders of the Sioux Nation.

Left: the unhappy President holds the equally unhappy Louise Sheaffer who has just presented him with a Buddy Poppy on behalf of the Veterans of Foreign Wars.

244

Above: Coolidge with members of the Jefferson Memorial Foundation. Above, right: opening the baseball season. Right: Cal with the Daughters of the War of 1812. Below: trout fishing (with worms). Below, right: Cal's message refusing a third term.

I do not choose to run for President in nineteen twenty eight

245

WHEN COOLIDGE WAS PRESIDENT:
Nathan Leopold and Richard Loeb (center and right), sons of wealthy Chicago families and postgraduate students at Chicago University, confessed the kidnapping and killing of fourteen-year-old Bobby Franks. The only motive for the crime was the "thrill of it." Ably defended by Clarence Darrow, they were saved from the gallows and got life imprisonment.

Shortly after Coolidge took office, the oil scandals of the previous administration came to light, thus supplying much material for cartoonist Rollin Kirby (below).

"UGH!"

Charles Ponzi, Boston's arch swindler, took in millions with his get-rich-quick scheme in the 1920's, wound up in federal prison.

Increasing auto accidents inspired the invention of a safety bumper (above), which was supposed to grasp a pedestrian and carry him to safety up to a speed of thirty m.p.h.

In July, 1925, John Thomas Scopes, a young biology teacher, was tried for teaching evolution in defiance of Tennessee law. Defended by (above, l. to r.) Clarence Darrow, Arthur Garfield Hayes and Dudley Field Malone, he was found guilty but later freed.

General William Mitchell (standing, center) who was first to sink a ship from a plane, stands trial for insubordination (1925).

The auto came of age in 1925 when traffic lanes were first painted on the Capitol Plaza.

Albert B. Fall (above) was finally brought to book in 1929 when he was sentenced to a year in prison and fined $100,000. Luckier was Harry Daugherty, shown right (in light coat) with his attorney, Max Steuer. He was freed by a hung jury. Fall was the highest government official ever convicted.

While Rudolph Valentino, the screen's first Latin lover, lay in state in Campbell's Funeral Parlor, New York, in 1926 (below), the crowds became so huge and unmanageable that police reserves had to be called out.

Congressman McMillan of South Carolina dances the Charleston on the Capitol grounds.

"IF I CATCH YOU INSIDE THE CITY LIMITS I'LL RUN YOU IN"

The Hollywood revolution began in 1927 when Warner Brothers released *The Jazz Singer*, a "talkie" starring Al Jolson, who sang several melodies in blackface (above).

Chicago's Anglophobe Mayor of the twenties, Big Bill Thompson, said he'd arrest King George if His Majesty ever came to town.

America's hero of the Coolidge era was Colonel Charles A. "Lucky" Lindbergh (right) who flew alone in his monoplane, *Spirit of St. Louis*, from New York to Paris in May, 1927. The nonstop flight of 3,610 miles took 33 hours, 29 minutes, 30 seconds.

HERBERT C. HOOVER 1874–1964
PRESIDENT 1929–1933

No president ever began an administration under more favorable skies than did Herbert Hoover when he took the oath of office in March, 1929. The country was basking in the sunshine of the "Coolidge Boom" and to its helm came the world's best-known citizen—a humanitarian of international reputation, an efficient engineer with a genius for organization. He also had a genius for making unfortunate utterances. "We in America today are nearer to the final triumph over poverty than ever before in the history of a land," he declared in his acceptance speech, and added that "the poorhouse is vanishing from among us." Everlasting prosperity was the Republican campaign theme—"a chicken in every pot and a car in every garage." When the crash came a few months after Hoover's inauguration, the glittering phrases were derisively quoted from every corner of the land. The hapless President was blamed for the depression although it was world-wide and as unstoppable as a hurricane. He was, in fact, the first president to intervene in a depression. But no man could stem it, though Hoover tried. He summoned to the White House for conferences industrial, commercial, financial and labor leaders and created several fact-finding bodies. He reassured the people that "Prosperity is just around the corner." The depression deepened and Hoover became its symbol. His appearance and actions heightened the impression—the cold, precise personality, the stiff, high collar and round face, his chilly relations with the press.

Hoover was the first president born west of the Mississippi, the first to enter the White House a multimillionaire. He was born in a modest home (above) at West Branch, Iowa, the son of a Quaker blacksmith. The Hoover success story is in keeping with the American tradition of poverty-to-riches by honest toil. Orphaned at nine, he was brought up by relatives in Oregon. At seventeen he entered Stanford University, worked his way through, and upon graduating in 1895 took a job as a common laborer in a Nevada mine. Shortly thereafter the young engineer went to Australia where there was a gold rush, and from there to various parts of the world. By the time he was forty he had a chain of offices encircling the globe and had amassed a fortune as a promoter and financier of mining properties from China, to Russia, Burma and to Africa.

Hoover was unknown outside of mining circles until 1914 when he was appointed head of the American Relief Society in London to help return to the United States many thousands of Americans who had been stranded abroad by the sudden outbreak of World War I. So efficiently did he carry out the job that he was named to organize the feeding of millions of Belgians in their devastated country. When we entered the war President Wilson appointed him United States Food Administrator (left, as he looked in 1917). After the war, as Chief of the Supreme Economic Council of the Allies, Hoover organized great food-relief projects in Europe. Billions of dollars passed through his hands during the seven-year period he was engaged in humanitarian work, but he declined compensation for his services. Back home again, he served as secretary of commerce under Harding and Coolidge.

Below, Hoover is sworn in as president by Chief Justice Taft (appointed by Harding).

Lou Hoover (above) was a freshman, Hoover a senior, when they met at Stanford University. After their marriage in 1899 Mrs. Hoover roamed the world with her husband for fifteen years. In the White House the Hoovers entertained lavishly, employed more people than ever before in its history (about 150 all told, of which some 80 were military aides, police and secret service men).

"DON'T MIND ME, GO RIGHT ON WORKING"

President Hoover once suffered the indignity of being publicly booed at a baseball game and of hearing hundreds chant in unison, "We want beer! We want beer!" as he left the park. There was no doubt about his stand on prohibition. In his acceptance speech for the nomination he said, "I do not favor repeal of the Eighteenth Amendment. I stand for the efficient enforcement of the laws enacted . . . Our country has deliberately undertaken a great social and economic experiment, noble in motive, far-reaching in purpose." The "noble experiment" was investigated by the Wickersham Commission, appointed by Hoover. It found, to no one's surprise, that enforcement had proved wholly inadequate, that the law was distasteful to the American people, that it was freely violated and gave rise to wholesale corruption. Nevertheless, the Commission did not recommend its repeal. This made the unpopular President more unpopular than ever, as the cartoon on this page indicates.

254

In the face of the depression and the repugnant prohibition law, Hoover made a desperate bid for re-election (above). There was little to say. He defended his position of local self-help to the un-employed (rather than federal aid) and warned that if the Democrats got in "the grass will grow in the streets" and "weeds will overrun the fields of millions of farms." He was defeated by a landslide.

255

WHEN HOOVER WAS PRESIDENT: The most momentous crash in Wall Street history took place (October 29, 1929) when over sixteen million shares were traded and averages fell nearly forty points. Above: panic outside the Exchange.

As unemployment rose (to over ten million in 1932) apple vendors appeared on the streets of all major United States cities.

Breadlines and bank failures (above) increased as Hoover's administration came to a close. The production index fell to its lowest point in the country's history and the whole banking structure seemed to be on the verge of utter collapse.

Scarface Al Capone, Chicago overlord of organized crime (below, with a United States Marshal) literally got away with murder for years, but was finally jailed for falsifying his income tax. After serving time at Alcatraz, Al lived royally at his Miami estate.

In July, 1932, a "Bonus Army" of some seven thousand men descended on Washington and refused to leave. On the 28th their shacks were burned on Hoover's orders and the army dispersed.

New York's playboy Mayor, Jimmy Walker, is shown here as he took the stand on May 4, 1932, to face Judge Samuel Seabury who was appointed to investigate crime in New York City politics. Jimmy did not do well. As a result of the investigation he was forced to resign, and the following year Fiorello La Guardia was elected on a reform platform. Jimmy went to England.

FRANKLIN DELANO ROOSEVELT
1882–1945
PRESIDENT 1933–1945

Franklin D. Roosevelt, the first President to serve more than two terms and the first to be inaugurated January 20, had much in common with his fifth cousin, Theodore Roosevelt. Both were born to considerable wealth (above, F.D.R.'s birthplace at Hyde Park, New York), both went to Harvard, both began their political careers in the New York legislature, both served as assistant secretaries of the Navy, as governors of New York, and both were nominated vice-president. (T.R. was elected, F.D.R., defeated.) Both became president. Both publicly vowed that they would refuse a third term and both broke their promises. As reformers and leaders of social and economic revolutions (T.R.'s "Square Deal" and F.D.R.'s "New Deal") they were both detested and adored. The parallel continues in their outspoken contempt of what T.R. called the "vested interests," "the malefactors of great wealth." This was the group that F.D.R. called "economic royalists," the "money changers" he would drive from the temple.

Today, more than a decade after Franklin Roosevelt's death, the man is still both revered and despised as intensely as if he were living. To attempt to evaluate him here would be presumptuous, for even the most qualified historians cannot agree on his ultimate place in American history.

For instance, Harvard Professor Arthur M. Schlesinger, Jr., a devoted New-Dealer and recipient of the Pulitzer Prize for History (1945), rates him as the third greatest president, behind Lincoln and Washington. On the other hand, there are the noted historians Dr. Harry Elmer Barnes and the late Charles A. Beard, to whom Roosevelt was a monumental charlatan.

Roosevelt, say his adherents, was president during the greatest depression and the greatest war in the history of the world, and he defeated them both. To this his critics reply that the depression was deepening in 1937 after four years of Roosevelt (which it was) and that prosperity was restored only because of European war orders. As for the war, while Roosevelt was promising again and again to keep us out of it, he was at the same time deliberately, secretly and unlawfully steering us into it. Furthermore, they say, everything gained in the war was lost at Yalta.

History's final verdict will not be known to this generation.

This photograph taken in June, 1883, shows the future President perched on his father's shoulder. The elder Roosevelt, then fifty-five, married twenty-six-year-old Sara Delano in 1880.

In the big mansion overlooking the Hudson River at Hyde Park, young Roosevelt was brought up like a little prince, leading the most sheltered life of any president. He had a nurse and governesses who taught him to speak French and German, and private tutors. He travelled abroad with his parents several times and did not attend school until he was fourteen, when he was conducted by his father to the Groton School in Massachusetts. (Above, the Groton football squad. Roosevelt, who did not win his letter, is in the front row, second from the left.)

F.D.R. went up to Harvard in 1900 and enjoyed a more successful career than he had at Groton. He joined the exclusive Fly Club and was president of the *Crimson*, the college newspaper. After graduating he attended Columbia Law School.

Right, F.D.R. and Eleanor Roosevelt, his fifth cousin once removed. The picture was taken at the Roosevelt home on Campobello Island, New Brunswick, in 1904, a year before they were married in New York. At the wedding Eleanor was given away by her uncle, President Theodore Roosevelt.

261

The pictures on this page show (above) the good-looking, robust young Roosevelt at twenty-five paddling a birch bark canoe at Campobello, and (left) eleven years later (1918), when he was assistant secretary of the Navy. This photograph was taken in Washington during a Liberty Loan Drive. On F.D.R's left are Douglas Fairbanks and Mary Pickford; crouching in front: Marie Dressler and Charlie Chaplin.

Just before paralysis struck him in August, 1921, the thirty-nine-year-old Roosevelt stood six feet, two inches, weighed about 175 pounds and was in vibrant health. One evening at Campobello after a day of vigorous exertion, followed by a swim in the icy waters of the Bay of Fundy, Roosevelt went to bed with a chill. The next morning he had a high temperature and complained of acute pain in the legs. In a few days they were paralyzed. He never again stood unaided.

Roosevelt's first inaugural medal (above), designating him as the thirty-first president, was supposed to establish the numerical order of the presidents once and for all. It did not, however. The order was originally upset by the split administrations of Cleveland who became the twenty-second president in 1885 and was followed by Harrison, the twenty-third. Then came Cleveland's second term. To still call him the twenty-second president after the twenty-third had served would lead to confusion, it was thought. So Cleveland was officially designated the twenty-second *and* the twenty-fourth—still confusing but perhaps less so than the other way. Despite the above medal, F.D.R. is the thirty-second president in practically all biographies, encyclopedias, almanacs and official records.

In the most complete reversal in American history Roosevelt was swept into office by a seven million majority. (Four years before, Hoover's majority had been over six million.) F.D.R. was fifty-one when he took the oath of office, a year younger than Lincoln when he was inaugurated. Like Lincoln, he faced a grave national crisis and immediately went into action. With the authority conferred on him, F.D.R. rushed through a series of measures with dazzling speed: the bank holiday; repeal of prohibition; vast appropriations to be used for relief, for work for the unemployed and to save homes and farms from foreclosure, and businesses from bankruptcy. "Action and action now" was F.D.R.'s inaugural promise, and action was what the country got.

The above photograph was taken in 1934 when the President and members of his family reviewed the fleet from the U.S.S. *Indianapolis* in New York harbor. Left to right: Eleanor, Mrs. James Roosevelt, F.D.R., James, and the President's mother. The elder Mrs. Roosevelt was the dowager head of Hyde Park where Eleanor and F.D.R. lived for many years. Strong-minded and imperious, she dominated the family home and was adored to an extraordinary degree by her only son.

The famed Roosevelt smile (left) drove some men to fury. Others found it irresistible. To his advocates it reflected Roosevelt's great personal charm. To his critics it characterized his insincerity and deviousness, traits which even his friends admitted he had. His bitter attacks on the well-to-do caused many to wonder how he could fraternize with people like Vincent Astor, on whose luxurious yacht *Nourmahal*, the President cruised many times.

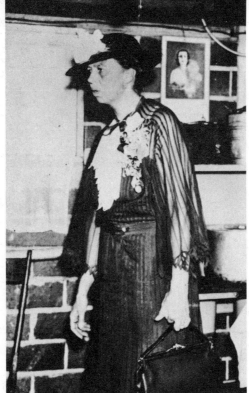

Eleanor Roosevelt, was the most active and ubiquitous wife of any president, is shown here pursuing some of her typical activities.

Across the top, left to right: speaking before the American Youth Congress in New York; inspecting the basement of a Homestead Home at Des Moines, Iowa; at Lowell Thomas' estate, Pawling, New York; Westbrook Pegler, who sits beside her, remained a bitter antagonist until her death in 1962. Standing are Deems Taylor and the late George Bye, literary agent. Below, left: working in her Val-Kill shop at Hyde Park; below, right: planting a tree in the Memory Garden of the Girl Scouts' "National Little House," Washington.

The tireless mother of five grown children and too many sons-in-law and daughters-in-law (ex and current) to count, Mrs. Roosevelt travelled some 500,000 miles in the United States alone, edited a magazine, wrote a daily and monthly column, gave innumerable lectures, laid countless cornerstones, descended a coal mine and rubbed noses with the New Zealand Maoris.

On December 8, 1941, the day after the attack on Pearl Harbor,
the President signed the Declaration of War against Japan.

The first president to leave the country during a war, Roosevelt conferred with Churchill at Casablanca, Morocco, in January, 1943, to plan military strategy following the North African invasion of the previous fall. It was at this conference that F.D.R. demanded unconditional surrender of the Axis powers. Churchill later stated that "the first time I heard that phrase used it was from the lips of President Roosevelt."

In November, 1943, Roosevelt again left the country for the Cairo and Teheran Conferences. At Teheran, Iran, F.D.R., Churchill and Stalin met together (for the first time) to discuss the invasion of Western Europe. "I believe he (Stalin) is truly representative of the heart and soul of Russia," said Roosevelt after the meeting, "and I believe that we are going to get along very well with him and the Russian people—very well indeed."

On this trip Roosevelt visited Sicily where he met General Eisenhower (below) on December 8, just two years to the day after the signing of the Declaration of War against Japan. By that time Italy had surrendered to the Allies and was at war with Germany.

WHEN ROOSEVELT WAS PRESIDENT: "Public Enemy Number One" John Dillinger, America's most notorious bandit, was considered a hero by some, as this billboard near Loretto, Pennsylvania, indicates. He was killed by the FBI in 1934.

A powerful weapon used by labor with great frequency in the '30's was the illegal sit-down strike. Below: workers take possession of the Fisher Body Plant, St. Louis, 1937.

Senator Huey (Kingfish) Long promised every family a five-thousand-dollar annual income, to be paid for by the rich.

The country was shocked in 1937 when F.D.R. tried (and failed) to "pack the Supreme Court" (above), *i.e.*, swell its numbers with members sympathetic to the New Deal.

At a cost of $150,000,000, New York's World Fair opened in April, 1939, ran until October, 1940. Over sixty countries were represented.

Defiant to the last, Sewell Avery (left), head of Mongomery Ward Company, was carried from his office by United States soldiers when he refused to leave the strike-bound plant.

The sixty-million-dollar French liner *Normandie*, burned and capsized at her pier in New York, February 9, 1942. Beyond salvage, she was scrapped.

WHAT DECISIONS?

Roosevelt was a sick man when he met Churchill and Stalin at Yalta, in the Crimean Peninsula, in February, 1945 (above). Uncle Joe—as F.D.R. often called the Russian dictator in his official communiques to Churchill—proved to be a shrewd bargainer at the conference. In return for his promise to fight Japan, Stalin was granted extraordinary rights in Asia and Eastern Europe, even though Roosevelt knew at the time that the atomic bomb would soon be tested. (As it turned out Russia did not enter the Japanese war until after the first atomic bomb had been dropped. She was at war with Japan for only six days. Later Stalin violated every Yalta agreement which guaranteed free elections in Europe.)

The secret agreements reached by the three leaders caused the man in the street to wonder about the decisions made at Yalta (note cartoon, left). So secret were they that even James F. Byrnes, a Roosevelt adviser at the conference, was kept in the dark.

The Franklin D. Roosevelt Library is at Hyde Park on land donated to the Government by F.D.R. during his lifetime. The building was raised by voluntary subscription (some $400,000) and is administered by the National Archives. Over half a million people annually pay twenty-five cents each to visit the library-museum which contains thousands of books, photographs, movie films and museum objects. At the main entrance (above) is a bust of the President which was presented by the International Ladies' Garment Workers' Union. In a rose garden nearby a plain white marble tombstone marks the grave of the thirty-second President.

HARRY S. TRUMAN 1884–
PRESIDENT 1945–1953

On April 12, 1945, less than three months after his inauguration to the Vice-Presidency, Harry Truman was summoned to the White House to receive the yet unreleased news that Roosevelt had died that afternoon at Warm Springs, Georgia, of a cerebral hemorrhage. That evening shortly after seven o'clock in the presence of his family (above, Mrs. Truman and daughter Margaret) and government officials, he was sworn in by Chief Justice Harlan Fiske Stone. Thus did Truman become the seventh accidental president. It was a dazed and humble President who said to friendly reporters the next day, "I've got the most awful responsibility a man ever had. If you fellows ever pray, pray for me." The fact that Truman carried out his responsibilities with courage and went on to win the Presidency virtually by himself was a wonder to many, considering his background.

A Missouri farmer with a high-school education,

Truman did not leave the family farm until he was thirty-three when he joined the army and went off to war in 1917. Two years later he returned with the rank of captain, and opened a haberdashery shop in Kansas City, which soon failed. Broke and without much future, Truman was picked up by Tom Pendergast, Kansas City's crooked political boss, who put him on his slate. Truman made a creditable record in local politics, kept his hands clean and was eventually awarded a United States senatorship by the Boss. In the Senate he had an undistinguished career until he formed the Truman War Investigating Committee which acted as a watchdog on government wartime expenditures. Its success brought his name to the foreground. In 1944, on the eve of the Democratic convention, Roosevelt decided to discard Henry Wallace, then vice-president, and suggested as a replacement either William O. Douglas or Truman, provided that the names were approved by Sidney Hillman, C.I.O. labor boss. Hence the phrase, "clear it with Sidney." Sidney thought Harry would do fine.

Gay Harry posed for this picture (left) with Lauren Bacall, "The Look," at the National Press Club Canteen in Washington in 1945, a year that was crowded with the most climactic events in our history: the battles of the Bulge and Iwo Jima, the Yalta and Potsdam Conferences, the first atomic bomb, the surrender of Germany and Japan, the deaths of Roosevelt, Mussolini and Hitler, and the United States acceptance of the United Nations Charter.

The presidential yacht, the U.S.S. *Williamsburg*, provided Truman and his friends many week ends of relaxation on the Potomac. It is shown below steaming into the harbor at St. Thomas, Virgin Islands, with the President and his party aboard.

Truman's frugal mode of living on his modest salary as senator—a salary augmented by that of his wife who served as his secretary—underwent a considerable change when he became president. In addition to the *Williamsburg*, he inherited from Roosevelt the *Sacred Cow* (above, with seven-man crew), a four-motored Douglas C-54 Skymaster equipped with a special elevator and deluxe interior.

Below right, the electronic control board in the $119,000 railroad communication car used by Truman. Its radio telephone, teletype, and code transmitters enabled the President to communicate instantly with the White House, ships at sea, military installations or any foreign capital. Below left, on his special campaign train Truman receives an ear of corn from an Iowa youngster.

During President Truman's term in office, the presidential salary was raised by Congress from $75,000 to $100,000 a year and the expense account of the office from $40,000 to $90,000 (tax free).

"GIVE 'EM HELL" CAMPAIGN

AT BASEMENT LEVEL

In the "Give 'em Hell" campaign of 1948 (left), the sixty-four-year-old Truman travelled 31,000 miles and made over 350 speeches, hammering away at every whistle stop at the Republican "do nothing" Eightieth Congress. Almost no one thought he could win, not even his supporters, and least of all the Republicans who were lulled to sleep by the results of the public-opinion polls. Everything indicated a walkover for his opponent, Governor Thomas E. Dewey of New York. But Dewey, cold and colorless, refused to roll up his sleeves and resorted to dignified platitudes. The result was the biggest upset in the history of presidential elections. The *Chicago Daily Tribune* was so confident of a Dewey victory that it announced his election before the final returns came in, much to Truman's glee.

The agreement made at Potsdam designating the thirty-eighth parallel as the dividing line between Soviet and American troops in Korea was broken when the North Korean Army crossed the line on June 25, 1950. Truman acted instantly. That same day he ordered General Douglas MacArthur to go to the aid of South Korea, and the war was on.

In October Truman flew to Wake Island to confer with MacArthur (above), then the United Nations commander in chief. MacArthur returned to Korea and opened a major offensive, but was prevented from following his advantage on orders from Washington. Truman dismissed him from his Korean and Japanese posts in 1951.

WHEN TRUMAN WAS PRESIDENT: The atomic age began with the destruction of the Japanese city of Hiroshima on August 6, 1945, when 78,000 non-combatants were killed with one blast (left). The billowing smoke rose twenty thousand feet above the city and spread over ten thousand feet at the base of the rising column. Three days later a second A-bomb was dropped on Nagasaki, killing 74,000.

Aboard the U.S.S. *Missouri* in Tokyo Bay on September 2, 1945, MacArthur watched General Umezu of Japan sign the Articles of Surrender.

New York's heaviest snowfall (25.8 inches) crippled the city, December 26, 1947, and brought all surface transportation to a standstill.

A five-man crime committee headed by Senator Estes Kefauver toured the country in 1951, investigating illegal operations of politicians, police, racketeers and gamblers in several cities. Among the five hundred witnesses interviewed was New York's underworld boss Frank Costello (right) who was later sent to jail. Kefauver's committee reported that gambling involved over twenty million dollars annually.

Alger Hiss (left) was sentenced to five years in jail in 1951 following his conviction of perjury in connection with the turning over of government secrets to the Soviets.

The American superliner *United States* broke the Atlantic record in 1952 by crossing to England in three days, ten hours, forty minutes.

The new White House (above) is not unlike the building of 1825 (left) in outward appearance, despite the addition of the ten-thousand-dollar balcony installed by Truman. (These pictures show the south front, the earlier one being a view from Tibre Creek, since filled in to make Constitution Avenue.) Late in 1948, when it was discovered that the White House was in danger of complete collapse, the Trumans moved to nearby Blair House where they stayed until the old building was strengthened and restored at a cost of $5,761,000. In March, 1952, the Trumans returned to a completely modernized White House with air conditioning and running ice water in every room. Counting storage and utility rooms, the building contains 132 rooms, twenty baths and showers and twenty-nine fireplaces. There are fifty-four rooms and sixteen baths in the part of the house used as living quarters.

Above: Lincoln's bedroom, which is used for high-ranking male guests. The long bed, covered by a spread crocheted by Mrs. Calvin Coolidge, was made especially for Lincoln.

Below: the all-electric modern kitchen equipped with stainless-steel utensils and opaque glass walls. Located on the ground floor, the room has dumb-waiters to transfer food to a pantry which connects with state and family dining rooms on the main floor.

The grandest and largest room in the White House is the East Room (above) which is used for State functions, Christmas parties, balls and musicales. It is seventy-nine feet long, thirty-six and three quarters feet wide with a twenty-two-foot-high ceiling, and has four fireplaces and three huge gold-plated and crystal chandeliers. In this room Abigail Adams, the first mistress of the White House, hung out her wash. Lincoln's soldiers were quartered here while the Confederates threatened Washington. In it Nellie Grant and Alice Roosevelt (T.R.'s daughter) were married, and funeral services were held for William Henry Harrison, Taylor, Lincoln, Harding and Franklin Roosevelt. On its walls, fitted into panels, are the portraits of George Washington (the one Dolley Madison saved) and Martha Washington. The grand piano, a gift from Steinway and Sons, has ornate gold eagles for legs and gilded scenes on its sides of American folk dancing.

DWIGHT D. EISENHOWER 1890–
PRESIDENT 1953–1961

Dwight David Eisenhower, America's hero of World War II, was the third regular army man to become president, the first to be born in Texas and the first of German ancestry. Over half of our presidents (twenty) have served their country in uniform, beginning with Washington, but all save three were citizen-soldiers. The three exceptions are Zachary Taylor, U. S. Grant and Eisenhower—dedicated Army men with no political experience when the Presidency called.

Eisenhower was born in Denison, Texas, on October 14, 1890, the third of seven sons (one died in infancy) of David and Ida Stover Eisenhower. Texas was the future President's birthplace by accident, for his parents came there from Kansas, stayed less than two years and then returned to Abilene when he was five months old. All the other Eisenhower boys were born in Kansas and all grew up in Abilene where their father earned a meager salary as a mechanic in a creamery. (He had previously failed in business in Kansas, and during the Texas interlude had worked in a railroad machine shop.)

The above picture of the Eisenhower family was taken when Dwight (extreme left) was eight years old. A quarter of a century later at a family reunion in Abilene the same group again posed for a picture, in the identical position they appear in above. At that time the Eisenhower boys were on their way to success. From them were to come a president, an engineer, a banker, a lawyer, a businessman and a college president—a remarkable record in view of their poor circumstances in the early days. The Eisenhower parents, members of the Church of the Brethren in Christ, reared their sons in a strict religious environment.

In high school Ike—as he was then called—played football and baseball, and after graduating worked around town for over a year. In 1910 he took a War Department competitive examination for appointment to the service schools. A candidate could then apply for either Annapolis or West Point, or he could list himself as an "either," i.e., no preference. Although Ike had his heart set on Annapolis, he put down "either" on his application in the belief that by so doing his chances of success would be increased. A few months later the twenty-year-old Ike found himself climbing the hill to the Point.

The picture on the opposite page shows Cadet Eisenhower in his second year at West Point (1912) as the halfback understudy of Geoffrey Keyes, the Army's star of the previous year. Ike played in six games and showed great promise as a hard-tackling, hard-running back. His biggest thrill was downing Jim Thorpe in the Carlisle game. A broken knee finished his football career.

In 1915 Ike graduated from West Point (slightly above average in scholarship; in conduct 95th in a class of 164) and was sent to Fort Houston in San Antonio. There he met Mamie Geneva Doud, the daughter of a Denver businessman. They were married in Denver on July 1, 1916 (above). Ike refused to sit down until after the ceremony for fear of spoiling the knife-like crease in his trousers.

Promotions were slow during the first twenty-five years of Ike's moderately distinguished army career. Although he rose to the rank of lieutenant colonel (temporary) in the first World War, he dropped back to captain in 1920, then up to major the same year and for the next sixteen years did not budge. The future did not seem promising—perhaps a colonelcy some day. He had been forced to spend World War I in this country and now, in 1936 at the age of forty-six, he was still a major. But things happened rapidly after that. From lieutenant colonel in March, 1941, Ike rose to the rank of full general in twenty-three months.

A few days after Pearl Harbor Eisenhower was summoned to Washington by Chief of Staff, George C. Marshall, and put to a test on the problem of Pacific strategy. How many other officers had been given that same assignment is not known, but it is known that Eisenhower's brilliant design stood out above all the others. He was subsequently made Chief of the War Plans Division and was sent to England to prepare a plan on American participation in Europe. Again Ike scored with a masterful directive. This led to his command of the European Theater and later to his appointment by Roosevelt as Supreme Commander for the invasion of Europe. Eisenhower's magnificent achievement in this role was due not only to his strategic planning but to his consummate tact, his engaging personality and his ability to be tough and forceful at the right time.

A man with such qualities ought to make a good president many people thought in the summer of 1947 when a boom was set off upon his announcement that he was leaving the army to become president of Columbia University. He was so popular that he probably could have had the nomination of either party for the asking, but Ike said no in terms that could not be mistaken. By 1952, however, there was such a demand for him to run that he could no longer refuse. While still in Europe on active service again he permitted his name to be used in the Republican ballot in some states where the delegates were chosen by ballot.

Below, Ike returns in glory to Abilene just before his campaign for the nomination. After a bitter contest between Taft and Eisenhower supporters over delegates, Ike was nominated on the first ballot.

Governor Adlai Stevenson of Illinois made witty campaign speeches and was an appealing candidate, but he was no match for the popular Ike. Moreover, he was handicapped by the Democratic record: the indecisive Korean war, Communist infiltration in Washington ("a red herring" to Truman), the inflated "Truman dollar," and crime and corruption in government. Even Stevenson referred to the state of affairs as the "mess in Washington." The Democrats were put on the defensive. They praised the F.D.R. record and warned that if the Republicans got in, a depression was sure to follow. Organized labor, the tail of the Democratic kite, endorsed Stevenson, but to no avail. Eisenhower won hands down. He polled nearly seven million more votes than Stevenson (442 electoral votes to 89) and broke the solid South by taking Virginia, Florida, Tennessee and Texas.

Above, President Truman and his wife greet the Eisenhowers at the White House, January 20, 1953, just before the President-elect left for the Capitol and the swearing-in ceremonies.

The petite and gracious Mamie Doud Eisenhower has her husband's gift for getting along with people, and was one of the more popular of the White House hostesses. She willingly performed the duties of a First Lady, but consistently avoided the spotlight and did not interfere with the business of government. Army assignments kept the Eisenhowers so much on the move that they had no permanent home until 1952 when the President bought a farm near Gettysburg.

Mamie's inaugural dress, which she wears in the above portrait, was added to the Smithsonian Institution's collection of dresses of the First Ladies when her White House regime ended.

The first presidential news conference covered by movie and TV cameras took place on January 19, 1955 (above), and was soon beamed to the nation's living rooms. The country saw the President answer a reporter's request for an "appraisal of your first two years." In his reply Eisenhower listed the end of the Korean war, and a more stable foreign situation in general. At home, taxes and spending had been cut, said the President, and the economy is sound and prosperous.

"Dynamic conservatism" is the apt phrase the President uses to define his administration. He said: "I believe we should be conservative. I believe we should conserve everything that is basic to our system. We should be dynamic in applying it to the problems of the day so that all 163 million Americans will profit from it."

'NEW ROLE'

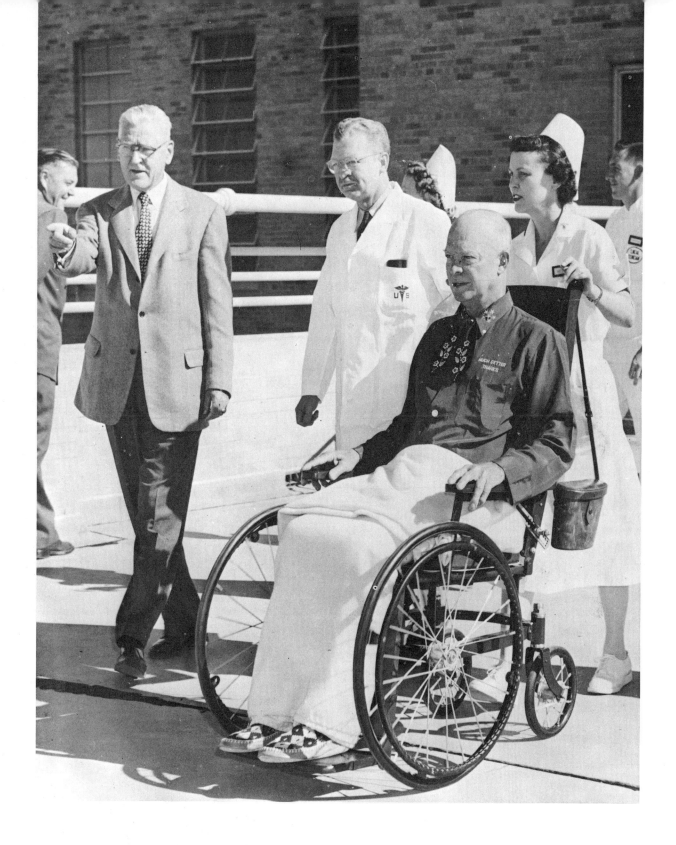

Early in the morning of September 24, 1955, the President suffered a heart attack in the home of his mother-in-law, Mrs. John S. Doud, in Denver. Two days later, at a press conference, Dr. Paul Dudley White of Boston described the attack as "moderate." Meantime a shocked nation talked of nothing else.

Stocks tumbled with a loss of some twelve billion dollars and Democratic leaders said that they would not make political capital out of Ike's illness.

Above, the President is wheeled onto the sun deck at Fitzsimmons Army Hospital in Denver on October 25th to pose for his first appearance since his attack.

Would Ike run for a second term, or wouldn't he? For five months, while the President remained silent the question was discussed throughout the country. Then, on the last day of February, 1956, came the announcement the Republicans had hoped would come, the Democrats had hoped would not . . . Ike *would* run. The decision had come after a long discussion with advisors and a thorough medical check-up.

As the Republican elephant Yahooed with joy, Adlai Stevenson, a good bet to win the Democratic nomination again, received the news with no great enthusiasm, as the above photo indicates.

A few months later the President had an attack of ileitis (inflammation of the ileum, a portion of the small intestine) and went under the knife. After his recovery he again had to face the decision, and once more the news came: he was physically fit and would be a candidate.

Herblock—Washington Post

"Yahooooo!"

292

"All the News That's Fit to Print"

The New York Times.

© 1956, by The New York Times Company.

LATE CITY EDITION
Condensation of U. S. Weather Bureau forecast:
Some cloudiness today; cloudy to-
night. Clearing, cooler tomorrow.
Temperature range today: 66—50.
Temperature range yesterday: 65.4—52.2.
Full U. S. Weather Bureau Report, Page 62.

VOL. CVI..No. 36,082.   Entered as Second-Class Matter. Post Office, New York, N. Y.   NEW YORK, WEDNESDAY, NOVEMBER 7, 1956.   Times Square, New York 36, N. Y. Telephone LAckawanna 4-1000   FIVE CENTS

EISENHOWER BY A LANDSLIDE;

Few men ever sought so hard to avoid a nomination for President as did Stevenson in 1952, or fought so hard to attain it four years later. But from the time the President began his campaign there was every indication that Stevenson and his running mate, Senator Estes Kefauver, were doomed.

Heralding an era of "new Republicanism," Ike made an exhaustive campaign tour throughout the country, building the confidence of voters in his health as well as his platform. Everywhere Ike went, he was wildly cheered and enthusiastic crowds turned out to greet him and to listen to the Republican campaign slogan: Peace, Progress, and Prosperity.

With a few exceptions, the Democrats did not make a direct issue of Ike's heart attack, but instead launched vigorous attacks on Ike's running mate, Richard Nixon, who had already survived a Republican party "split" to win the vice-presidential nomination in a landslide. Final death blow to the Democrats waning hopes came close to election eve when Stevenson proposed immediate cessation of all nuclear bomb tests.

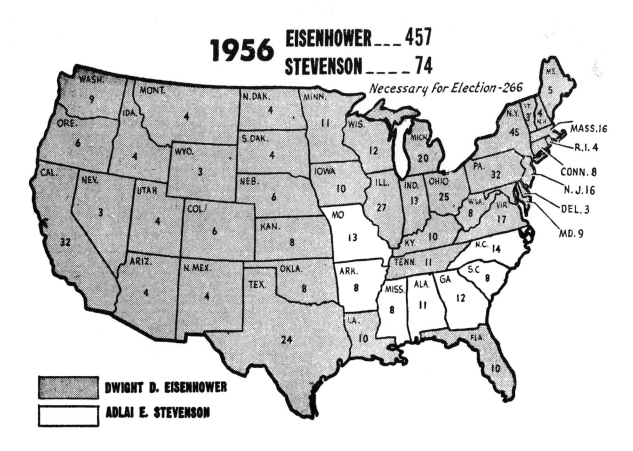

1956 EISENHOWER ___ 457 STEVENSON ___ 74

Necessary for Election -266

DWIGHT D. EISENHOWER
ADLAI E. STEVENSON

Here, at one of the four inaugural balls held in the Capital in January, 1957, the President and the First Lady, their son, Major John, and his wife, Barbara Anne, wave to a crowd of 9,000 celebrants.

Because Ike's term expired at noon on Sunday, January 20th, he was inaugurated that morning at a private ceremony in the East Room of the White House. Nixon preceded him (by tradition the Vice President is sworn in first) and the next day the two men went through the same ritual again. This time the ceremony was performed on the steps of the Capitol before thousands of people.

Dwight Eisenhower could look back with satisfaction on his four years in office. His administration had ended a hopeless and inconclusive war and had kept new wars from these shores. It had helped guide the country to new heights of prosperity, had cut taxes, balanced the budget and had shown concern for the welfare of its people rather than for the special interests of "big business," as labor and Democratic politicians perennially charge. It looked as if the honeymoon might go on forever when Ike began his second term, but this was not to be. Too many things started to turn the wrong way.

Even as Ike took the oath of office there were soft spots showing in the nation's economy, and before the year was up the recession was under way. As unemployment increased and the cost of living climbed steadily, tight money policies and dire predictions of things to come caused production and inventory cutbacks in most businesses.

The administration urged a "Look Ahead, Go Ahead" philosophy in an effort to build confidence in the future. Throughout the country, drives such as the "You Auto Buy Now" campaign helped some, but unemployment continued to rise as the downward trend continued.

As the economic unrest grew, so did closely-allied political unrest. The people's faith in Eisenhower which had produced his landslide second term victory gave way to attacks on his policies, his associates, and Ike, himself.

John Foster Dulles, a traveling Secretary of State, (left), arriving in Paris, was criticized for his "brink of war" speech which indicated the State Department was playing a dangerous, cat-and-mouse game with America's future as the stakes.

The resignation of Ezra Taft Benson, Secretary of Agriculture, was demanded by Democrats and Republicans alike who were alarmed by the animosity of the farm vote toward Benson's steadfast refusal to support full parity prices.

Finally, in mid-summer 1958, came the episode of Sherman Adams, Ike's most trusted advisor. Whether or not Adams was guilty of influencing government actions to favor any one firm, he had erred greatly in accepting the favors of Boston industrialist, Bernard Goldfine.

Although Ike refused to accept Adams's resignation, saying "he is too valuable," the damage to the President's prestige had been done and Ike's overwhelming popularity had slipped considerably according to public opinion polls.

On November 25, 1957, Mrs. Anne Wheaton (below), assistant to White House press secretary James Hagerty (who was in Paris arranging an NATO council meeting), called reporters into her office and announced what she had been told to announce by the decision of Sherman Adams, Ike's top assistant, and Major General Howard McC. Snyder, the President's personal physician. This was that Ike had been put to bed with a chill and that his ailment was not serious. Mrs. Wheaton thought she was releasing all the facts and did not then know that a team of medical specialists had diagnosed Ike's illness as a cerebral occlusion, or stroke.

The fact that an anxious nation was not precisely informed for twenty-four hours increased the growing feeling that the nature of the President's illness was being shielded by his White House staff, and that he was losing contact with the public.

Not until the afternoon of the day after the attack was a medical bulletin issued to newsmen: It was a blockage of a brain artery and the President had also suffered a slight impairment of speech. When reporters asked for a clarification ("Is this a heart attack or a stroke?") Mrs. Wheaton was unable to say. She called General Snyder on the telephone and after conferring with him announced that the General was unwilling to call the President's attack a stroke. Thus did the country get a botched and erroneous account of the true nature of the President's illness.

There was much speculation as to whether Ike would resign but his recovery was rapid. Four days after his seizure he felt well enough to attend church, and the next day he went to his Gettysburg farm looking as sound as ever. But the feeling remained that he was not as close to the people as before,

Looking as healthy as ever, the President flashes his famous smile as he signs the Alaskan Statehood Bill, adding a 49th state to the Union on July 7, 1958.

In spite of the setbacks of 1957, there were many bright spots in Ike's second term. As the summer of 1958 drew to a close, the nation's farmers were producing record crops, unemployment, though still high, was falling, and a definite upswing was in sight.

The President's own rating of the Democratic 85th Congress, second division, was: "A pretty good record of accomplishment." Among the bills passed which he considered imperative, were: Reciprocal Trade, Mutual Security and Defense Reorganization.

On the other side of the ledger was the ever increasing cost of living, creeping inflation, the failure of the House to pass the Kennedy-Ives labor reform bill which the Senate, by contrast, had passed by an overwhelming 88-1 vote.

Then, too, there was the recurrent question of the President's health and the suggestion that he was being shielded by a "palace guard." As the upswing progressed, Ike's popularity rose again, but it did not climb back to its previous height.

WHEN EISENHOWER WAS PRESIDENT: The White House was picketed for twelve days by sympathizers of Julius and Ethel Rosenberg, convicted atom spies. The couple died in the electric chair at Sing Sing on June 19, 1953.

The three-year inconclusive Korean War came to an end in July, 1953, with the signing of the Armistice at Panmunjom. United States casualties: 33,237 dead; 103,376 wounded.

FBI Chief Edgar Hoover (above), testified that he had informed President Truman on three occasions that government official Harry Dexter White, was a member of a Communist spy ring. The result of Hoover's report: White was promoted.

5 CONGRESSMEN SHOT BY 3 GALLERY GUNMEN

Headlines like this spread across the newspapers of the country on March 1, 1954, when Puerto Rican extremists blazed away with automatic pistols from the House gallery, and wounded five Congressmen.

The President's favorite cartoon of himself (below) appeared in the Washington *Star*. It shows Ike with his signals crossed, about to drive a baseball from the White House lawn as Clark Griffith, owner of the Washington Senators, rushes to halt him.

Controversy between Senator Joseph R. McCarthy and Army Secretary Robert T. Stevens over the promotion of an officer suspected of being a Communist, led to the 36-day-long Army-McCarthy hearings in 1954. (Above, McCarthy and counsel Roy M. Cohn.) Later, McCarthy was condemned by the Senate for undignified conduct.

The most sports-minded president since Teddy Roosevelt, Eisenhower was an accomplished dry-fly fisherman, a fine shot with both pistol and shotgun, and a better than fair golfer. Like many an ex-athlete, Ike got relaxation out of competitive sports, especially golf—by far his favorite game—which he played hard and to win. The stakes were nominal, usually a dollar Nassau. (Above left, he goes around with Vice-President Nixon at the Cherry Hills Country Club, Denver, Colorado.) Ike once said that the C.I.O. kept tabs on the number of his golf outings.

Like Churchill, Ike was an amateur painter. In his studio in the White House he worked with great concentration on his landscapes and while he is painting (the periods lasted anywhere from fifteen minutes to two hours) he would not talk to anyone. After golf and painting, his favorite relaxations were, in order: playing with his three grandchildren, bridge, TV, movies, reading (mostly Westerns), cooking (he never washes the dishes), fishing and shooting.

Dr. Jonas E. Salk in his Pittsburgh laboratory (above) made one of the greatest advancements in medical history by successfully isolating the polio virus thus producing the Salk vaccine. Soon after children, expectant mothers and many others were receiving a series of three shots that made feared epidemics of this crippling disease a thing of the past.

It was a confident, smiling public that read the stories of the success of Explorer I (above), America's first satellite launched into orbit between 187 and 1,800 miles above the earth, circling the globe at approximately 18,000 miles per hour.

An electrifying achievement was the feat of the nuclear-powered submarine, *Nautilus* (below), which astounded the world by sailing under the Arctic ice cap directly beneath the North Pole on August 3, 1958. Advanced submarine design and superior navigating combined to make this big "first" possible.

JOHN F. KENNEDY, 1917–1963
PRESIDENT 1961–1963

John Fitzgerald Kennedy, decorated hero of World War II, a shrewd politician, brilliant intellectual, statesman, and author of two best-selling books, broke precedents right and left when he took the oath of office to become our thirty-fifth President.

At forty-three he was the youngest man ever elected to the presidency, the first of Roman Catholic faith, the first of Irish ancestry on both sides of his family and the first President born in the Twentieth Century. He was also the richest man ever chosen for the White House. (Several Presidents have been wealthy men but Kennedy was probably the first one who had a million dollars of his own at the age of twenty-one.)

This was made possible by the generosity of his father, Joseph P. Kennedy, one-time New Dealer of the Franklin Roosevelt days who started with nothing and amassed an incredible fortune. It is generally rated at more than two hundred million dollars.

Father Kennedy sired nine children and gave them a million dollars outright apiece when they became old enough to vote.

The above aerial view shows the Kennedy family winter palace at Palm Beach, Florida, where the President spent his vacations away from the White House. The red-tiled ocean-front home which father Joe Kennedy bought in 1933 for $100,000, has a swimming pool flanked by palm trees, a tennis court, six bedrooms, separate servants' quarters, a four-car garage and enough space on the adjacent 200-foot lot for expansion—if needed.

The palace is a far cry from the modest frame house with a mortgage in a lower-class neighborhood in Brookline, a Boston suburb, where John F. Kennedy was born on May 29, 1917.

The Kennedys and the Fitzgeralds (the family of the President's mother who was born Rose Fitzgerald) came to Boston over a hundred years ago in the great wave of immigration that followed the famine in Ireland caused by the failure of the potato crop. Both families lived in East Boston, where one of the Kennedys ran a saloon. Both grandfathers of the President, John F. "Honey Fitz" Fitzgerald and Patrick J. Kennedy, went into politics. Honey Fitz served three terms in Congress and was a mayor of Boston. His daughter Rose, the eldest of six children, married Joe Kennedy, a bank president at

twenty-five, and the young couple moved into the Brookline home.

This photograph of the Kennedy family which was taken in 1934 shows eight of the nine children. Not shown is Joseph, Jr., the first born, who was then alive but was later killed as a Naval pilot in World War II. *Front row* (left to right): Patricia (10), Mrs. Kennedy, Teddy (3), Father Joe, Kathleen (14, died in a plane crash in 1948), Eunice (13), Rosemary (16). *Back row:* John F. (17), Jean (6), Bobby (9).

An earlier picture of the future President (left) shows him as a football player on the Dexter School team in 1926. As a youngster Jack was not very rugged. He was skinny, inclined to be sickly and liked books as much as sports. He played some football at Choate and Harvard but did not make his letter. "I wasn't a terribly good athlete but I participated," he once said. He graduated from Harvard *cum laude* in 1940.

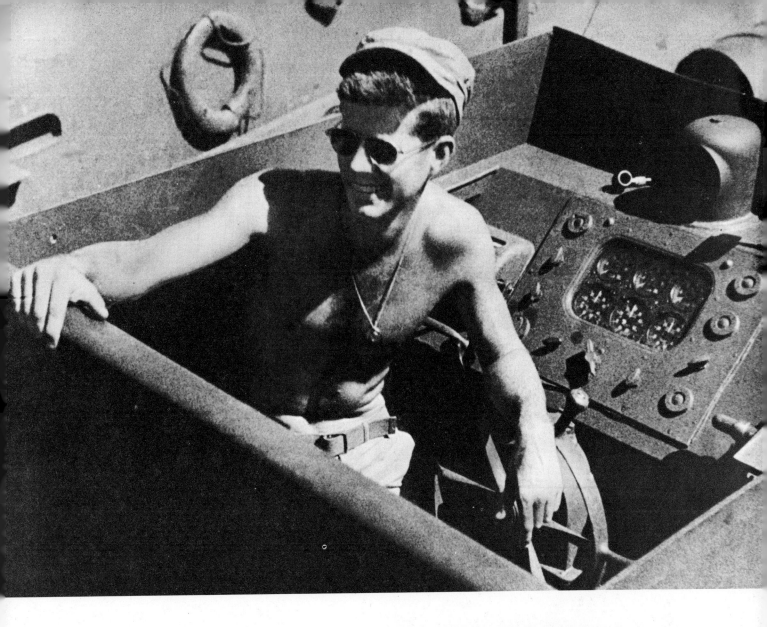

Naval Lieutenant Kennedy (above, as skipper of a PT boat) emerged from the war a genuine hero. Although he had a chronically ailing back, he passed the Navy's fitness test by taking special exercises and saw service in the South Pacific. In the Solomons a Jap destroyer ran down his boat and sliced it in two, slamming Kennedy to the deck. Despite agonizing pain from his bad back, Kennedy rescued his crew. With the strap of one man's life jacket in his teeth, Kennedy swam for five hours and towed him to the nearest land. Days later the stranded group was found and brought to safety. Discharged in 1945 after the Navy gave him a back operation, Kennedy came home and decided to go into politics. He served three terms in Congress and was elected to the U. S. Senate in 1953.

That year he married the cultured and lovely Jacqueline Lee Bouvier (right) at Newport, Rhode Island.

JULY 2nd
"Kennedy hasn't matured yet."

HST

Oct. 2nd
"Kennedy is my man."

Out of each side of a big mouth.

Kennedy served in the Lower House for six years and did not do much. He avoided the big issues and missed more than a quarter of the 604 roll call votes. In the Senate, however, he matured and took his place among the northern Democratic leaders. In 1956 at the Chicago Democratic convention he made a run for the vice-presidential nomination and almost made it. (He was defeated by Estes Kefauver of Tennessee by less than forty votes.) From that moment on Kennedy set his sights on the White House for 1960. He let it be known that he would like the nomination and then went to work with a well-oiled, skillful and sometimes ruthless organization to get the prize. He ran hard and successfully in the primaries and came to the Los Angeles convention in July, 1960, with a wagon load of votes.

Would Kennedy's youth be against him? Many thought so, including Harry Truman (left) who publicly challenged him on that score. Kennedy replied that he thought he could handle the job. He got the nomination and then Harry changed his tune.

It was a foregone conclusion that the Republicans would nominate Richard Nixon who is shown below with his wife Pat and their two daughters.

At the start of the campaign the odds were in Nixon's favor. He was four years older than Kennedy, more experienced in the executive branch of the government as an active Vice-President and was an outspoken foe of Communism and the Welfare State. He was a Protestant, and in Henry Cabot Lodge, U. S. Ambassador to the United Nations, he had an attractive and capable running mate.

Many thought that Kennedy's religion would hurt him but, as it turned out, just the opposite was true. The Senator promised everything to everybody, hammered at our loss of national prestige and the "missile gap" in Russia's favor. He staged a tireless campaign.

The turning point came when the candidates went on TV in a series of four debates. Nixon made the mistake of going on the defensive, holding his punches and trying to be a good sport about it all. The brilliant, forceful Kennedy weakened Nixon's public image.

In the cartoon (right) both candidates exclaim in unison: "I have difficulty recognizing myself."

Below: V-P candidate Lyndon B. Johnson, Senator from Texas, and his smiling wife, "Lady Bird."

All the News
That's Fit to Print"

The New York Times.

CITY EDITION

U S Weather Bureau Report - Page 34: Forecasts
Cloudy, chance of late rain today.
Rain, clearing and colder tomorrow.
Temp. range : 56—40, yesterday: 46 4 31 8

VOL. CX.... No. 37,546.   © 1960 by The New York Times Company.   NEW YORK, WEDNESDAY, NOVEMBER 9, 1960.   10 cents bereud 50 gules some from New York City except on Long Island higher in air delivery cities   M   FIVE CENTS

VOTING IS HEAVY THROUGHOUT THE NATION; TURNOUT IN NEW YORK STATE SETS RECORD; DEMOCRATS EXPECTED TO RETAIN CONGRESS

Everybody knew that the election was going to be close but no one dreamed it would be as close as it was. The day after the voting *The New York Times* (above) cautiously refrained from naming the winner. However, it looked like Kennedy—by a hair. And by a hair it was. Kennedy won by the narrowest popular vote margin in history—112,801 ballots, or less than one per cent of the total major party vote. But he won, and here (below) on the White House porch he leaves with Ike for the inauguration.

This picture was taken the moment after Kennedy had taken the oath of office (on Jan. 20, 1961). It shows good loser Nixon congratulating him as Lyndon Johnson beams between them.

Kennedy's inaugural address was hailed throughout the nation as a literary masterpiece. It comprised only 1,355 words, far fewer than the average of the forty-four previous inaugurations of 2,499 words. The new President pledged support to our Allies and the United Nations and urged the people of the world to "explore the stars, conquer the deserts, eradicate disease, tap the ocean depths and encourage the arts and commerce." His most quoted passage is: "And so, my fellow Americans: ask not what your country can do for you—ask what you can do for your country."

Although the Republicans had lost, it was by no means a crushing defeat and certainly no clear mandate from the people in view of Kennedy's tissue-thin margin of victory.

In losing the election, in which nearly 69 million votes were cast, Nixon carried twenty-six states with 219 electoral votes; Kennedy won twenty-three states with 303—and that is what counted. However, of the eight major geographical regions, Nixon carried five and Kennedy three (New England, Middle Atlantic and South). Kennedy's main strength was in the big cities and the suburbs.

The most pronounced switch was the Catholic vote. Gallup's poll revealed that sixty-two per cent of the Catholics who had voted Republican for President in 1956 switched to Democratic in 1960.

Most of the hundred or so key appointments to the New Frontier (Kennedy's name for his administration) met with general approval. Taken as a whole, the appointees were intelligent, resourceful and hardworking. A great many were intellectuals associated with Harvard; some were Kennedy's political cronies who helped him win the election; a few were hard-headed businessmen.

One appointment that did not sit very well with the American people was the one given Bobby Kennedy, the President's thirty-five-year-old brother, as Attorney General of the United States (note cartoon, left). Bobby was the first relative of a President to hold Cabinet office and the youngest Attorney General in the history of the country. He had never practiced law in any state or Federal court.

Kennedy was the first President to stage an un-rehearsed, live TV press conference (below). (Eisenhower's conferences were taped, then edited before being televised.) Often appearing before more than 300 press correspondents, the President displayed flawless skill in answering the many questions thrown at him.

J. F. K.

John F. Kennedy.

The problems that faced the President from the moment he took office were huge and manifold, as this cartoon from the London Sunday Express indicates. Here, crowding the "IN" box are a few of the items that demand his immediate attention: the missile race with Russia, Communist China, the emergence of new nations in Africa and, topping everything, the threat of Communism in Cuba.

Kennedy enjoyed the traditional post-Inaugural honeymoon that all new Presidents enjoy. The press adulated him to excess; public opinion polls showed him reaching heights of popularity that even Ike never achieved. In time, however, the honeymoon waned—which was expected, and people began to take a harder look at the attractive young man.

The main criticism of the New Frontier was that its goals were not being achieved. There was no program to put them in effect. Nothing was being done. As one prominent member of the Democratic party put it, "We are like the Harlem Globetrotters, passing forward, behind, sidewise and underneath. But nobody has made a basket yet."

The Kennedys moved into the White House with two children—Caroline, three, and John Fitzgerald Kennedy, Jr., shown above with his mother at the age of thirteen days. This is the first photograph of the new baby. It was taken on December 8, 1960, after the christening in Georgetown University Chapel. The gown worn by the infant is the same one the President wore forty-three years before.

A reason for Kennedy's popularity was his informal approach to the presidency. It made people feel that they were close to him. He gave the impression of being available at all times, that he could never become the prisoner of a tight little White House staff shielding him from the public.

An example of the President's personal touch was illustrated in the heart-warming scene portrayed in the picture below. Here, at the Andrews Air Force Base in Maryland, Kennedy greeted the freed RB-47 fliers upon their return from Russia.

Millions of Americans knew the story of the six-foot, 175-pound President's rise to power but few knew the inner man. The picture presented by his biographers and friends revealed a complex person. He was, first of all, a man who took command with complete assurance and went after what he wanted with an all-out effort. He was cool-headed, clear-minded, tireless and precise. He was no backslapper; many found him distant and calculating. He had a fine sense of humor and liked to laugh but he never laughed from the belly.

WHEN KENNEDY WAS PRESIDENT:
His administration suffered one of the most humiliating setbacks in American history only ninety days after it took power. This was the Bay of Pigs fiasco on April 17, 1961, when a force of Cuban exiles, secretly trained and equipped by U.S. agencies and with JFK's approval, came to grief on Cuba's south shore. This telephoto shows a few of the more than 3,000 prisoners (later ransomed for $50,000,000 worth of drugs and medicine) captured by the vastly superior forces of Fidel Castro, Cuba's Prime Minister.

John H. Glenn, shown below being fitted into his silver space suit, orbited the earth three times on February 20, 1962, to become the first American to go into orbit. Although the Russians had previously done this, Glenn's feat gave America a psychological lift.

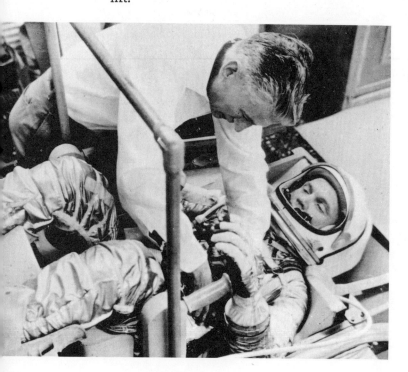

A different kind of flight brought sadness to America on June 3, 1962, when a chartered jetliner crashed in Paris killing 114 Georgians, almost all of whom were members of the Atlanta Art Association. Above, Atlanta Mayor Ivan Allen, who flew to Paris after the disaster, inspects the wreckage.

THE HEAVY SOVIET INVOLVEMENT IN CUBA

Where Russians are operating: ▲ Camps | Missile sites ⛴ Ports of entry

Kennedy, who loved popularity and applause, enjoyed himself greatly on his trip to Germany in June, 1963. Above, he receives a tumultuous welcome in West Berlin with the Mayor of the city, Willie Brandt, at his side.

The American people were stunned when Kennedy went on the air on October 22, 1962, and told them that the Russians had built several missile bases in Cuba capable of carrying warheads 2,000 miles. He announced a blockade of Cuba. Faced with war, the Russians backed down and removed the missiles. Many of their troops remained, however.

The largest civil rights demonstration in the nation's history took place in Washington, D.C., on August 28, 1963, when an estimated 210,000 Negroes and whites assembled at the Washington Monument and marched up Constitution Avenue (below) to the Lincoln Memorial.

Kennedy had been in office two years, ten months and two days when this picture was taken on November 22, 1963, a few minutes before his rendezvous with death.

In the big blue presidential limousine, which had been flown from Washington for the motorcade through Dallas, were the Kennedys and Texas Governor John Connally and his wife. The Connallys sat in the jump seats. Jacqueline Kennedy, radiant in a pink suit and pillbox hat, held a bouquet of red roses in her lap. It was a warm, sunny day. The temperature was in the seventies. Because of the fine weather, the plastic bubble top of the limousine was removed.

At 11:50 a.m. the twelve-car motorcade began to move. In front of the presidential limousine and following it were cars bristling with armed Secret Service escorts—thirty-six in all. In the fourth car rode Vice-President Lyndon Johnson and his wife.

It had been a gratifying political week for the President. He had been well received by audiences in Tampa and Miami Beach, and just the day before by crowds of Texans in San Antonio, Houston and Fort Worth. And now, pleased by the greeting at Love Field, the Dallas airport, and the friendly crowds lining the streets, Kennedy responded warmly. Several times he stood up and waved as the motor procession cruised slowly through the city toward the Dallas Trade Mart, where he was scheduled to speak at a civic luncheon.

The crowds were thinner once the motorcade left Main Street and took a turn on to Elm Street in front of a seven-story warehouse called the Texas School Book Depository. Through an open window on the sixth floor a lone spectator watched the President's car approach, then picked it up through the telescopic sight of the rifle in his hands. "Look at that FBI man up there," said a boy on the street. "He sure is on the job."

What the sniper saw is shown in the reconstructed scene (right). What actually happened is shown below. At the first shot Kennedy's smile vanished and he clutched his neck. Governor Connally turned toward the President and *crack!* he was himself hit. As he fell into his wife's arms the third shot split the air and the back of Kennedy's head exploded in blood. The terrifying sequence was all over in less than six seconds.

Immediately Secret Service agents swarmed around the limousine. But no one knew where the shots had come from. The car roared away for the Parkland Hospital, 3.5 miles distant, with the Johnson car following inches behind. About five minutes later the President was brought into Emergency Room One. The first physicians to see him knew it was too late. They did everything possible to revive him but it was no use. Lyndon Johnson probably had become President while speeding to the hospital at seventy miles an hour.

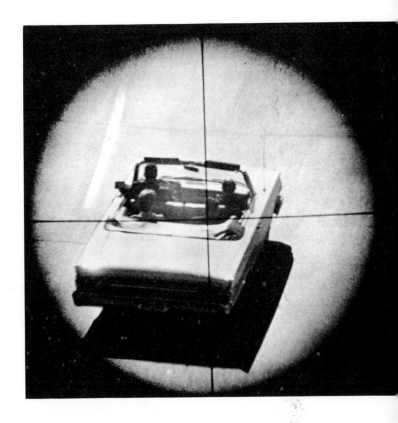

Officially he became President at 2:38 p.m., Central Standard Time, two hours after the assassination, when he took the oath of office (shown below) aboard the presidential jet plane, Air Force One. In the plane, which was on the ground in Dallas, was the body of John F. Kennedy.

The oath was administered by Federal Judge Sarah T. Hughes, the first woman in history to swear in a United States President. About thirty people were crowded in the hot and stuffy cabin of the plane as the new President raised his right hand and repeated after the Judge:

"I do solemnly swear that I will faithfully execute the office of the President of the United States, and will, to the best of my ability, preserve, protect and defend the Constitution of the United States. So help me God."

Johnson then turned and kissed Mrs. Kennedy, whose suit and stockings were still streaked with blood. The crowd began to disperse. "Let's get this plane back to Washington," said the President firmly.

Before the big jet arrived in Washington the Dallas police had a prime suspect in custody charged with the murder of John F. Kennedy. He was Lee Harvey Oswald, a twenty-four-year-old malcontent with a bad record who had been labeled a "potentially dangerous schizophrenic" by a pyschiatrist. The evidence against him was overwhelming: his finger prints were on the murder rifle, paraffin tests on his hands proved that he had fired a weapon, and an order for the rifle was in his handwriting. Furthermore, he worked in the warehouse from which the shots were fired and he was seen there at the time of the shooting. His wife later identified the rifle as his.

The senseless murder of the President fitted perfectly the pattern of Oswald's warped personality. Nevertheless, he did not confess the crime. Two days later while in the hands of the Dallas police, a night club operator named Jack Ruby gunned him down. The killing was seen by millions on television.

A tidal wave of disgust swept across the nation— a nation already shocked, stunned and saddened by the violent death of John F. Kennedy.

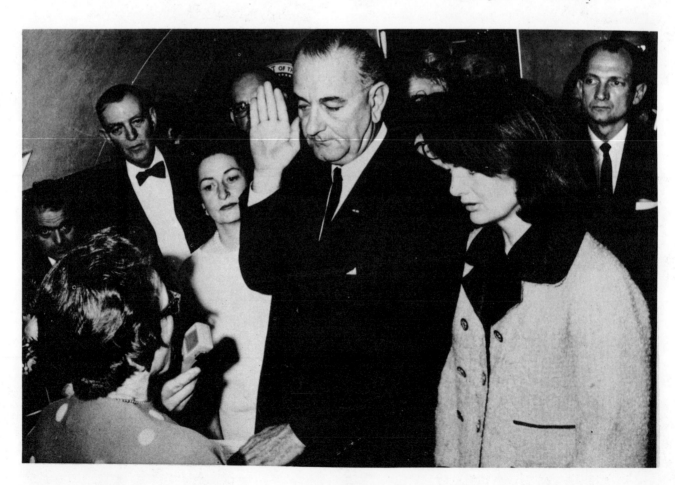

On Sunday afternoon, November 24, the President's casket was placed in the Capitol rotunda, where it lay until the next morning. All afternoon and through the night huge crowds filed by the bier, perhaps 250,000 people in all. It was one of the most impressive demonstrations Washington had ever seen.

On Monday the flag-draped casket was taken to St. Matthews Cathedral and then to Arlington National Cemetery for burial. Untold thousands lined the streets of the city and watched the funeral procession in silence (above). Behind the caisson bearing the President's body was a riderless horse, symbol of a lost leader. Then on foot followed Jacqueline Kennedy, her head high and clear-eyed, in company with other members of the family. Behind them came heads of state and dignitaries of ninety-two foreign nations. (Right) "John-John" Kennedy salutes his father's coffin at the Cathedral.

319

LYNDON BAINES JOHNSON 1908–
PRESIDENT 1963–

President Johnson (above, sitting for his first "formal" portrait at his White House desk a few days after the assassination) was fully aware of his responsibilities from the moment he took the oath of office. He realized that the first thing to be done was to give the nation confidence. "I want the world to know," he said to his aides on Air Force One as the big jet was flying from Dallas to Washington, "that while the leader has fallen, the nation isn't prostrate."

At Andrews Air Force Base in Washington, where the plane landed after a flight of two hours and thirteen minutes, Johnson made his first address as President of the United States. He spoke briefly of the sorrow the tragedy had brought to everyone, then closed with these simple words: "I will do my best. That is all I can do. I ask for your help—and God's."

Johnson did not get to bed until 3:30 a.m. (in his own house, The Elms) but he was up early the next morning and the world was soon told that the new regime would continue the policies of the Kennedy Administration.

That night Johnson, heavily under guard, consulted a procession of advisors, aides, Cabinet members and Congressional leaders. On the phone he spoke to former Presidents Truman and Eisenhower, and numerous high-ranking government officials.

He told the Congressional leaders that he needed their help, that they must put aside party differences for a while. From others he sought advice and listened intently to what they had to say, but at the same time he let them know what he intended to do. It was, he said, to make the transition of power as smooth and orderly as possible. This was his main theme. He kept repeating that there must be unity and continuity in this time of crisis.

321

Although the whole nation mourned, the American people had confidence in the new President and the effortless way in which he assumed the world's most powerful office. They knew he was well qualified for the job, having served in the House and Senate, and as Vice-President. This represented a total of twenty-seven years in Washington.

John F. Kennedy always had a high opinion of him. In 1960 when the two were rivals for the Democratic nomination, Kennedy said: "I know all the other candidates and I think I'm as able to handle the Presidency as any of them, or abler—all except Lyndon, and he hasn't got a chance."

Johnson inherited his interest in politics. His father and grandfather were members of the Texas legislature. The day Lyndon was born (August 27, 1908) in a small frame house on the banks of the Pedernales River near Stonewall, Texas, his grandfather mounted his horse and raced around the county, crying: "A United States Senator has been born today!"

Lyndon went to local public schools, then entered Southwest Texas State Teachers College. After his graduation in 1930, the tall gangling youth taught in Houston's public schools for two years. He came to Washington as secretary to Congressman Richard Kleberg of the famed King Ranch and there met Claudia Taylor (called Lady Bird after a nurse's nickname). He married her in 1934 and quickly started up the political ladder as Congressman and Senator with seven months time out during the war when he saw action in the South Pacific as a Lieutenant Commander in the U.S. Naval Reserve. He came home with a silver star.

A master politician, Johnson became the most powerful and most effective Majority Leader in the history of the Senate. He was a cyclone of energy and it was perhaps because of his unceasing drive that he suffered a near-fatal heart attack in 1955. "It was as bad an attack as a man could have and still live," he said.

Below, the President holds an informal press conference with a small group of reporters in his office.

This picture of the Johnson family was taken shortly after they moved into the White House. The teenage daughters flanking the President and his wife are: Lynda Bird (left) and Luci Baines.

As First Lady of the land, Mrs. Johnson has proved to be a charming and capable hostess. A vivacious, pretty woman with black hair, black eyes and a slim figure, she entertains with a friendly warmth that has delighted Washington. She is a tireless, down-to-earth person and completely natural. A friend has described her as having "the touch of velvet and the stamina of steel."

President Johnson, shown below in a rare moment of relaxation on his LBJ ranch in Texas, moved with swiftness and confidence in his first 100 days in office. He made full use of his boundless energy to project himself as a strong leader, an economizer and a liberal who is determined to save Government money. He successfully achieved this image.

One of his triumphs was the passage of the tax-cutting bill. Johnson drastically cut back the foreign aid program, closed a few military bases and ordered several Government Departments to go on a strict economy basis.

In foreign affairs he exercised caution (note cartoon, right) and relied heavily on the judgements of his aides and Cabinet members. "Swiftness at home, caution abroad," perhaps summarizes his administration. According to polls and political commentators, he gained the approval of the American people.

It was a foregone conclusion that LBJ would be his party's choice for President in the 1964 race, but it was a different story in the Republican camp, where there were several possibilities. As the year got under way, however, it became apparent that the strongest candidate for the nomination was Barry Goldwater, an outspoken conservative and United States Senator from Arizona since 1952.

To the dismay of many Republican moderates, but not to their surprise, Goldwater won the nomination on the first ballot at the party's convention in San Francisco in July (above). The Vice-Presidential candidate was William E. Miller (left), former Congressman of New York and ex-chairman of the Republican National Committee.

325

Above is the scene in the Presidential box overlooking Convention Hall in Atlantic City on August 27, 1964, as Hubert H. Humphrey, LBJ's choice for Vice-President, accepts the nomination on the floor below. In the box (left to right) are: Mrs. Robert F. Kennedy, her husband (who wanted the V-P nomination badly), Lady Bird Johnson, the President (who had been nominated for the Presidency by acclamation), Mrs. Humphrey, and the two Johnson daughters.

Hubert Humphrey, fifty-three-year-old United States Senator from Minnesota since 1948, had made a name for himself as a far-left liberal, an ebullient optimist of great energy and a torrential talker (250 words a minute in his formal speeches) who would willingly discourse on any subject at any time to any audience. Right, the exuberant Humphrey holds aloft an eight-month-old infant.

As the champion of conservatism Goldwater presented his case against deficit spending, the monster paternalistic state, the military draft and the moral corruption of the present administration.

Although his speaking style was flat and unexciting, he aroused a fanatical enthusiasm in his followers. On the other hand — as the above photo indicates — he aroused fear in the hearts of many Americans who saw his fierce anti-Communistic zeal leading us into nuclear war. His opponents made the most of this and also of his unfortunate habit of spouting some ill-chosen words at times (later denied by Goldwater). This undoubtedly lost him millions of votes. Many who agreed with his views lost confidence in him as the campaign progressed. In October all the national polls showed President Johnson an easy winner.

The President had many advantages over Gold-water. He had the prestige of his office and he had made a good record (by trimming the budget and getting the tax reduction and the civil rights bills unsnarled in Congress and finally passed). Furthermore, there was peace and prosperity throughout the country.

As a campaign personality, however, LBJ was uninspiring. He came to life only when he mingled with crowds shaking every hand within reach (shown on the following page). His antics, however, displeased many people.

More serious was the uneasy feeling some people had about his character. Two of his closest associates, Bobby Baker (his former protegé) and Walter W. Jenkins, LBJ's right-hand man, were forced to resign their respective jobs in utter disgrace. This was not the President's fault, of course, but still, people wondered.

Fischetti

'Who else you got?'

They wondered, too, how a man could become a multi-millionaire, as LBJ did, while he was serving the country on the public payrolls. There was never any question about the legality of his fortune, however.

In many quarters there was disenchantment with both candidates, as this cartoon points out. But as the election approached it was obvious that most Americans believed LBJ to be the better qualified of the two.

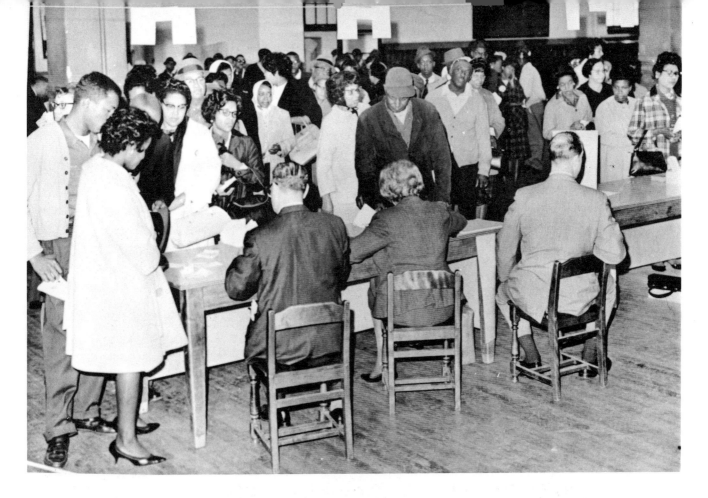

On November 3, 1964, Washington, D.C., residents voted for President (above) for the first time since 1800.

On the same day the President and Lady Bird marked their ballots at Johnson City, Texas, at 8:07 A.M.

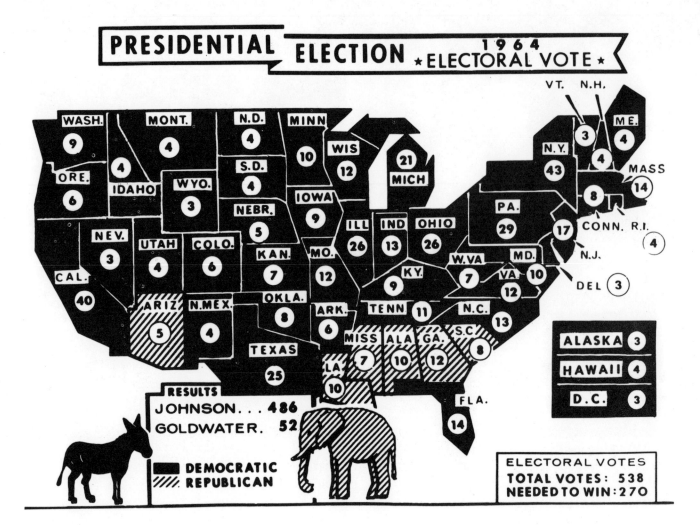

PRESIDENTIAL ELECTION 1964 ★ELECTORAL VOTE★

WASH. 9
ORE. 6
MONT. 4
IDAHO 4
N.D. 4
S.D. 4
WYO. 3
MINN 10
WIS 12
MICH 21
VT. 3
N.H.
N.Y. 43
ME. 4
MASS 14
NEV. 3
UTAH 4
COLO. 6
NEBR. 5
IOWA 9
ILL 26
IND 13
OHIO 26
PA. 29
CONN. 8
R.I. 4
CAL. 40
ARIZ. 5
N.MEX. 4
KAN. 7
MO. 12
KY. 9
W.VA 7
VA 12
MD. 10
N.J. 17
DEL 3
OKLA. 8
ARK. 6
TENN. 11
N.C. 13
S.C. 8
TEXAS 25
LA. 10
MISS 7
ALA 10
GA. 12
FLA. 14

ALASKA 3
HAWAII 4
D.C. 3

RESULTS
JOHNSON... 486
GOLDWATER. 52

DEMOCRATIC
///// REPUBLICAN

ELECTORAL VOTES
TOTAL VOTES: 538
NEEDED TO WIN: 270

Several hours before the Johnsons marked their paper ballots in Texas, the eight registered voters of Dixville Notch, New Hampshire, met and cast their votes. It was one minute after midnight, Election Day morning, when the first returns in the United States were announced from the tiny New Hampshire village: Goldwater 8, Johnson 0. But from there on it was Johnson all the way, all day long.

His smashing victory made history. He won every one of the East's 142 electoral votes, thus becoming the first Democratic President ever to carry Vermont, and the first to win Maine since Woodrow Wilson won it in 1912. He swept the Midwest, the Rocky Mountain States and the Pacific Coast. Only in the deep South and in Arizona, Goldwater's home state, did he fail.

The above map showing his landslide electoral victory is strikingly similar to the 1956 pattern (see page 293) when Republican Dwight Eisenhower won.

The President received more popular votes than any candidate in the nation's history, and his electoral vote margin (486 to 52) was exceeded only by Franklin Roosevelt's record 523-to-8 victory over Alf Landon in 1936.

The smashing victory was what the President had asked for. "I want the mandate of this election to be written strong and clear," he said, "so that none will mistake its meaning."

The meaning was clear to the more than 42,000,-000 voters who supported him, an untold number of whom were Republicans who had defected.

The reason for the landslide was. obvious. The American citizenry knew what they had in President Johnson. They were not so sure what they would get with Goldwater and his suspect trigger finger. They did not want to take that gamble. Basically, it was a vote for peace.

President Lyndon B. Johnson began the year 1965 with one of the most overwhelming mandates the American people had ever given a President. He at

once showed that he meant to use this mandate to accomplish a sweeping change in the American nation and its way of life—a change that would establish what he called the Great Society.

The President told his Cabinet that the Great Society would be achieved both through "imaginative new ideas and programs" and "hard-hitting, tough-minded reforms in existing programs." Then, in his State of the Union Message on January 4, he told the nation that in building the Great Society his aim would be "To keep our economy growing; to open for all Americans the opportunities now enjoyed by most Americans; to improve the quality of life for all."

Lyndon Johnson wasted no time in launching his program—and in doing so he made the American Presidency his own. He moved out from under the shadow of his predecessor, John F. Kennedy, and demonstrated in many ways that he wanted to become one of the nation's great Presidents.

Setting briskly to work, LBJ displayed an amazing, inexhaustible energy that seemed to have all of official Washington running to keep up with him. He sent the new Congress an awesome flood of messages calling for a wide range of legislation touching on every conceivable matter. In just the first six months of 1965, for example, he sent Congress 75 bills, 300 reports, and 200 messages.

To cope with this avalanche, the President had a

331

willing body of legislators in the 89th Congress. At the same time that it elected Lyndon Johnson President, the nation had sent solid Democratic majorities to both houses of Congress. Now LBJ made effective use of these majorities. The photograph shows Mr. Johnson thanking Senator Robert F. Kennedy, brother of the late President, for his help with a part of the Administration program.

And the President was able to add something important of his own—a remarkable arsenal of political and legislative abilities that he had developed during more than two decades spent on both sides of Congress, in the Vice Presidency, and in the White House. All the political know-how, the persuasiveness, the shrewdness that had made LBJ one of the most effective Senate majority leaders in U.S. history now were applied to the problem of getting his legislative program enacted into law.

As LBJ busied himself proposing, urging, prodding, imploring, persuading (his opponents called it "arm-twisting") through the use of talks, speeches,

messages, telephone calls, and personal contacts, Congress acted. By the time the First Session of the 89th Congress adjourned in the fall of 1965, enough far-reaching new laws had been passed to take the nation a fair distance along the path toward the President's cherished Great Society.

Few American Congresses had ever made such a record. It was an impressive achievement by any standard. While opposition voises were labeling the First Session of the 89th a "rubber-stamp" Congress, LBJ, proud and beaming, called it "the fabulous 89th."

Here are a few highlights from the long list of legislation enacted by the First Session of the 89th Congress: In the field of education (the cornerstone of LBJ's Great Society), Federal financing of college scholarships and grants of nearly $4 billion in aid to schools and colleges; in the field of civil rights, a voting-rights law to help Negro citizens take their places on the voting rolls; for the "war on poverty," nearly $3 billion in aid to depressed areas; for the nation's elderly, a $6,500,000,000 Federal health-insurance program (Medicare); for the nation's cities, a new Cabinet post, the Department of Housing and Urban Development; in the field of housing, some $8 billion in financing for new and existing housing

programs; in the field of immigration, a new, liberalized law doing away with the old national-origins quota system; for taxpayers, a $4 billion cut in excise taxes.

But despite this spectacular success in getting his legislative program into the statute books, Mr. Johnson's path was not all smooth. Perhaps the biggest source of anguish and bewilderment for the President and the nation in 1965 was the war in Vietnam. America's participation in this bitter, confusing conflict was stepped up sharply during the year, with the President authorizing a far greater involvement of U.S. troops—such as those seen going ashore, above —and also a greatly expanded campaign of bombing attacks on Communist targets. Bombers were sent over North Vietnam on the President's orders, with LBJ hovering over the entire operation—even to approving the targets and calling the White House war room at 3 a.m. to find out if all planes had returned.

Much criticism was directed at the Administration and the President concerning the war in Vietnam. Demonstrations like the one shown below took place all over the country. And in the field of civil rights, too, Mr. Johnson came in for a good deal of censure,

LOVE... NOT HATE!
BREAD... NOT BOMBS!

At left, Gemini VII is photographed from Gemini VI as the two record-breaking American space ships orbit the earth together. Below, astronauts emerge from Gemini VI after the successful splashdown.

from voices at both ends of the political spectrum. The record of his actions in this field, however, showed that LBJ was putting himself squarely behind the effort to guarantee Negro Americans their full constitutional rights—to "overcome the crippling legacy of bigotry and injustice."

The President put himself and the prestige of his office behind other American efforts as well—notably, the nation's ambitious space program. With vigorous support from the Administration, American space scientists and astronauts made some remarkable achievements during 1965. In July the space-probe rocket Mariner IV, which had been launched in November of 1964, passed within 5,000 miles of the planet Mars and sent back some 20 photographs, enabling man to examine the mysterious red planet from a vantage point 30 miles closer than that provided by the best modern telescopes. In December the United States set a new endurance record for manned space flight when the spacecraft Gemini VII, with two astronauts aboard, orbited the earth for 14 days. During the historic flight a second two-man spacecraft, Gemini VI, was orbited and its pilot flew it to within a few feet of Gemini VII. The nation thus passed a vital milestone in its program to send men to the moon.

President Johnson found time during the year not only for the space program, the war in Vietnam, and the nation's domestic and foreign affairs, but also for important discussions with visiting dignitaries from all parts of the world. His most famous visitor in 1965 was Pope Paul VI (left), who came to New York City to address the U.N. General Assembly.

In sum, Lyndon Johnson showed that he was becoming a forceful President who was not afraid to break new ground and would not hesitate to involve himself directly in the great issues and controversies of our day.

REFERENCE GUIDE

to the

PRESIDENTS OF THE UNITED STATES

★ ★ ★ ★ ★ ★ ★ ★ ★ ★ ★ ★ ★ ★ ★

The Office and Powers of the Presidency
Biographies and Chronologies
Records of Cabinet Members
and Presidential Elections

★ ★ ★ ★ ★ ★

THE OATH OF
THE PRESIDENT

★ ★

★ ★ ★ ★ ★ ★

The Oath of the President was first administered on April 30, 1789, before a cheering crowd in New York City, the nation's first capital. General George Washington listened gravely to the words of the

Oath: "I do solemnly swear (or affirm) that I will faithfully execute the Office of President of the United States, and will to the best of my ability, preserve, protect and defend the Constitution of the United States." Then, holding his right hand on a Bible and his left on his heart, Washington (above) said: "I swear . . . so help me God," and officially became the first President of the United States.

The White House

The official home of the Presidents of the United States stands on a site chosen by George Washington himself. Our first President also approved the architect's plans for the structure, which was to become the first public building constructed in the nation's new capital, the "Federal City" of Washington in the newly created District of Columbia. A French engineer and landscape architect, Major Pierre L'Enfant, produced an imposing plan for the new capital city, and an Irish-born architect named James Hoban was responsible for the design of the White House. Said to be modeled upon the home of the Duke of Leinster in Dublin, Ireland, the Executive Mansion, built of sandstone quarried on Aquia Creek, Va., has a simplicity and an unassuming dignity that seem to belong more to the New World than to the Old.

Although the cornerstone of the mansion he had approved was laid on October 13, 1792, President Washington never lived in the White House. The honor of being the first Chief Executive to occupy it fell to John Adams, who moved into the mansion—which was still not quite finished—in November of 1800. Since that time, under the direction of the nation's Presidents and First Ladies, the White House has become—in the words of Jacqueline Kennedy, wife of President John F. Kennedy—"a showcase of American art and history." Renovated, 1948-52, the White House reflects the good taste and symbolizes the high ideals of the Founding Fathers, as well as of the generations of American Presidents since then.

Powers and Duties of the President

The Presidency of the United States is a many-sided office. The President derives his powers as Chief Executive from the Constitution, but his position as national leader is the most striking feature of the American political system. The President, it has been said, holds eight different positions. He is:

1. Chief of State—the ceremonial head of the U.S. government.

2. Chief Executive—the head of the government, charged with responsibility for the execution of Federal laws and the administration of the government departments and agencies.

3. Chief of foreign affairs—the director of the foreign affairs of the United States and the nation's only representative authorized to negotiate with foreign countries.

4. Chief of the armed forces—the commander-in-chief in war and peace of all U.S. military forces.

5. Chief of legislation—the leader of the nation in whom executive and political power is invested, by custom but not by the Constitution. He proposes to Congress individual measures necessitated by current emergencies or a complete set of laws to achieve the program on which he won election.

6. Chief of his party—the director of the party's political activities and mediator of factional differences, who determines important political appointments.

7. Umpire of national aims and policies—with the Vice-President, he is the only political leader nationally elected; once in the White House, he assumes the role of representative of all the people, formulating a consensus of public opinion.

8. Chief of the free world—the leader of the mightiest power on earth. After World War II, the U.S. President was projected into the leadership of the free world and often was obliged to send American forces into battle without a declaration of war by Congress (constitutionally the prerogative of both Houses) to help defend established governments against Communist aggression.

The specific powers of the President and the responsibilities that relate to the office are set forth in Article II of the Constitution, as follows:

Section 1. The executive Power shall be vested in a President of the United States of America. He shall hold his Office during the Term of four Years, and, together with the Vice President, chosen for the same term, be elected, as follows:

Each State shall appoint, in such Manner as the Legislature thereof may direct, a Number of Electors, equal to the whole Number of Senators and Representatives to which the State may be entitled in the Congress: but no Senator or Representative, or Person holding an Office of Trust or Profit under the United States, shall be appointed an Elector.

The Electors shall meet in their respective States, and vote by Ballot for two Persons, of whom one at least shall not be an Inhabitant of the same State with themselves. And they shall make a List of all the Persons voted for, and of the Number of Votes for each; which List they shall sign and certify, and transmit sealed to the Seat of the Government of the United States, directed to the President of the Senate. The President of the Senate shall, in the Presence of the Senate and House of Representatives, open all the Certificates, and the Votes shall then be counted. The Person having the greatest Number of Votes shall be the President, if such Number be a Majority of the whole Number of Electors appointed; and if there be more than one who have such Majority, and have an equal Number of Votes, then the House of Representatives shall immediately chuse by Ballot one of them for President: and if no Person have a Majority, then from the five highest on the List the said House shall in like Manner chuse the President. But in chusing the President, the Votes shall be taken by States, the Representation from each State having one Vote; A quorum for this Purpose shall consist of a Member or Members from two thirds of the States, and a Majority of all the States shall be necessary to a Choice. In every Case, after the Choice of the President, the Person having the greatest Number of Votes of the Electors shall be the Vice President. But if there should remain two or more who have equal Votes, the Senate shall chuse from them by Ballot the Vice President.

The Congress may determine the Time of chusing the Electors, and the Day on which they shall give their Votes; which Day shall be the same throughout the United States.

No Person except a natural born Citizen, or a Citizen of the United States, at the time of the Adoption of this Constitution, shall be eligible to the Office of President; neither shall any Person be eligible to that Office who shall not have attained to the Age of thirty five Years, and been fourteen Years a Resident within the United States.

In Case of the Removal of the President from Office, or of his Death, Resignation, or Inability to discharge the Powers and Duties of the said Office, the Same shall devolve on the Vice President, and the Congress may by Law provide for the Case of Removal, Death, Resignation or Inability, both of the President and Vice President, declaring what Officer shall then act as President, and such Officer shall act accordingly, until the Disability be removed, or a President shall be elected.

The President shall, at stated Times, receive for his Services, a Compensation, which shall neither be encreased nor diminished during the Period for which he shall have been elected, and he shall not receive within that Period any other Emolument from the United States, or any of them.

Before he enter on the Execution of his Office, he shall take the following Oath or Affirmation:—"I do solemnly swear (or affirm) that I will faithfully execute the Office of President of the United States, and will to the best of my Ability, preserve, protect and defend the Constitution of the United States."

Section 2. The President shall be Commander in Chief of the Army and Navy of the United States, and of the Militia of the several States, when called into the actual Service of the United States; he may require the Opinion, in writing, of the principal Officer in each of the executive Departments, upon any Subject relating to the Duties of their respective Offices, and he shall have Power to grant Reprieves and Pardons for Offences against the United States, except in Cases of Impeachment.

He shall have Power, by and with the Advice and Consent of the Senate, to make Treaties, provided two thirds of the Senators present concur; and he shall nominate, and by and with the Advice and Consent of the Senate, shall appoint Ambassadors, other public Ministers and Consuls, Judges of the supreme Court,

335

and all other Officers of the United States, whose Appointments are not herein otherwise provided for, and which shall be established by Law: but the Congress may by Law vest the Appointment of such inferior Officers, as they think proper, in the President alone, in the Courts of Law, or in the Heads of Departments.

The President shall have Power to fill up all Vacancies that may happen during the Recess of the Senate, by granting Commissions which shall expire at the End of their next Session.

Section 3. He shall from time to time give to the Congress Information of the State of the Union, and recommend to their Consideration such Measures as he shall judge necessary and expedient; he may, on extraordinary Occasions, convene both Houses, or either of them, and in Case of Disagreement between them, with Respect to the Time of Adjournment, he may adjourn them to such Time as he shall think proper; he shall receive Ambassadors and other public Ministers; he shall take Care that the Laws be faithfully executed, and shall Commission all the Officers of the United States.

Section 4. The President, Vice President and all civil Officers of the United States, shall be removed from Office on Impeachment for, and Conviction of, Treason, Bribery, or other High Crimes and Misdemeanors.

Special Powers of the President

Many Federal posts, such as judgeships, cabinet offices, and directorships of agencies, are filled by Presidential nomination but require confirmation by the Senate. Members of the President's "official family," his aides and advisers, however, are appointed by him.

During recess of Congress, the President may recall either or both houses as he deems necessary.

Along with the obligation to sign laws passed by Congress, the President has the right to return any measure he disapproves of to the house of Congress that originated it, outlining his reasons for vetoing it. A two-thirds vote of both houses, however, overrides a Presidential veto, and the measure becomes law without his consent. A measure passed by Congress becomes law without Presidential signature if he takes no action on it within ten days after passage while Congress is in session. A pocket veto is a congressional measure not signed by the President after adjournment of Congress; such a bill does not become law.

Congress may empower the President to take law-making action in certain specific instances without requesting individual measures. Such a right, however, is usually limited to specific powers; and like all laws, such measures are subject to judicial review if challenged.

The President has the power of pardon, which extends to all persons convicted of a Federal offense except one who has been impeached. Absolute pardon forgives all charges; conditional pardon retains certain liabilities; reprieve delays execution of the death sentence.

Emergency Powers of the President

If a situation arises that calls for immediate action to avert a catastrophe, the President can declare a state of emergency. Such cases are rare, however, and limited to—for instance—a threatened invasion by a hostile power, or Federal action in case of a natural disaster. When public order is endangered, the President may at his own discretion federalize the National Guard, send Federal marshals into the affected area, or dispatch units of the armed forces.

Electing the President and Vice-President

Every four years there is an election for President and Vice-President of the United States. The election, actually for members of an electoral college, is held on the Tuesday after the first Monday in November.

Early in an election year—years that are divisible by four—party committees meet (by custom, not by law) to determine the date of their national convention to nominate candidates for President and Vice-President. Later, usually during the spring, primaries are held to choose delegates to the conventions. Presidential aspirants at this time travel through the country to meet with delegates and seek their support at the convention.

Party nominating conventions are usually held in the latter part of the summer, and nominees for the two highest posts are selected by majority vote, which sometimes requires many ballots to achieve. At the same conventions, so-called platforms are written and accepted by the delegates, expounding the party's goals and policies, to which the Presidential and Vice-Presidential nominees are bound, and on which they will seek popular support on Election Day.

After the election, the candidates for President and Vice-President who received the majority of the popular vote are usually elected by the electors, meeting at their respective state capitals on the first Monday after the second Wednesday in December. A majority of electoral votes is required. The votes are counted officially at a joint session of Congress on January 6 following the November election.

On January 20 (formerly on March 4) the President and Vice-President are inaugurated. The Inauguration is usually made an occasion for festivities such as parades, balls, and other celebrations.

Amendments Governing the Presidency

Amendment 12 (Adopted September 25, 1804)

The Electors shall meet in their respective states and vote by ballot for President and Vice-President, one of whom at least, shall not be an inhabitant of the same state with themselves; they shall name in their ballots the person voted for as President, and in distinct ballots the person voted for as Vice-President, and they shall make distinct lists of all persons voted for as President, and of all persons voted for as Vice-President, and of the number of votes for each, which lists they shall sign and certify, and transmit sealed to the seat of the government of the United States, directed to the President of the Senate;—The President of the Senate shall, in the presence of the Senate and House of Representatives, open all the certificates and the votes shall then be counted;—The person having the greatest number of votes for President, shall be the President, if such number be a majority of the whole number of Electors appointed; and if no person have such majority, then from the persons having the highest numbers not exceeding three on the list of those voted for as President, the House of Representatives shall choose immediately, by ballot, the President. But in choosing the President, the votes shall be taken by states, the representation from each state having one vote; a quorum for this purpose shall consist of a member or members from two-thirds of the states, and a majority of all the states shall be necessary to a choice. And if the House of Representatives shall not choose a President whenever the right of choice shall devolve upon them, before the fourth day of March next following, then the Vice-President shall act as President, as in the case of the death or other constitutional disability of the President.—The person having the greatest number of votes as Vice-President, shall be the Vice-President, if such number be a majority of the whole number of Electors appointed, and if no person have a majority, then from the two highest numbers on the list, the Senate shall choose the Vice-President; a quorum for the purpose shall consist of two-thirds of the whole number of Senators, and a majority of the whole number shall be necessary to a choice. But no person constitutionally ineligible to the office of President shall be eligible to that of Vice-President of the United States.

Amendment 20 (Adopted February 6, 1933)

Section 1. The terms of the President and Vice President shall end at noon on the 20th day of January, and the terms of Senators and Representatives at noon on the 3d day of January, of the years in which such terms would have ended if this article had not been ratified; and the terms of their successors shall then begin.

Section 2. The Congress shall assemble at least once in every year, and such meeting shall begin at noon on the 3d day of January, unless they shall by law appoint a different day.

Section 3. If, at the time fixed for the beginning of the term of the President, the President elect shall have died, the Vice President elect shall become President. If a President shall not have been chosen before the time fixed for the beginning of his term, or if the President elect shall have failed to qualify, then the Vice President elect shall act as President until a President shall have qualified; and the Congress may by law provide for the case wherein neither a President elect nor a Vice President elect shall have qualified, declaring who shall then act as President, or the manner in which one who is to act shall be selected, and such person shall act accordingly until a President or Vice President shall have qualified.

Section 4. The Congress may by law provide for the case of the death of any of the persons from whom the House of Representatives may choose a President whenever the right of choice shall have devolved upon them, and for the case of the death of any of the persons from whom the Senate may choose a Vice President whenever the right of choice shall have devolved upon them.

Section 5. Sections 1 and 2 shall take effect on the 15th day of October following the ratification of this article.

Section 6. This article shall be inoperative unless it shall have been ratified as an amendment to the Constitution by the legislatures of three-fourths of the several States within seven years from the date of its submission.

Amendment 22 (Adopted March 1, 1951)

Section 1. No person shall be elected to the office of the President more than twice, and no person who has held the office of President, or acted as President, for more than two years of a term to which some other person was elected President shall be elected to the office of the President more than once. But this Article shall not apply to any person holding the office of President when this Article was proposed by the Congress, and shall not prevent any person who may be holding the office of President, or acting as President, during the term within which this Article becomes operative from holding the office of President or acting as President during the remainder of such term.

Section 2. This article shall be inoperative unless it shall have been ratified as an amendment to the Constitution by the legislatures of three-fourths of the several States within seven years from the date of its submission to the States by the Congress.

Succession to the Presidency

The question of Presidential disability has often been debated, especially at the time of President James Garfield's assassination (almost three months elapsed before his death after he was shot in 1881); President Woodrow Wilson's illness of almost six months; and more recently, President Dwight D. Eisenhower's illnesses. In 1947 Congress passed the Presidential Succession Law in order to bring elected officials first in line to assume Presidential powers. In case of removal, resignation, death, inability, or disqualification of both President and Vice-President, the Act provides that the Speaker of the House of Representatives (after resignation from his elected office) should be next in succession. In case the Speaker could not qualify, succession would devolve (1) upon the President pro tempore of the Senate (after resignation from the Senate), and (2) upon the Cabinet, beginning with the Secretary of State.

In order to clarify succession to the Presidency and Vice-Presidency on a Constitutional basis, Congress, on July 6, 1965, passed and submitted to the States for ratification the following Amendment to the Constitution:

Section 1. In case of the removal of the President from his office or his death or resignation, the Vice President shall become President.

Section 2. Whenever there is a vacancy in the office of the Vice President, the President shall nominate a Vice President who shall take the office upon confirmation by a majority vote of both houses of Congress.

Section 3. Whenever the President transmits to the President pro tempore of the Senate and the Speaker of the House of Representatives his written declaration that he is unable to discharge the powers and duties of his office, and until he transmits to them a written declaration to the contrary, such powers and duties shall be discharged by the Vice President as Acting President.

Section 4. Whenever the Vice President and a majority of either the principal officers of the executive departments or of such other body as Congress may by law provide, transmit to the President pro tempore of the Senate and the Speaker of the House of Representatives their written declaration that the President is unable to discharge the powers and duties of his office, the Vice President shall immediately assume the powers and duties of the office as Acting President.

Thereafter when the President transmits to the President pro tempore of the Senate and the Speaker of the House of Representatives, his written declaration that no inability exists, he shall resume the powers and duties of his office unless the Vice President and a majority of either the principal officers of the executive department or of such other body as Congress may by law provide, transmit within four days to the President pro tempore of the Senate and the Speaker of the House of Representatives their written declaration that the President is unable to discharge the powers and duties of his office. Thereupon Congress shall decide the issue, assembling within 48 hours for that purpose, if not in session. If the Congress, within 21 days after receipt of the latter written declaration, or, if Congress is not in session, within 21 days after Congress is required to assemble, determines by two-thirds vote of both houses that the President is unable to discharge the powers and duties of his office, the Vice President shall continue to discharge the same as Acting President; otherwise, the President shall resume the powers and duties of his office.

★ **GEORGE WASHINGTON (1732-99)** ★ *First President (April 30, 1789-Mar. 3, 1797)*

Born in Westmoreland County, Va., Feb. 22 (Feb. 11, Old Style), 1732. Descendant of John Washington, who emigrated to Virginia from England in 1658. Fifth child and fourth son (in a family of 7 boys and 3 girls) of Augustine Washington (1694-1743), a planter. Father had 3 sons and 1 daughter by his first wife, who died in 1728; George Washington was first child and first son by Mary Ball (1708-89), second wife of Augustine Washington. Educated principally by father and older brother. Episcopalian in religion. Took training as surveyor; was appointed official surveyor of Culpeper County, Va., 1749. Accompanied older brother to island of Barbados, in Caribbean; contracted and survived smallpox there; returned to Virginia; inherited estate of Mount Vernon after older brother's death, 1752. Appointed adjutant of military district in Virginia, 1752; sent by governor of Virginia on hazardous mission into western wilderness; commissioned lieutenant colonel, 1754, and campaigned against French; in 1755 served as aide-de-camp to British General Braddock; as colonel, became commander-in-chief of all Virginia forces in French and Indian War. Returned to civilian life. On Jan. 6, 1759, married Martha Dandridge Custis, 27, a widow, daughter of a planter. Had no children; wife had 4 children by her first marriage, 2 of whom died before her marriage to George Washington. Served in Virginia House of Burgesses, 1758-75; was justice of the peace, Fairfax County, Va., 1760-74. Early associated with the cause of American independence, he served in the Continental Congress; on June 15, 1775, he was elected commander-in-chief of the Continental Army. The ultimate success of the American Revolution, achieved against all probability and despite crushing opposition and discouragements from without and within, was very largely the result of Washington's generalship and his remarkable abilities as a leader of men. After the war's end, he retired to Mount Vernon, 1783. Served as president of Constitutional Convention, 1787; unanimously elected first President of U.S., 1789, John Adams becoming Vice-President. Inaugurated in New York, N.Y., April 30, 1789, at the age of 57. Re-elected for a second term, 1792; inaugurated in Philadelphia, Pa., Mar. 4, 1793, John Adams continuing as Vice-President. As President, Washington devoted himself to consolidating the gains of the Revolution and achieving for the young country both stability at home and stature abroad; when he left the Presidency the U.S. was a firm union, its central government was strong, and its name and credit had begun to command international respect. Declining to serve for a third term, he retired to Mount Vernon; contracting a respiratory infection, he died there on Dec. 14, 1799, at the age of 67. He is buried at Mount Vernon. Washington was tall (6 feet 2 inches) and powerful, with large hands and feet; he was impressive in his poise and dignity. In addition to the famous "Father of His Country," he was called "Sword of the Revolution" and "Sage of Mount Vernon." His wife, born in New Kent County, Va., June 21, 1732, survived him by 2 years. She died on May 22, 1802, at Mount Vernon, and is buried there.

★ **JOHN ADAMS (1735-1826)** ★ *Second President of the United States (Mar. 4, 1797-Mar. 3, 1801)*

Born in Braintree (now Quincy), Mass., Oct. 30, 1735. Great-grandson of Henry Adams, who emigrated to America from England in 1636. Eldest son (in a family of 3 boys) of John Adams (1691-1760), a farmer, and Susanna Boylston (1699-1797). Attended Harvard College; graduated 1755. On Oct. 25, 1764, married Abigail Smith, 19, daughter of a Congregational minister (who performed the marriage). Had 3 sons and 2 daughters; eldest son, John Quincy Adams, became sixth President of U.S. After college, taught school and considered entering Unitarian ministry, but finally studied law. Rose steadily in the legal profession, and just as steadily allied himself with the growing movement for American independence. Led opposition to the Stamp Act; applauded the Boston Tea Party; was a delegate to the Continental Congress, 1774-77, and a signer of the Declaration of Independence. Influential in the choice of George Washington to head Continental Army, Adams was a commissioner to France (along with Benjamin Franklin) during the Revolutionary War, and also was American minister to Holland. At end of war, helped negotiate treaty of peace. Became first U.S. ambassador to England. Elected Vice-President under Washington, 1789, and re-elected with him for second term, 1792. On Washington's retirement, ran for Presidency against Thomas Jefferson, 1796, winning by narrow margin. Inaugurated in Philadelphia, Pa., Mar. 4, 1797, at the age of 61, becoming first President to be sworn in by a Chief Justice. On Nov. 1, 1800, became first President to occupy White House. Adams' term of office (during which, under the existing electoral laws, Jefferson was his Vice-President) was marked by constant political strife. He used great intelligence and resourcefulness to avert a threatening major war with France; he appointed the first Secretary of the Navy and laid the foundations of U.S. sea power. But the repressive Alien and Sedition laws passed, 1798, during his administration were widely unpopular, angered the libertarian opposition, and led to his defeat when he ran for re-election against Jefferson, 1800. He then retired from political life, devoting himself to writing. Years later, had famous correspondence with Jefferson, which lasted until both died on the same day, July 4, 1826. Adams was then nearly 91; no U.S. President has lived longer. He died in Quincy, Mass., and is buried at the First Unitarian Church there. Adams was short (5 feet 7 inches) and plump, and had a somewhat irascible manner. Among his nicknames were "The Atlas of Independence" and "The Father of the American Navy." His wife, a woman of strong and witty character, was born in Weymouth, Mass., Nov. 11, 1744. She died in Quincy, Mass., Oct. 28, 1818; Adams survived her by 7 years. She is buried in Quincy.

★ THOMAS JEFFERSON (1743-1826) ★ *Third President (Mar. 4, 1801-Mar. 3, 1809)*

Born at "Shadwell," Goochland (now Albemarle) County, Va., April 13 (April 2, Old Style), 1743. Welsh in ancestry (according to a family tradition); descendant of Thomas Jefferson, who settled in Virginia before 1677. Third child and eldest son (in a family of 4 boys and 6 girls) of Peter Jefferson (1708-57), a surveyor and land-owner, and Jane Randolph (1720-76). Attended College of William and Mary; graduated 1762. Adhered to no specific religious denomination. Studied law; began practice, 1767. On Jan. 1, 1772, married Martha Wayles Skelton, 23, a widow, daughter of a lawyer and planter. Had 1 son and 5 daughters; wife had 1 son, who died in infancy, by her first husband. Served in Virginia House of Burgesses, 1769-75; gained reputation for literary abilities; served on Virginia Committee of Correspondence and in Continental Congress; wrote first draft of Declaration of Independence, 1776. Served in Virginia House of Delegates, 1776-79; was governor of Virginia, 1779-81. Retired to private life; wrote *Notes on Virginia;* drafted Virginia constitution. Served in Continental Congress, 1783-85; as U.S. minister to France, 1785-89; as first U.S. Secretary of State under Constitution, 1790-93. Retired again to private life. In 1796, ran for President; was defeated by John Adams but, receiving second greatest total of electoral votes, became Vice-President under existing law. Wrote *Manual of Parliamentary Practice,* still basis for U.S. Senate procedure. Ran for President, 1800, and was elected, with Aaron Burr of New York becoming Vice-President. Inaugurated at Washington, D.C., Mar. 4, 1801, at the age of 57. Re-elected for a second term, 1804, with George Clinton of New York becoming Vice-President; inaugurated Mar. 4, 1805. Jefferson's two terms as President saw great territorial expansion of the U.S., notably by acquisition of Louisiana Territory, 1803. Retired once more to "Monticello," his Virginia estate; was principal founder of University of Virginia, 1819, as well as architect of its buildings; served as president of American Philosophical Society, 1797-1815; pursued his lifelong interests of philosophy, science, agriculture, education, and archi-tecture; corresponded at great length with John Adams, the letters ending only with the death of both men on July 4, 1826. Jefferson died at the age of 83, at Monticello, and is buried there. Thomas Jefferson was tall (6 feet 3 inches) and lanky, with reddish hair. He was called "The Father of the University of Virginia," "Old Sachem," and "The Sage of Monticello." His wife, born in Charles City County, Va., Oct. 19, 1748, died Sept. 6, 1782, at Monticello, and is buried there. She was 33; Jefferson survived her by 43 years, never remarrying.

★ JAMES MADISON (1751-1836) ★ *Fourth President (Mar. 4, 1809-Mar. 3, 1817)*

Born in Port Conway, Va., Mar. 16 (Mar. 5, Old Style), 1751. Descendant of James Madison, who emigrated to Virginia from England in 1653. First child and eldest son (in a family of 6 boys and 4 girls) of James Madison (1723-1801), a landowner and farmer, and Eleanor Rose Conway (1731-1829). Attended College of New Jersey (now Princeton University); graduated 1771. Episcopalian in religion. Became active in independence movement in Virginia; was elected to Orange County, Va., Committee of Safety, 1774; served in Virginia Convention, 1776; in Continental Congress, 1780-83. Studied law. Served in Virginia House of Delegates, 1784-86; again in Continental Congress, 1787. Contributed importantly to Federal Constitution, dominating Constitutional Convention of 1787. Served in U.S. House of Representatives, 1789-97; was influential in adoption of Bill of Rights. On Sept. 15, 1794, married Dorothea ("Dolley," or "Dolly") Dandridge Payne Todd, 26, a widow, daughter of a planter. Had no children; wife had 2 sons, one of whom died in infancy, by first marriage. Served as U.S. Secretary of State, 1801-09, during entire Jefferson administration. Upon retirement of President Jefferson, was elected President, 1808, with George Clinton of New York as his Vice-Presidential running mate. Inaugurated Mar. 4, 1809, at the age of 57. Madison's time in office was marked by the War of 1812 and the events leading up to it, and also by the brilliant social seasons conducted by the President's wife. Renominated and re-elected, 1812, with Elbridge Gerry of Massachusetts becoming Vice-President; inaugurated for the second time, Mar. 4, 1813. At the end of his second term, Madison retired to private life. He was active, together with Thomas Jefferson, in founding the University of Virginia; became rector of the university after the death of Jefferson, 1826. Devoting himself to writing, worked on his famous *Journal of the Federal Convention.* He died June 28, 1836, at the age of 85, on his estate of "Montpelier," Va., and is buried there. Madison was small (5 feet 4 inches) and frail, with a wrinkled countenance. He was called "The Father of the Constitution" and "The Sage of Montpelier." His celebrated wife, born in Guilford County, N.C., May 20, 1768, survived him by 13 years. She died in Washington, D.C., July 12, 1849, and is buried at Montpelier.

★ JAMES MONROE (1758-1831) ★ *Fifth President (Mar. 4, 1817-Mar. 3, 1825)*

Born in Westmoreland County, Va., April 28, 1758. Descendant of Andrew Monroe, who emigrated to Virginia from Scotland before 1647. First child and eldest son (in a family of 4 boys and 1 girl) of Spence Monroe (?-1774), a farmer and jurist, and Elizabeth Jones. Attended College of William and Mary; left before graduation to enlist in Continental forces; was wounded in action at Battle of Trenton, 1776; rose to rank of major. Episcopalian in religion. Studied law, 1780-83, under Thomas Jefferson, at that time governor of Virginia; formed lifelong friend-ship with Jefferson. Served in Virginia legislature, 1782-83; in Continental Congress, 1783-86. On Feb. 16, 1786, married Elizabeth Kortright, 17, daughter of a merchant. Had 1 son and 2 daughters. Served in U.S. Senate, 1790-94; was U.S. minister to France, 1794-96; governor of Virginia, 1799-1802. Performed various U.S. diplomatic missions in Europe, 1803-08. Ran for President, 1808; was unsuccessful. Served in Virginia legislature, 1810; was governor of Virginia, 1811; resigned to serve as U.S. Secretary of State, 1811-17; served also as Secretary of War, 1814. Ran for President, 1816, with Daniel D. Tompkins of New York as running mate, and was elected, defeating Rufus King. Inaugurated Mar. 4, 1817, at the age of 58. Re-elected without opposition, 1820, and inaugurated for the second time on Mar. 4, 1821. Monroe's administration was notable for the peace and prosperity the U.S. enjoyed (the "Era of Good Feeling") and for the promulgation of the Monroe Doctrine, 1823. Monroe retired to private life in Loudon County, Va., after leaving the Presidency; joined Board of Visitors, University of Virginia, 1828; served as president of Virginia constitutional convention, 1829. He moved to New York City in 1830; died there, July 4, 1831, at the age of 73. He is buried in Richmond, Va. Monroe was tall (6 feet) and muscular, with large features. The last President of the U.S. to come from the "Virginia Dynasty," he was called "The Last of the Cocked Hats." His wife, born in New York, N.Y., June 30, 1768, died in Oak Hill, Va., Sept. 30, 1830; Madison survived her by less than a year. She is buried in Richmond, Va.

★ JOHN QUINCY ADAMS (1767-1848) ★   *Sixth President (Mar. 4, 1825-Mar. 3, 1829)*

Born in Braintree (now Quincy), Mass., July 11, 1767. Great-great-grandson of Henry Adams, who emigrated to America from England in 1636. Second child and eldest son (in a family of 3 boys and 2 girls) of John Adams (1735-1826), second President of the U.S., and Abigail Smith (1744-1818). Spent much of youth traveling in Europe with his father; attended Harvard College; graduated in 1787. Unitarian in religion. Studied law; began practice, 1790; wrote political pamphlets. Served as U.S. minister to Netherlands, 1794-97. On July 26, 1797, in London, England, married Louisa Catherine Johnson, 22, daughter of U.S. consul in London. Had 3 sons and 1 daughter. Served as U.S. minister in Berlin, Prussia, 1797-1801; returned to practice of law in Boston, Mass.; served in Massachusetts state senate, 1802; in U.S. Senate, 1803-08. Independent in politics. Became professor of rhetoric and oratory, Harvard College, 1806. Served as U.S. minister to Russia, 1809-14. Nominated, 1811, to U.S. Supreme Court; declined. In 1814, served on commission negotiating peace with England to end War of 1812. Served as U.S. minister to England, 1815-17; as U.S. Secretary of State under Monroe, 1817-25. In 1824 Presidential election, was one of 4 candidates; when none received majority in Electoral College, Adams was elected President by U.S. House of Representatives. Inaugurated Mar. 4, 1825, at the age of 57; John Caldwell Calhoun of South Carolina became Vice-President. As President, the nonpartisan Adams involved himself in practically no maneuvering for political advantage, but attempted instead to expand and centralize Federal powers. Ran for re-election, 1828, with Richard Rush of Pennsylvania as running mate; defeated by Andrew Jackson, Adams retired to private life in Massachusetts. Returned to Washington, D.C., to represent his Massachusetts district in U.S. House of Representatives, 1831-48; with his independence, integrity, and formidable intellectual powers, he had one of the most distinguished careers of anyone who ever served in the House of Representatives. Felled by a stroke while on the floor of the House, he died Feb. 23, 1848, at the age of 80, and is buried, with his father, at the first Unitarian Church in Quincy. John Quincy Adams was short (5 feet 7 inches), pudgy, and bald; a forthright, passionate speaker, he was sometimes called "Old Man Eloquent." His wife, born in London, England, Feb. 12, 1775, survived him by 4 years. She died in Washington, D.C., May 14, 1852, and is buried in Quincy, Mass.

★ ANDREW JACKSON (1767-1845) ★   *Seventh President (Mar. 4, 1829-Mar. 3, 1837)*

Born in Waxhaw district, South Carolina, Mar. 15, 1767. Third child (posthumous) and third son of Andrew Jackson (?-1767), a farmer who emigrated to America from Ireland in 1765, and Elizabeth Hutchinson (?-1780). Orphaned by his mother's death when he was 14, he had little formal schooling. Presbyterian in religion. Studied law; began practice, 1787; in 1788 became prosecuting attorney of district in western North Carolina (now Tennessee). In August of 1791, married Rachel Donelson Robards, 24, a divorcee, daughter of a land speculator. Had no children. (Had marriage performed a second time, 1794, upon learning that first ceremony inadvertently had preceded the divorce.) Prospered in land speculation as well as in legal profession; was delegate to Tennessee state constitutional convention, 1796; served in U.S. House of Representatives, 1796-97; in U.S. Senate, 1797-98; was judge of supreme court of Tennessee, 1798-1804; in 1802 became major general of Tennessee militia. In War of 1812, won decisive victory over Creek Indians, 1814; repelled British attempt to take New Orleans, January 1815. Served as first U.S. governor of Florida, 1821; as U.S. Senator from Tennessee, 1823-25. In 1824, ran unsuccessfully for President. Ran again, 1828, with John Caldwell Calhoun of South Carolina as running mate, and was elected, defeating incumbent President John Quincy Adams. Inaugurated Mar. 4, 1829, at the age of 61. Renominated in 1832, with Martin Van Buren of New York as running mate, and re-elected, defeating Henry Clay. Inaugurated for the second time Mar. 4, 1833. During his two terms in office, Jackson greatly enlarged the powers of the Presidency, instituted the "spoils system" of political rewards, increased the influence of the common people in government, and formed what was to become the modern Democratic party. After the end of his second term, he retired to private life at his Nashville, Tenn., estate, "The Hermitage." He died there, of tuberculosis, on June 18, 1845, at the age of 78. He is buried at The Hermitage. Jackson was tall (6 feet 1 inch) and slender, weighing only 140 pounds, with bushy hair. "Old Hickory" was his most famous nickname; he was also called "The Hero of New Orleans" and "The People's President." His wife, born in Halifax County, Va., June 15, 1767, died Dec. 22, 1828, in Nashville, Tenn.; Jackson survived her by 16 years. She is buried at The Hermitage.

★ MARTIN VAN BUREN (1782-1862) ★   *Eighth President (Mar. 4, 1837-Mar. 3, 1841).*

Born in Kinderhook, N.Y., Dec. 5, 1782. Descendant of Cornelis Van Buren, who emigrated to New Netherland from Holland in 1631. Third child and second son (in a family of 4 boys and 1 girl) of Abraham Van Buren (1737-1817), a farmer and innkeeper, and Maria Goes Hoes Van Alen Van Buren (1747-1817). Became law clerk at age of 14; began his own practice in 1803. Dutch Reformed in religion. On Feb. 21, 1807, married Hannah Hoes, 23, a relative of his mother. Had 4 sons. Entered Republican politics; served as county surrogate, 1808-13; New York state senator, 1812-20; U.S. Senator, 1821-28; governor of New York, 1829; U.S. Secretary of State, 1829-31. As Jacksonian Democrat, was nominated for Vice-President, 1832, and elected as running mate of re-elected President Andrew Jackson; served throughout Jackson's second term, March 4, 1833-March 3, 1837. With Richard Mentor Johnson of Kentucky as running mate, ran for President, 1836, and was elected. Inaugurated Mar. 4, 1837, at the age of 54. As President, Van Buren showed great skill at political maneuver and compromise, but he could not overcome the fiscal problems connected with the Panic of 1837, nor could he cope with the slavery question. Ran for re-election, 1840; defeated by William Henry Harrison. Sought Democratic Presidential nomination in 1844, but lost out to James K. Polk. In 1848, as candidate of the Free Soil party (antislavery Democrats), ran for President again; lost to Zachary

Taylor. Retired to Kinderhook, N.Y.; supported Lincoln's policies during Civil War. He died of asthma on July 24, 1862, at the age of 79, in Kinderhook, and is buried there. Van Buren was small (5 feet 6 inches) and erect, with a courtly manner. Among his many nicknames were "Old Kinderhook" and "Wizard of the Albany Regency." His wife, born in Kinderhook, Mar. 8, 1783, died in Albany, N.Y., Feb. 5, 1819; Van Buren survived her by 43 years. She is buried in Kinderhook.

★ WILLIAM HENRY HARRISON (1773-1841) ★ *Ninth President (Mar. 4-April 4, 1841)*

Born at "Berkeley," Charles City County, Va., Feb. 9, 1773. Descendant of Benjamin Harrison, who emigrated to America from England in 1633. Father of John Scott Harrison (1804-78), U.S. Congressman. Grandfather of Benjamin Harrison (1833-1901), twenty-third President. Seventh child and youngest son (in a family of 3 boys and 4 girls) of Benjamin Harrison (1726-91), Revolutionary statesman and signer of Declaration of Independence, and Elizabeth Bassett (1730-92). Episcopalian in religion. Attended Hampden-Sydney College, Va.; later studied medicine; in 1791 entered U.S. army, taking part in action against Indians in Northwest Territory. On Nov. 25, 1795, married Anna Tuthill Symmes, 20, daughter of a judge. Had 6 sons and 4 daughters. In 1800 became governor of Indiana Territory; in 1811 fought famous, though indecisive, engagement with Shawnee Indians of Chief Tecumseh at Tippecanoe. In War of 1812, commanded Army of the Northwest; won important Battle of the Thames against Indians and British in 1813; rose to rank of major general. Elected to Congress from Ohio and served in House of Representatives (1816-19) and Senate (1825-28). Served as U.S. envoy to Colombia, 1828-29. Chosen as Whig party candidate for President, 1836, but lost election to Democrat Martin Van Buren. Nominated again by Whigs in 1840 and, with John Tyler as running mate, defeated President Van Buren; Whig campaign was marked by excesses of wild enthusiasm that set new style for Presidential election campaign. Inaugurated Mar. 4, 1841, at the age of 68. Gave longest inaugural speech in U.S. history. Contracted pneumonia almost immediately and died in the White House on April 4, 1841, after a term of only one month, the shortest served by any President. He is buried in North Bend, Ohio. Harrison was of medium build (5 feet 8 inches), with a narrow, elongated face. "Tippecanoe" was his most famous nickname. His wife, born in Morristown, N.J., July 25, 1775, survived him by 22 years. She died Feb. 25, 1864, in North Bend, Ohio, and is buried there.

★ JOHN TYLER (1790-1862) ★ *Tenth President (April 6, 1841-Mar. 3, 1845)*

Born at "Greenway," Charles City County, Va., Mar. 29, 1790. Descendant of Henry Tyler, who emigrated to Virginia from England before 1650. Sixth child and second son (in a family of 3 boys and 5 girls) of John Tyler (1747-1813), Revolutionary statesman and governor of Virginia, and Mary Marot Armistead (1761-97). Attended (from age of 12) College of William and Mary; graduated 1807. Episcopalian in religion. Studied law under father; began practice at age of 19. Served in Virginia state legislature, 1811-16. On Mar. 29, 1813, married Letitia Christian, 22, daughter of a planter. Had 3 sons and 5 daughters. Elected to U.S. House of Representatives, 1816, and served until 1821; returned to Virginia legislature, 1823-25; was governor of Virginia, 1825-27; served as U.S. Senator, 1827-36. In 1836 was unsuccessful Whig candidate for Vice-Presidency; returned to Virginia legislature in 1839. As running mate of Whig candidate William Henry Harrison, was elected Vice-President, 1840. On death of President Harrison, was sworn in as President, April 6, 1841, at the age of 51. First man ever to succeed to Presidency by death of incumbent, Tyler found many reluctant to accept him as full President, but he firmly asserted his right to the office. As President, he alienated his cabinet and the Whig party by vetoing legislation. Held strong states'-rights views; was morally opposed to slavery but believed that as long as it existed slaveowners were legally entitled to their "property." During term of office his wife, born at "Cedar Grove," New Kent County, Va., Nov. 12, 1790, died in the White House, Sept. 10, 1842. She is buried in Cedar Grove, Va. On June 26, 1844, Tyler married Julia Gardiner, 24, daughter of a New York legislator. Had 5 sons and 2 daughters. At end of term, retired to private life in Virginia. Returned to Washington in 1861 as chairman of states' convention seeking way to avert approaching Civil War. Later, supported secession of Virginia from Union and was elected to Confederate Congress. Died on Jan. 18, 1862, at the age of 71, in Richmond, Va., and is buried there. A tall, thin man, Tyler was called "Young Hickory" and "The Accidental President." His second wife, born in Gardiners Island, N.Y., May 4, 1820, survived him by 27 years. She died July 10, 1889, in Richmond, Va., and is buried there.

★ JAMES KNOX POLK (1795-1849) ★ *Eleventh President (Mar. 4, 1845-Mar. 3, 1849)*

Born in Mecklenburg County, N.C., Nov. 2, 1795. Descendant of Robert Bruce Polk, of Scotch-Irish ancestry, who emigrated to Maryland from Ireland before 1700. First child and eldest son of Samuel Polk (1772-1827), a farmer, and Jane Knox (1776-1852). Attended University of North Carolina; graduated 1818. Studied law; in 1820 began practice in Columbia, Tenn. Presbyterian in religion. On Jan. 1, 1824, married Sarah Childress, 20, daughter of a planter. Had no children. Member of Tennessee house of representatives, 1823-25; in U.S. House of Representatives, 1825-39; was Speaker of House, 1835-39. Left Congress to serve as governor of Tennessee, 1839-41. Ran for re-election as governor in 1841 and 1843; was defeated both times. In 1844, received Democratic nomination for Presidency as "dark horse," breaking convention deadlock. With George Mifflin Dallas of Pennsylvania as running mate, defeated Whig Henry Clay in Presidential election. Inaugurated Mar. 4, 1845, at the age of 49, becoming youngest Chief Executive up to that time. As President, Polk set himself four major goals and accomplished all of them: settlement of Oregon boundary question; reduction of tariff; creation of independent U.S. Treasury; and acquisition of California. At the end of his term of office, having no desire to seek re-election, he retired to private life. He died a few months later, of an intestinal disorder, at the age of 53, in Nashville, Tenn., and is buried there. Polk was about medium height (5 feet 8 inches), with sensitive, fine features. "Napoleon of the Stump" was one of his nicknames. His wife, born in Murfreesboro, Tenn., Sept. 4, 1803, survived him by 42 years. She died Aug. 14, 1891, in Nashville, Tenn., and is buried there.

★ **ZACHARY TAYLOR (1784-1850)** ★ *Twelfth President (Mar. 4, 1849-July 9, 1850)*

Born at "Montebello," Orange County, Va., Nov. 24, 1784. Descendant of James Taylor, who emigrated to America from England before 1640. Third child and third son (in a family of 6 boys and 3 girls) of Richard Taylor (1744-1829), a Revolutionary officer and farmer, and Sarah Dabney Strother (1760-1822). Educated by tutor on father's plantation, Jefferson County, Ky. Episcopalian in religion. In 1808 received appointment as first lieutenant of infantry; became captain in 1810. On June 21, 1810, married Margaret Mackall Smith, 21, daughter of a planter. Had 1 son and 5 daughters. In War of 1812, fought successful engagement with Indians at Fort Harrison on the western frontier and was made major. Served in Illinois and Indiana territories; rose to rank of colonel; led troops in Black Hawk War, 1832; campaigned against Seminole Indians in Florida, 1837-40; became brigadier general, 1838. In Mexican War, won several important early battles, 1846; was promoted to major general by President Polk. On Feb. 23, 1847, though outnumbered 4 to 1, defeated forces of Mexican general Santa Anna at Buena Vista to end war. Nominated for Presidency by Whig party, 1848. With Millard Fillmore as running mate, won election, defeating Lewis Cass, candidate of Democratic party, and Martin Van Buren, candidate of Free Soil party. Inaugurated Mar. 4, 1849, at the age of 64. Originally pro-slavery in his views, Taylor as President opposed the extension of slavery, alienating his Southern supporters. On July 4, 1850, a hot day, he drank copiously of iced water and milk, and ate cherries; contracting cholera morbus, he died on July 9, in the White House, at the age of 65. He is buried in Springfield, Ky. Taylor was of about medium height (5 feet 8 inches) and of stocky build, with black hair. Along with his most famous nickname, "Old Rough and Ready," he was called "Old Zack." His wife, born in Calvert County, Md., Sept. 21, 1788, survived him by 2 years; she died on Aug. 18, 1852, in Pascagoula, La. She is buried in Springfield, Ky.

★ **MILLARD FILLMORE (1800-74)** ★ *Thirteenth President (July 10, 1850-Mar. 3, 1853)*

Born in Locke, N.Y., Jan. 7, 1800. Descendant of James Fillmore, of English ancestry, who lived in Massachusetts about 1700. Second child and eldest son (in a family of 6 boys and 3 girls) of Nathaniel Fillmore (1771-1863), a farmer, and Phoebe Millard (1780-1831). Studied law; in 1823 was admitted to bar and began practice. Unitarian in religion. On Feb. 5, 1826, married Abigail Powers, 27, daughter of a Baptist clergyman. Had 1 son and 1 daughter. Entering politics, was elected in 1828 to New York legislature; in 1832 was elected to U.S. House of Representatives on Anti-Mason ticket; served one term. Became Whig, serving again in U.S. House of Representatives, 1837-43; in 1844 ran unsuccessfully for governor of New York. Elected Vice-President, 1848, as running mate of Zachary Taylor. On the death of President Taylor, was sworn in as President, July 10, 1850, at the age of 50. Fillmore's administration was marked by his attempts to achieve compromise between pro-slavery and anti-slavery positions. These attempts won him the approval of neither side, and he failed to achieve renomination by the Whig party in 1852. His wife, born in Stillwater, N.Y., Mar. 13, 1798, died in Washington, D.C., Mar. 30, 1853; she is buried in Buffalo, N.Y. Fillmore ran for Presidency in 1856 as candidate of American, or Know-Nothing, party; was badly defeated. Retired from politics. On Feb. 10, 1858, married Caroline Carmichael McIntosh, 44, a widow. Had no children. Became chancellor of University of Buffalo; helped found Buffalo General Hospital. Died Mar. 8, 1874, at age of 74, in Buffalo, and is buried there. Fillmore was of medium height (5 feet 9 inches) and extremely distinguished appearance. "Louis Philippe" was one of his nicknames. His second wife, born in Morristown, N.J., Oct. 21, 1813, survived him by 7 years. She died Aug. 11, 1881, in Buffalo, N.Y., and is buried there.

★ **FRANKLIN PIERCE (1804-69)** ★ *Fourteenth President (Mar. 4, 1853-Mar. 3, 1857)*

Born in Hillsborough (now Hillsboro), N.H., Nov. 23, 1804. English in ancestry. Seventh child and fourth son (in a family of 5 boys and 4 girls) of Benjamin Pierce (1757-1839), Revolutionary soldier and statesman. Father had 1 girl by first wife, who died in 1788; Franklin Pierce was sixth child and fourth son by Anna Kendrick (1768-1838), second wife of Benjamin Pierce. Attended Bowdoin College, Brunswick, Me.; graduated 1824. Episcopalian in religion. Studied law; was admitted to New Hampshire bar, 1827. Entered politics as Democrat, in 1829, during father's term of office as governor of New Hampshire; served in state legislature, 1829-33. On Nov. 19, 1834, married Jane Means Appleton, 28, daughter of a Congregational minister and educator. Had 3 sons. Served in U.S. House of Representatives, 1833-37; U.S. Senate, 1837-42. Returning to New Hampshire, practiced law and was active in local Democratic politics. In 1846, declined appointment by President Polk as U.S. Attorney General. In Mexican War, rose to rank of brigadier general. Became Democratic party candidate for Presidency in 1852 and, with William Rufus De Vane King of Alabama as his running mate, was elected. Inaugurated Mar. 4, 1853, at the age of 48, becoming youngest man to serve as President up to that time, and also first President to be born in nineteenth century. As chief executive, Pierce took a generally pro-Southern course. Campaigned for renomination but was unsuccessful; retired to New Hampshire. In Civil War, opposed Federal policies. He died of a stomach disorder, Oct. 8, 1869, at the age of 64, in Concord, N.H., and is buried there. Pierce was of medium build (5 feet 10 inches) and extremely attractive appearance; one of his nicknames was "Handsome Frank." His wife, born in Hampton, N.H., Mar. 12, 1806, died in Andover, Mass., Dec. 2, 1863; Pierce survived her by 5 years. She is buried in Concord, N.H.

★ **JAMES BUCHANAN (1791-1868)** ★ *Fifteenth President (Mar. 4, 1857-Mar. 3, 1861)*

Born near Mercersburg, Pa., April 23, 1791. Scotch-Irish in ancestry. Second child and eldest son (in a family of 5 boys and 6 girls) of James Buchanan (1761-1821), a storekeeper and farmer who emigrated to America from Ireland in 1783, and Elizabeth Speer (1767-1833). Attended Dickinson College; graduated 1809. Presbyterian in religion. Studied law; began practice in 1812 and rose swiftly in legal profession, prospering and acquiring reputation as orator. Entered politics as Federalist; served in Pennsylvania house of representatives, 1814-15; in U.S. House of Representatives, 1821-31. In 1824 joined Democratic party. Served as U.S. minister to Russia, 1832-33; U.S. Senator, 1834-45; U.S. Secretary of State, 1845-49; U.S. minister to Great Britain, 1853. Made several attempts,

1844-56, to gain Democratic nomination for Presidency; received the nomination in 1856 and, with John Cabell Breckinridge of Kentucky as his running mate, was elected President. Inaugurated Mar. 4, 1857, at the age of 65. As President, Buchanan carried on a strong foreign policy and, among other measures, negotiated a treaty of commerce with China. Domestically, however, he attempted to appease both Northern and Southern elements, with a marked lack of success. Not renominated in 1860; supported unsuccessful campaign of his Vice-President. Retired to Pennsylvania farm; supported the Union in Civil War. He died of rheumatic gout on June 1, 1868, at the age of 77, in Lancaster, Pa., and is buried there. Buchanan was tall (6 feet) and burly. Among his nicknames were "Old Buck" and "The Bachelor President." He was the only President who never married.

★ **ABRAHAM LINCOLN (1809-65)** ★   *Sixteenth President (Mar. 4, 1861-April 15, 1865)*

Born in a log cabin on "Sinking Spring Farm," Hardin (now Larue) County, Ky., Feb. 12, 1809. Descendant of Samuel Lincoln, who emigrated to Massachusetts from England in 1637. Second child and first son (in a family of 2 boys and 1 girl) of Thomas Lincoln (1778-1851), a farmer and carpenter, and Nancy Hanks (1784-1806). Father's second wife, Sarah Bush Johnston (1784-1818), had an important, loving influence on the young boy. Lincoln had less than a year of formal schooling; adhered to no specific religious denomination. Family moved to Indiana (1816) and then Illinois (1830). As boy and young man, Lincoln worked at various frontier occupations; strove to educate himself through reading; made two river-flatboat trips to New Orleans, 1828 and 1831. Worked as rail-splitter, mill manager, storekeeper, handyman, village postmaster, surveyor. Served in Black Hawk War, 1832, as captain of militia company. Studied law in spare time; was admitted to bar, 1836. Served in Illinois state legislature, as Whig, 1834-41. Courtship of Ann Rutledge (1816-35) in New Salem, Ill., has become legendary. On Nov. 4, 1842, married Mary Todd, 23, daughter of a banker. Had four sons. Served in U.S. House of Representatives, 1847-49; campaigned for Zachary Taylor in Massachusetts, 1848. Retired to Springfield, Ill., law practice, 1849-54, gaining prominence as lawyer. Re-entered politics, 1854; failed in attempt to receive Whig party nomination for U.S. Senator, 1855. Became Republican, 1856; rose to leadership of party in Illinois; received considerable support for Vice-Presidential nomination, 1856, though failed to be nominated. Running for U.S. Senate, 1858, had famous series of debates with Democratic opponent, Stephen A. Douglas. Although unsuccessful in the ensuing election, he achieved national stature through the debates. In 1860 received Republican party nomination for Presidency. Was elected with Hannibal Hamlin of Maine as his running mate, defeating Stephen A. Douglas, candidate of Northern Democrats, John C. Breckinridge, candidate of Southern Democrats, and John Bell, Constitutional Union party candidate. Inaugurated Mar. 4, 1861, at the age of 52. Civil War broke out very soon thereafter; Lincoln coped with it first as an "insurrection," then as a full-scale war, expanding his executive powers to control the situation. Confronted with resistance and dissension within the government and with discouraging losses by Northern armies, Lincoln strove tirelessly and brilliantly for a victory of arms and a reunification of the divided nation. Extremist demands for complete emancipation of the slaves, without compensation to slaveholders, he countered with a preliminary proclamation on slavery Sept. 22, 1862; nominally freed 4,000,000 slaves with Emancipation Proclamation, Jan. 1, 1863. Before and during his time as President, he produced in his speeches and writings some of the most memorable literary expressions in the English language, including famous Gettysburg Address, Nov. 19, 1863, in which he eloquently expressed the meaning of the national struggle. As a man, Lincoln became a peculiarly American symbol of dedication to the cause of humanitarian justice, freedom, and true democracy. He was renominated in 1864, with Andrew Johnson of Tennessee as his running mate, and was re-elected, defeating Democrat George B. McClellan and Independent Republican candidate John C. Frémont. Inaugurated Mar. 4, 1865, for the second time. On April 14, 1865, less than a week after the final Confederate surrender at Appomattox, he was shot by John Wilkes Booth while attending a theatrical performance in Washington, D.C. He died the next morning, at the age of 56. He is buried in Oak Ridge Cemetery, Springfield, Ill. Lincoln was very tall (6 feet 4 inches) and gaunt, with black hair and beard, sunken eyes, and a deeply lined face. In addition to the famous "Honest Abe," Lincoln had many nicknames, including "The Rail-splitter," "The Great Emancipator," "Father Abraham," "The Man of the People," and "The Martyr President." His wife, born in Lexington, Ky., Dec. 13, 1818, survived him by 17 years. She died July 16, 1882, in Springfield, Ill., and is buried there.

★ **ANDREW JOHNSON (1808-75)** ★   *Seventeenth President (April 15, 1865-Mar. 3, 1869)*

Born in Raleigh, N.C., Dec. 29, 1808. English in ancestry. Third child and second son (in a family of 2 boys and 1 girl) of Jacob Johnson (1778-1812), a sexton, and Mary McDonough (1783-1856). Never attended any school. Served apprenticeship to tailor; worked at tailoring trade in North Carolina, then moved to Tennessee. Adhered to no specific religious denomination. On May 17, 1827, married Eliza McCardle, 16, daughter of a shoemaker. Had 3 sons and 2 daughters. Attempted to educate himself, aided by his wife; entered politics; was alderman of Greeneville, Tenn., 1828-30; mayor, 1830-33. Served in Tennessee state legislature, 1835-37, 1839-43; in U.S. House of Representatives, 1843-53. Was governor of Tennessee, 1853-57; served in U.S. Senate, 1857-62; was military governor of Tennessee, 1862-65. Although a Democrat, he received the 1864 Republican party nomination for the Vice-Presidency, as running mate of Abraham Lincoln. After Lincoln's re-election in 1864, Johnson was inaugurated as Vice-President, Mar. 4, 1865, at the age of 56. Upon the death of President Lincoln, he was sworn in as President, April 15, 1865. Johnson made an effort to carry forward Lincoln's programs, but his time as President was marked by bitter political strife, culminating in his impeachment and trial in the U.S. Senate, 1868. He was acquitted by one vote and served out his term. Receiving no party's nomination for the Presidency in the coming election, he returned to Tennessee, 1869, and entered local politics. In 1872, he ran unsuccessfully for the U.S. House of Representatives; in 1874, he was re-elected to the U.S. Senate, where he served until his death, of a paralytic attack, on July 31, 1875, at the age of 66. He died at Carter's Station, Tenn., and is buried in the Andrew Johnson National Cemetery, Greeneville, Tenn. Johnson was of medium height (5 feet 10 inches) and build, with dark hair and complexion. Among his nicknames were "The Father of the Homestead Act" (he was influential in the drafting and passage of the law in 1862), "The Tennessee Tailor," and "Old Andy." His wife, born in Leesburg, Tenn., Oct. 14, 1810, survived him by less than 6 months. She died in Greene County, Tenn., Jan. 15, 1876, and is buried in Greeneville.

★ **ULYSSES SIMPSON GRANT (1822-85)** ★ *Eighteenth President (Mar. 4, 1869-Mar. 3, 1877)*

Born in Point Pleasant, Ohio, April 27, 1822, and named Hiram Ulysses Grant. Descendant of Matthew Grant who emigrated to Massachusetts from England in 1630. First child and eldest son (in a family of 3 boys and 3 girls) of Jesse Root Grant (1794-1873), a tanner, and Hannah Simpson (1798-1883). Changed name to Ulysses Hiram Grant; attended U.S. Military Academy, West Point, N.Y., changing name again, to Ulysses Simpson Grant; graduated 1843. Served in Mexican War under generals Zachary Taylor and Winfield Scott; rose by 1853 to rank of captain. Methodist in religion. On Aug. 22, 1848, married Julia Boggs Dent, 22, daughter of a judge. Had 3 sons and 1 daughter. Resigned from army, 1854; followed various occupations. After outbreak of Civil War, returned to military service, becoming brigadier general, 1861. Commanding Union troops in a series of important victories, he was elevated to major general; given command over a larger area of operations, he further distinguished himself and was made lieutenant general. On Mar. 9, 1864, President Lincoln appointed him commander of all Union armies. Grant's strategy resulted in the fall of Richmond and the final surrender of Robert E. Lee, commander-in-chief of Confederate forces, April 9, 1865. Commissioned General of the Army after the war, Grant supervised troop demobilization and administered Reconstruction Acts; served as ad interim U.S. Secretary of War (under President Johnson), 1867-68. In 1868, was nominated for Presidency by Republican party and, with Schuyler Colfax of Indiana as running mate, defeated Democrat Horatio Seymour. Inaugurated Mar. 4, 1869, at the age of 46, becoming youngest President up to that time. Renominated and re-elected, in 1872, with Henry Wilson of Massachusetts as running mate, defeating Horace Greeley, candidate of Democratic and Liberal Republican parties. Grant's two terms in office were flawed by scandals; though no scandal touched him personally, he has been criticized for appointing little-qualified or unworthy persons to public office. Refusing to run for a third term, he retired to private life; traveled widely in Europe; on his return in 1879, figured briefly in third-term movement, which collapsed. In later life suffered financial reverses; wrote memoirs (published posthumously). He died of cancer of the throat on July 23, 1885, at the age of 63, in Mount McGregor, N.Y. He is buried in New York City, in Grant's Tomb. Grant was a heavy-featured, unkempt man of about medium height (5 feet 9 inches), wearing a full beard. "Unconditional Surrender" and "Hero of Appomattox" were among his nicknames. His wife, born in St. Louis, Mo., Jan. 26, 1826, survived him by 17 years. She died in Washington, D.C., Dec. 14, 1902, and is buried with her husband in Grant's Tomb.

★ **RUTHERFORD BIRCHARD HAYES (1822-93)** ★ *Nineteenth President (Mar. 3, 1877-Mar. 3, 1881)*

Born in Delaware, Ohio, Oct. 4, 1822. Descendant of George Hayes, who emigrated to Connecticut from Scotland in 1680. Fifth child (posthumous) and youngest son (in a family of 3 boys and 2 girls) of Rutherford Hayes (1787-1822), a farmer, and Sophia Birchard (1792-1866). Attended private schools in Ohio and Connecticut, then attended Kenyon College; graduated 1842. Methodist in religion. Went to Harvard Law School; was admitted to Ohio bar; from 1845 practiced law in Lower Sandusky (later Fremont), Ohio; in 1850 moved practice to Cincinnati, Ohio. Entered politics in 1851 as Whig; in 1855 became Republican. On Dec. 30, 1852, married Lucy Ware Webb, 21, daughter of a physician. Had 7 sons and 1 daughter. Elected city solicitor of Cincinnati, 1858. In Civil War, made recruiting speeches for Union Army, then entered army in 1861 as major; rose to rank of major general. Served in U.S. House of Representatives, 1864-67; elected governor of Ohio, 1867; re-elected, 1869. Ran unsuccessfully for Congress in 1872, but in 1875 was re-elected governor. In 1876, with William Almon Wheeler of New York as Vice-Presidential candidate, ran for Presidency against Democrat Samuel J. Tilden. First disputed Presidential election in U.S. history; Tilden appeared the winner, but his triumph was converted by partisan control of Electoral Commission into Hayes victory. Inaugurated Mar. 3, 1877, at the age of 54. As President, Hayes withdrew Federal occupation troops from South, pressed for civil-service reform, and followed conservative fiscal policies. Declining to serve more than one term, retired to his Ohio home and devoted rest of his life to educational and philanthropic pursuits. He died of a heart attack on Jan. 17, 1893, at the age of 70, in Fremont, Ohio, and is buried there. Hayes was of medium height (5 feet 9 inches) and thick-set, with dark hair and a full beard. "Granny" was one of his nicknames. His wife was known as "Lemonade Lucy," because of her policy of serving no alcohol in the White House. Born in Chillicothe, Ohio, Aug. 28, 1831, she died three years before her husband, on June 25, 1889, in Fremont, Ohio, and is buried there.

★ **JAMES ABRAM GARFIELD (1831-81)** ★ *Twentieth President (Mar. 4, 1881-Sept. 19, 1881)*

Born in a log cabin at Orange, Ohio, Nov. 19, 1831. Descendant of Edward Garfield, who emigrated· to America from England in 1630. Fifth child and youngest son (in a family of 3 boys and 2 girls) of Abram Garfield (1799-1833), a farmer-pioneer, and Elizabeth Ballou (1801-88). Fatherless from age of 2, he grew up under conditions of poverty and hardship. Held various frontier jobs, including working on Ohio canal. Studied at Western Reserve Eclectic Institute (later Hiram College), then attended Williams College; graduated 1856. Returned to Eclectic Institute as teacher of classics; became principal. On Nov. 11, 1858, married Lucretia Rudolph, 26, daughter of a farmer, and a friend since childhood. Had 5 sons and 2 daughters. Member of Disciples of Christ Church; practiced as lay preacher. Elected, as Republican, to Ohio state senate, 1859. Studied law; was admitted to bar, 1860. In Civil War, distinguished himself as recruiter of troops, field commander, strategist, and high staff officer in Union Army; rose to rank of major general. While still in army, ran successfully for Congress from Ohio; served in U.S. House of Representatives, 1863-80. Gained fame as orator and advocate of "sound money" policies; grew in influence, becoming Republican leader of House and even surviving suspicion of wrongdoing in Crédit Mobilier scandal. Was elected to the U.S. Senate in 1880, but before taking seat attended Republican Presidential nominating convention and unexpectedly was chosen as compromise candidate, breaking a 35-ballot deadlock. With Chester A. Arthur as running mate, was elected President in 1880, defeating Democrat Winfield Scott Hancock. Immediately became involved in stormy conflict within party over political patronage. Inaugurated Mar. 4, 1881; a few months later was shot, July 2, 1881, by a possibly demented office-seeker, Charles J. Guiteau. Died 11 weeks later, Sept. 19, 1881, in Elberon, N.J., at the age of 49. He is buried in Cleveland, Ohio. Garfield was burly, 6 feet tall, and heavily bearded. "Canal Boy" was one of his nicknames. His wife's nickname was "Crete." Born in Hiram, Ohio, April 19, 1832, she survived him by 36 years, never remarrying. She died March 13, 1918, in Pasadena, Calif., and is buried in Cleveland, Ohio.

★ **CHESTER ALAN ARTHUR (1830-86)** ★ *Twenty-first President (Sept. 20, 1881-Mar. 3, 1885)*

Born in Fairfield, Vt., Oct. 5, 1830. Fifth child and eldest son (in a family of 3 boys and 6 girls) of William Arthur (1797-1875), a Baptist clergyman who emigrated to America from Ireland about 1815, and Malvina Stone (1802-69). Attended Union College; graduated 1848. Baptist in religion. Taught school, then studied law. Achieved considerable success as lawyer; became active in Republican politics. On Oct. 25, 1859, married Ellen Lewis Herndon, 22, daughter of U.S. naval officer. Had 2 sons and 1 daughter. During Civil War, performed important administrative duties in N.Y. State. Appointed Collector of Port of New York, 1871, by President Grant; removed in 1878 by President Hayes, who thus sought to diminish influence of Senator Roscoe Conkling, political boss of New York State. After Garfield received Republican Presidential nomination, 1880, Arthur became Vice-Presidential candidate in party move to retain Conkling's support. As product of New York political machine, lacked public respect, but was admired for his dignified conduct during 11-week period of President Garfield's lingering death after assassin's attack. Sworn in as President Sept. 20, 1881, at the age of 50, Arthur conducted an administration of integrity, disavowing his earlier and less admirable political associations. Prosecuted "Star Route" postal frauds; attempted to eradicate spoils system in Federal government; sponsored thoroughgoing civil-service reform; launched long-needed modernization of U.S. Navy. Sought a second term as President, but 1884 Republican nominating convention chose James G. Blaine instead. Retired from politics, intending to resume law practice, but died of cerebral hemorrhage in New York City on Nov. 18, 1886, at age of 56. He is buried in Albany, N.Y. Arthur was tall (6 feet 2 inches) and of imposing appearance, with mustache and side whiskers. Addicted to fashionable clothes, he was called "Elegant Arthur" and "The Dude." As his wife (born in Fredericksburg, Va., Aug. 30, 1837) had died in New York City on Jan. 12, 1880, before he assumed the Presidency, a married sister, Mary Arthur McElroy, acted as official White House hostess.

★ **GROVER CLEVELAND (1837-1908)** ★ *Twenty-second and Twenty-fourth President (Mar. 4, 1885-Mar. 3, 1889 and Mar. 4, 1893-Mar. 3, 1897)*

Born in Caldwell, N.J., Mar. 18, 1837, and named Stephen Grover Cleveland. Descendant of Moses Cleveland, who emigrated to Massachusetts from England in 1635. Fifth child and third son (in a family of 4 boys and 5 girls) of Richard Falley Cleveland (1804-53), a Presbyterian clergyman, and Anne Neal (1806-82). Dropped "Stephen" from his name. Studied law; was admitted to bar, 1859; served as assistant district attorney of Erie County, N.Y., 1863-65; sheriff of Erie County, 1871-74; mayor of Buffalo, N.Y., 1882; governor of New York, 1883-85. In 1884 he received the Democratic nomination for the Presidency; with Thomas Andrew Hendricks of Indiana as running mate, defeated Republican James G. Blaine in Presidential election. Inaugurated Mar. 4, 1885, at the age of 47. As President, Cleveland added to the reputation he already enjoyed for forthright, nonpartisan integrity. On June 2, 1886, he married (in the White House) Frances Folsom, 21, daughter of a lawyer. Had 2 sons and 3 daughters. Running for re-election in 1888, Cleveland was defeated by Republican Benjamin Harrison. He then retired to private life. In 1892 he was again nominated for the Presidency by the Democratic party; with Adlai Ewing Stevenson of Illinois as his running mate, he defeated incumbent President Harrison and re-entered the Presidency. Inaugurated for the second time, Mar. 4, 1893, at the age of 55. Cleveland's second term was marked by financial problems and labor unrest, notably the Panic of 1893 and the 1894 Pullman Company strike. At the end of his term he retired a second time to private life. He settled in Princeton, N.J., devoting himself to lecturing and writing; became a trustee of Princeton University, 1901. He died on June 24, 1908, at the age of 71, in Princeton, N.J., and is buried there. Cleveland was of slightly more than medium height (5 feet 11 inches) and of great bulk, weighing 260 pounds. Among his nicknames were "Grover the Good" and "The Buffalo Sheriff." His wife, born in Buffalo, N.Y., July 21, 1864, survived him by 39 years. She died in Baltimore, Md., Oct. 29, 1947, and is buried in Princeton, N.J.

★ **BENJAMIN HARRISON (1833-1901)** ★ *Twenty-third President (Mar. 4, 1889-Mar. 3, 1893)*

Born in North Bend, Ohio, Aug. 20, 1833. Descendant of Benjamin Harrison, who emigrated to Virginia from England in 1633; great-grandson of Benjamin Harrison (1726-91), Revolutionary statesman, signer of Declaration of Independence; grandson of William Henry Harrison (1773-1841), ninth president of U.S. Fifth child and third son (in a family of 8 boys and 5 girls) of John Scott Harrison (1804-78), a farmer and U.S. Congressman. Father had 1 boy and 2 girls by his first wife, who died in 1830; Benjamin Harrison was second child and second son by his father's second wife, Elizabeth Ramsey Irwin (1810-50). Attended Miami University; graduated 1852. Presbyterian in religion. On Oct. 20, 1853, married Caroline Lavinia Scott, 21, daughter of a Presbyterian minister and educator. Had 1 son and 1 daughter. Studied law in Cincinnati, Ohio; became active in Republican politics. In 1854 settled in Indianapolis, Ind.; was city attorney and court reporter. During Civil War, commanded infantry units in Union Army; rose to rank of brigadier general. Prospered as lawyer after war; in 1876 ran for governor of Indiana but was defeated; in 1881 was elected to U.S. Senate. Received Republican nomination for President in 1888 and, with Levi Parsons Morton of New York as running mate, was elected; defeated Democratic incumbent President Cleveland in electoral college, though Cleveland's popular vote was the greater by 100,000. Inaugurated Mar. 4, 1889, at the age of 55. During his term of office his wife, born in Oxford, Ohio, Oct. 1, 1832, died in the White House, Oct. 25, 1892. She is buried in Indianapolis, Ind. Honest but not very effective as President, Harrison ran for re-election in 1892 but was defeated by Democratic ex-President Cleveland. Returned to practice of law; campaigned for Republican party; spoke and wrote about problems of government and the Presidency; published *This Country of Ours* (1897). On April 6, 1896, married Mary Scott Lord Dimmock, 37, a widow, the niece of his first wife. Had 1 daughter. Contracted pneumonia and died on Mar. 13, 1901, at the age of 67, in Indianapolis, Ind., and is buried there. Harrison was short (5 feet 6 inches) and wore a full beard; among his nicknames were "Little Ben" and "Kid Gloves." His second wife, born in Honesdale, Pa., April 30, 1858, survived him by 46 years, never remarrying. She died Jan. 5, 1948, in New York City, and is buried in Indianapolis, Ind.

★ **WILLIAM McKINLEY (1843-1901)** ★ *Twenty-fifth President (Mar. 4, 1897-Sept. 14, 1901)*

Born in Niles, Ohio, Jan. 29, 1843. Scotch-Irish in ancestry. Seventh child and third son (in a family of 4 boys and 5 girls) of William McKinley (1807-92), an iron-founder, and Nancy Campbell Allison (1809-97). Attended Allegheny College; did not graduate. Methodist in religion. In Civil War, enlisted in Union Army as private; rose to rank of major. Studied law; began practice, 1867; served as prosecuting attorney of Stark County, Ohio, 1869-71. On Jan. 25, 1871, married Ida Saxton, 23, daughter of a banker. Had 2 daughters. Entered Republican politics; served in U.S. House of Representatives, 1877-84, 1885-91. Served as governor of Ohio, 1892-96. Received Republican nomination for Presidency, 1896; with Garret Augustus Hobart of New Jersey as running mate, defeated Democrat William Jennings Bryan in Presidential election. Inaugurated Mar. 4, 1897, at the age of 54. As President, McKinley endeavored to put into practice the high protective-tariff policies he had espoused as a member of Congress. In an era that saw the U.S. become both prosperous and (with victory in the Spanish-American War) a world power, McKinley gained great popularity; nominated for re-election in 1900, he defeated Bryan a second time. Inaugurated Mar. 4, 1901, together with his Vice-Presidential running mate, Theodore Roosevelt of New York. On Sept. 6, 1901, while attending a Pan-American exposition in Buffalo, N.Y., he was shot by Leon F. Czolgosz, an anarchist. He died Sept. 14, 1901, in Buffalo, at the age of 58. He is buried in Canton, Ohio. McKinley was short (5 feet 7 inches), erect, and of dignified appearance. One of his nicknames was "Napoleon of Protection." His wife, born in Canton, Ohio, June 8, 1847, survived him by 5 years. She died May 26, 1907, in Canton, and is buried there.

★ **THEODORE ROOSEVELT (1858-1919)** ★ *Twenty-sixth President (Sept. 14, 1901-Mar. 3, 1909)*

Born in New York, N.Y., Oct. 27, 1858. Descendant of Claas Martenszen van Roosevelt, who emigrated to New Amsterdam from Holland before 1650. Second child and eldest son (in a family of 2 boys and 2 girls) of Theodore Roosevelt (1831-78), a merchant, and Martha Bulloch (1834-84). Attended Harvard University; graduated 1880. Dutch Reformed in religion. On Oct. 27, 1880, married Alice Hathaway Lee, 19. Had 1 daughter. Studied law briefly; turned to writing, producing historical works. Entered politics as Republican; served in New York state legislature, 1882-84. His wife, born in Chestnut Hill, Mass., July 29, 1861, died in New York, N.Y., Feb. 14, 1884; she is buried in Cambridge, Mass. Roosevelt invested in and operated a ranch in Dakota Territory, 1883-87; continued writing, producing autobiographical works; ran unsuccessfully for mayor of New York City, 1886. Went to England; was married there, Dec. 2, 1886, to Edith Kermit Carow, 25. Had 4 sons and 1 daughter. Served on U.S. Civil Service Commission, 1889-95; continued historical writings; served as president of New York City board of police commissioners, 1895-97; was U.S. Assistant Secretary of the Navy, 1897-98. Resigned to form "Rough Riders" regiment in Spanish-American War; rose to rank of colonel. Served as governor of New York, 1899-1901; in 1900 was nominated by Republican party as Vice-Presidential running mate of President McKinley, running for re-election. Became Vice-President at second inauguration of McKinley, 1901. Succeeded to Presidency upon President McKinley's death, Sept. 14, 1901. Sworn in on same day at the age of 42, becoming youngest President in U.S. history. Nominated and elected again, 1904, with Charles Warren Fairbanks of New York as his running mate, defeating Democrat Alton Brooks Parker. Inaugurated Mar. 4, 1905. As President, Roosevelt vigorously supported programs of social reform, regulation of trusts, and conservation; pushed construction of the Panama Canal; mediated war settlement between Russia and Japan. Declining to run for re-election, he devoted himself to literary pursuits after leaving Presidency; went big-game hunting in Africa, 1910. Disapproving of policies of his successor (and former disciple), President Taft, he accepted nomination for Presidency by insurgent, progressive Republicans who came to be known as Bull Moose party. In three-way election of 1912, received more votes than incumbent President Taft, but was defeated by Democrat Woodrow Wilson. Returned to writing; in 1914 went on exploring expedition to South America; in 1916 supported Presidential campaign of Republican Charles Evans Hughes, who was defeated by Wilson. Offered his military services to President Wilson after U.S. entry into First World War; was refused; devoted himself to speeches and writings. He died of inflammatory rheumatism, Jan. 6, 1919, at the age of 60, in Oyster Bay, Long Island, N.Y., and is buried there. Roosevelt was medium in height (5 feet 10 inches) and notably vigorous in manner, with a bushy mustache and prominent teeth. Besides "Bull Moose," he was also called "Rough Rider" and "Trust Buster." His second wife, born in Norwich, Conn., Aug. 6, 1861, survived him by 29 years. She died Sept. 30, 1948, in Oyster Bay, and is buried there.

★ **WILLIAM HOWARD TAFT (1857-1930)** ★ *Twenty-seventh President (Mar. 4, 1909-Mar. 3, 1913)*

Born in Cincinnati, Ohio, Sept. 15, 1857. Descendant of Robert Taft, who emigrated to America from England before 1700. Seventh child and sixth son (in a family of 8 boys and 2 girls) of Alphonso Taft (1810-91), a lawyer and jurist. Father had 4 boys and 1 girl by first wife, who died in 1852; William Howard Taft was second child and second son by Louisa Maria Torrey (1827-1907), second wife of Alphonso Taft. Attended Yale College; graduated 1878. Unitarian in religion. Studied law; was admitted to Ohio bar, 1880. Served as court reporter; entered Republican politics; served as assistant prosecuting attorney, Hamilton County, Ohio, 1881-82. On June 19, 1886, married Helen Herron, 25, daughter of a judge. Had 2 sons and 1 daughter. Appointed to superior court of Ohio, ad interim, 1887-88; elected, 1888, to 5-year term on court. Served as U.S. Solicitor General, 1890-92; U.S. Circuit Court judge, 1892-1900. Served as president of U.S. Philippine Commission, 1900-01; governor general of Philippines, 1901-04; U.S. Secretary of War, 1904-08. Received Republican nomination for Presidency, 1908; with James Schoolcraft Sherman of New York as running mate, defeated Democrat William

Jennings Bryan in Presidential election. Inaugurated Mar. 4, 1909, at the age of 51. As President, Taft continued many of the policies of his predecessor and political mentor, Theodore Roosevelt, but ultimately fell out with Roosevelt over interpretation of powers of Presidency. Quarrel between the two men led to separate candidacy of Roosevelt (as "Bull Moose" Republican) when Taft sought re-election in 1912 as regular Republican candidate; election was won by Democratic party candidate Woodrow Wilson. Taft then retired from politics; served on faculty of Yale as professor of law, 1913-21. Served as Chief Justice of U.S. Supreme Court, 1921-30. He died in Washington, D.C., Mar. 8, 1930, and is buried in Arlington National Cemetery. Taft was an enormous man, 6 feet tall and weighing more than 300 pounds. "Big Bill" was one of his nicknames. His wife, born in Cincinnati, Ohio, Jan. 2, 1861, survived him by 13 years. She died in Washington, D.C., May 22, 1943, and is buried in Arlington National Cemetery.

★ WOODROW WILSON (1856-1924) ★   *Twenty-eighth President (Mar. 4, 1913-Mar. 3, 1921)*

Born in Staunton, Va., Dec. 28, 1856, and named Thomas Woodrow Wilson. Scotch-Irish in ancestry. Third child and eldest son (in a family of 2 boys and 2 girls) of Joseph Ruggles Wilson (1822-1903), a Presbyterian minister and professor, and Jessie Janet Woodrow (1826-1888). Attended Davidson College, then attended College of New Jersey (now Princeton University); graduated 1879. Dropped "Thomas" from name. Presbyterian in religion. Studied law; practiced briefly, 1882-83. Left law for academic career, 1883; wrote *Congressional Government* (published 1885); taught history at Bryn Mawr College, 1885-88. On June 24, 1885, married Ellen Louise Axson, 25, daughter of a Presbyterian minister. Had 3 daughters. Received Ph.D. from Johns Hopkins University, 1886; taught history and political economy at Wesleyan University, 1888-90; was professor of jurisprudence and political economy, Princeton University, 1890-1902; president of Princeton University, 1902-10. Nominated for governor of New Jersey by Democratic party, and elected, 1910; served as governor, 1911-13. Received Democratic nomination for Presidency and, with Thomas Riley Marshall of Indiana as running mate, was elected in 1912, defeating Republican incumbent President Taft and former President Theodore Roosevelt, Progressive party (Bull Moose) candidate. Inaugurated Mar. 4, 1913, at the age of 56. Wilson's administration was marked initially by the vigorous liberal reforms of the President's New Freedom program, and by the attempt to maintain U.S. neutrality in the face of the European war. His wife, born in Savannah, Ga., May 15, 1860, died in Washington, D.C., Aug. 6, 1914; she is buried in Rome, Ga. On Dec. 18, 1915, Wilson married Edith Bolling Galt, 43, a widow, daughter of a judge. Had no children. Wilson was renominated and re-elected, 1916, defeating Republican Charles Evans Hughes; inaugurated for the second time, Mar. 4, 1917. His second term was marked by U.S. participation in the First World War, and by Wilson's dramatic but unsuccessful attempts to bring the U.S. into the League of Nations, which was founded, upon his insistence, after the war. On Sept. 26, 1919, while on a speaking tour to muster U.S. popular support for his peace aims, he collapsed of nervous exhaustion at Pueblo, Colo., and was rushed back to Washington, D.C., where on Oct. 2 he suffered a paralytic stroke. Although he served out his term, he was thenceforward an invalid, and his ability to perform the functions of the Presidency was severely curtailed. After his term in office, he lived in near-seclusion in Washington, D.C. He died Feb. 3, 1924, at the age of 67, in the capital, and is buried there, in the National Cathedral. A man of high moral purpose and integrity, with great intellect and impressive literary abilities, Wilson was of slightly more than medium height and had an ascetically handsome face. His second wife, born in Wytheville, Va., Oct. 15, 1872, survived him by 37 years. She died in Washington, D.C., Dec. 28, 1961.

★ WARREN GAMALIEL HARDING (1865-1923) ★   *Twenty-ninth President (Mar. 4, 1921-Aug. 2, 1923)*

Born in Corsica (now Blooming Grove), Ohio, Nov. 2, 1865. First child and eldest son (in a family of 3 boys and 5 girls) of George Tryon Harding (1843-1928), a farmer and physician of English and Scotch ancestry, and Phoebe Elizabeth Dickerson (1843-1910), of English and Dutch ancestry. Attended Ohio Central College, 1879-82; later worked on Marion, Ohio, weekly *Democratic Mirror*. In 1884 became part owner of Marion weekly *Star;* subsequently became sole owner. Baptist in religion. On July 8, 1891, married Florence Kling De Wolfe, 30, a divorcee (whose former husband had died), daughter of a banker. Had no children; wife had 1 son by her first marriage. Changed *Star* from weekly to daily; prospered as both newspaper and town grew. Entered politics as Republican; became county auditor, 1895; served in Ohio state senate, 1899-1903; was lieutenant-governor of Ohio, 1904-05. In 1910 ran unsuccessfully for governor; in 1914 was elected to U.S. Senate. Chosen by Republican party as Presidential candidate, 1920; with Calvin Coolidge as running mate, defeated Democratic ticket of James M. Cox and Franklin D. Roosevelt. Inaugurated Mar. 4, 1921, at the age of 55. Harding's administration was characterized by the genial mediocrity of its chief executive and the incompetence and corruption of many of its other high officials; scandals, including early inklings of the Teapot Dome affair, mounted steadily throughout 1922 and 1923. On July 28, 1923, in San Francisco, Calif., during a transcontinental speaking tour, he contracted bronchopneumonia, and he died of an embolism on Aug. 2, 1923. He was 57. He is buried in Marion, Ohio. Harding was 6 feet tall and impressively handsome. His wife, born in Marion, Ohio, Aug. 15, 1860, survived him by a year. She died Nov. 21, 1924, in Marion, Ohio, and is buried there.

★ CALVIN COOLIDGE (1872-1933) ★   *Thirtieth President (Aug. 3, 1923-Mar. 3, 1929)*

Born in Plymouth Notch, Vt., July 4, 1872, and named John Calvin Coolidge. Descendant of John Coolidge, who emigrated to America from England about 1630. First child and only son (in a family of 1 boy and 1 girl) of John Calvin Coolidge (1845-1926), a storekeeper, and Victoria Josephine Moor (1846-85). Attended Amherst College; graduated 1895. Dropped "John" from his name. Congregationalist in religion. Studied law; was admitted to bar, 1897; began practice in Northampton, Mass., 1898. On Oct. 4, 1905, married Grace Anna Goodhue, 26. Had 2 sons. Became active in Republican politics; was mayor of Northampton, Mass., 1910-11; served in Massachusetts state senate, 1911-15; was lieutenant-governor of Massachusetts, 1916-18; governor, 1919-20. His firmness during Boston police strike in early part of administration brought him nationwide attention. As running mate of Warren G. Harding, was elected Vice-President in 1920. On death of President Harding, succeeded to Presidency; sworn in on Aug. 3, 1923, at the age of 51. In 1924, with Charles G. Dawes of Illinois as his running mate, was elected to Presidency, defeating Democrat John W. Davis and Progressive party candidate Robert M. LaFollette. Inaugurated Mar. 4, 1925. Although he enjoyed great popularity with the electorate, Coolidge as President was ineffectual with Congress and in foreign affairs; but he recalled U.S. marines from the Dominican Republic, 1924. Asked by his party to run for another term, he declined, Aug. 2, 1927. Retired to Northampton, Mass.; wrote articles; published *Autobiography*, 1929. He died of a coronary thrombosis in Northampton on Jan. 5, 1933, at the age of 60. He is buried in Plymouth, Vt. Coolidge was of medium height (5 feet 10 inches) and slender build, with thin features. "Silent Cal" was one of his nicknames. His wife, born in Burlington, Vt., Jan. 3, 1879, survived him by 24 years. She died in Northampton, Mass., July 8, 1957, and is buried in Plymouth, Vt.

★ **HERBERT CLARK HOOVER (1874-1964)** ★   *Thirty-first President (Mar. 4, 1929-Mar. 3 1933)*

Born in West Branch, Iowa, Aug. 10, 1874. Descendant of Andrew Hoover, who emigrated to Pennsylvania from the Palatinate district in Germany in 1738. Second child and second son (in a family of 2 boys and 1 girl) of Jesse Clark Hoover (1846-80), a blacksmith, and Hulda Randall Minthorn (1848-83). Attended Stanford University; graduated (as mining engineer) 1895. Quaker in religion. On Feb. 10, 1899, married Lou Henry, 23, daughter of a banker. Had 2 sons. Forged extremely successful career as mining engineer with offices and interests all over the world, 1895-1913. During and after First World War, gained international reputation as chairman of American Relief Commission, London, 1914-15, and creator and chairman of Commission for Relief, Belgium, 1915-19; supervised distribution of medicines, food, and clothing to some 10 million victims of the war. Served as U.S. food administrator, 1917-19; as director of American Relief Administration, 1918-23, helping some 16 million needy children in 18 countries. Served, with great distinction, as U.S. Secretary of Commerce, 1921-28; promoted expansion of foreign trade, President's Conference on Unemployment, 1923, and construction of dam (named after him) across Colorado River, completed 1935. Received Republican nomination for Presidency, 1928; with Charles Curtis of Kansas as his running mate defeated Democrat Alfred E. Smith in Presidential election. Inaugurated Mar. 4, 1929, at the age of 54. His considerable abilities in the areas of administration and organization were unfortunately not equal to the task of coping with the economic depression that swept the U.S. and the world during his term of office. Ran for re-election, 1932; defeated by Democrat Franklin D. Roosevelt. Retired to private life. After Second World War, was coordinator of European Food Program, 1946-47; chairman of bipartisan commissions on organization and operation of Federal government, 1947-49 and 1953-55; founder, Hoover Library of War, Revolution and Peace, Stanford University. He died in New York, N.Y., Oct. 20, 1964, at the age of 90, and is buried in West Branch, Iowa. Hoover was tall (5 feet 11 inches), with a full, ruddy face. "Friend of Helpless Children" and "The Chief" were among his nicknames. His wife, born in Waterloo, Iowa, Mar. 29, 1875, died in New York, N.Y., Jan. 7, 1944; Hoover survived her by 20 years. She is buried in Palo Alto, Calif.

★ **FRANKLIN DELANO ROOSEVELT (1882-1945)** ★   *Thirty-second President (Mar. 4, 1933-April 12, 1945)*

Born in Hyde Park, N.Y., Jan. 30, 1882. Descendant of Claas Martenszen van Roosevelt, who emigrated to New Amsterdam from Holland before 1650, and from whom Theodore Roosevelt, twenty-sixth President, was also descended; Franklin D. Roosevelt was fifth cousin of Theodore Roosevelt. Second child and second son (in a family of 2 boys) of James Roosevelt (1828-1900), a lawyer and financier. Father had 1 son by first wife, who died in 1876; Franklin Delano Roosevelt was only child by Sara Delano (1854-1941), second wife of James Roosevelt. Attended Harvard University; graduated 1903. Episcopalian in religion. On Mar. 17, 1905, married Anna Eleanor Roosevelt, 20, a niece of President Theodore Roosevelt. Had 5 sons and 1 daughter. Studied law; began practice in 1907. Entering Democratic politics, served in New York state senate, 1911-13; was U.S. Assistant Secretary of the Navy, 1913-20. Ran for Vice-Presidency, 1920, as running mate of Democratic Presidential candidate James M. Cox; election was won by Republican Warren G. Harding. Returned to practice of law in New York City; maintained political connections during recuperation from attack of infantile paralysis; served as governor of New York, 1929-33. In 1932 he received the Democratic nomination for the Presidency and, with John Nance Garner of Texas as running mate, defeated Republican incumbent President Herbert Hoover. Inaugurated Mar. 4, 1933, at the age of 51. As President, Roosevelt launched an ambitious program designed to alleviate the economic depression that gripped the U.S. Calling his program the New Deal, he effected a redistribution of wealth through changes in taxation; tried to alleviate unemployment through public works sponsored by government; attempted to help industrial labor and farmers; strove for widespread social benefits and improvement of the economically underprivileged. Renominated and re-elected in 1936, defeating Republican Alfred M. Landon, he was inaugurated for a second term on Jan. 20, 1937; John N. Garner was again Vice-President. Much of his second term was spent in alerting U.S. to need for preparedness for possible involvement in coming European war. In 1940 he defeated Republican Wendell L. Willkie and became first President in U.S. history to be re-elected for third term; he was inaugurated Jan. 20, 1941, Henry A. Wallace of Iowa becoming Vice-President. This term saw U.S. entry into Second World War; before and during U.S. participation in war, Roosevelt exerted dynamic leadership in the international effort to curb and defeat German and Japanese fascism. On Jan. 20, 1945, after defeating Republican Thomas E. Dewey, he was inaugurated for a fourth term, with Harry S. Truman of Missouri becoming Vice-President. Attended several international conferences during war: with British Prime Minister Winston Churchill, at mid-Atlantic, Aug. 14, 1941, proclaiming Atlantic Charter; Crimea Conference with Churchill and Soviet Premier Joseph Stalin, at Yalta, Feb. 4-11, 1945, laying groundwork for United Nations charter conference and agreeing on some postwar arrangements; agreements frequently criticised for seemingly appeasing Soviet government. On April 12, 1945, shortly before final victory was achieved in Europe, he died of a cerebral hemorrhage, at the age of 63, in Warm Springs, Ga. He is buried at Hyde Park, N.Y. Roosevelt was tall (6 feet 2 inches) and well-built; he was athletic until illness deprived him of the full use of his legs. His many nicknames included "The Squire of Hyde Park" and "The Boss." His wife, born in New York, N.Y., Oct. 11, 1884, survived him by 17 years, going on to earn worldwide esteem for her humanitarian efforts and social vision. She died in New York, N.Y., Nov. 7, 1962, and is buried at Hyde Park.

348

★ **HARRY S. TRUMAN (1884-   )** ★ *Thirty-third President (April 12, 1945-Jan. 20, 1953)*

Born in Lamar, Mo., May 8, 1884. English-Scotch-Irish in ancestry. Middle initial does not stand for a name, but is simply the letter "S". First child and eldest son (in a family of 1 boy and 2 girls) of John Anderson Truman (1851-1914), a farmer, and Martha Ellen Young (1852-1947). Baptist in religion. Did not attend college. After leaving school, worked at various jobs, 1901-06; managed family farm, 1906-17. In First World War, served in artillery, 1917-19; saw action in France, 1918; rose to rank of major; returned to Missouri. On June 28, 1919, married Elizabeth Virginia Wallace, 34, daughter of a farmer, who bore him 1 daughter. Conducted haberdashery business in Kansas City, Mo., 1919-21. Entered Democratic politics; served as county judge (administrative, not judicial), 1922-24. Studied law. Served as presiding judge of Jackson (Mo.) County Court, 1926-34; in U.S. Senate, 1935-45; chairman of special Senate committee investigating national defense program, 1941-44. Chosen by Democratic party to be running mate of President Franklin D. Roosevelt in election of 1944, he became Vice-President, 1945. Upon the death of President Roosevelt, he was sworn in as President, April 12, 1945, at the age of 60. As President, Truman vigorously carried forward Franklin D. Roosevelt's programs. He encouraged establishment of the U.N. and pursued the war against Japan to a successful conclusion. In the postwar era, he established the Atomic Energy Commission, 1946; enunciated the Truman Doctrine of international assistance in combating Communism, 1947; launched the Marshall Plan for European rehabilitation, 1948; supported the establishment of NATO, 1949. In 1949 he was inaugurated President for another term, having unexpectedly defeated Republican Thomas E. Dewey in the 1948 Presidential election. Alben William Barkley of Kentucky became Vice-President. Truman's 1949-53 term was marked by the Berlin blockade and the Korean war, which was still in progress when Truman retired from the Presidency, Jan. 20, 1953, on the inauguration of his successor. Settling in Independence, Mo., he devoted himself principally to writing his memoirs, but from time to time engaged in political campaigning for Democratic candidates. Truman is of about medium height (5 feet 9 inches) and build, and has an energetic bearing. Among his nicknames are "Give 'em Hell Harry" and "The Man of Independence." His wife was born in Independence, Mo., Feb. 13, 1885.

★ **DWIGHT DAVID EISENHOWER (1890-   )** ★ *Thirty-fourth President (Jan. 20, 1953-Jan. 20, 1961)*

Born in Denison, Texas, Oct. 14, 1890, and named David Dwight Eisenhower. Descendant of German emigrants to Pennsylvania from the Rhineland before 1740. Third son (in a family of 7 sons) of David Jacob Eisenhower (1863-1942), a mechanic and gas company manager, and Ida Elizabeth Stover (1862-1946). Reversed given names, becoming Dwight David Eisenhower. Attended U.S. Military Academy, West Point, N.Y.; graduated 1915. Presbyterian in religion. On July 1, 1916, married Mamie Geneva Doud, 19, daughter of a businessman. Had 2 sons. In First World War, commanded tank training center; did not leave U.S. Served in Panama Canal Zone, 1922-24; attended Command and General Staff School, 1925-26; Army War College, 1928. Attained rank of major; served as assistant to Gen. Douglas MacArthur in Philippines, 1935-39. In Second World War, became chief, 1942, of War Plans Division, War Department General Staff; served as commanding general of European Theater of Operations and commander-in-chief of Allied forces in North Africa, 1942-43; became, 1943, Supreme Commander of Allied Expeditionary Forces and directed invasion of Europe; received German surrender, 1945. Commanded U.S. occupation forces in Germany, 1945; returned to U.S. and served as Army Chief of Staff, 1945-48. Retired from active duty, 1948; served as president of Columbia University, 1948-53. Took leave of absence from Columbia to serve, 1950-52, as Supreme Commander of NATO forces in Europe. Received Republican nomination for Presidency, 1952; with Richard Milhous Nixon of California as running mate, defeated Democrat Adlai E. Stevenson in Presidential election. Inaugurated Jan. 20, 1953, at the age of 62. Renominated and re-elected in 1956 (again with Nixon, and again defeating Stevenson), he was inaugurated for his second term on Jan. 20, 1957. During Eisenhower's 8 years in office the Korean war ended, 1953; the Southeast Asia Treaty Organization (SEATO) was formed, 1954; the U.S. occupation of Germany was ended, 1955; the U.S. suffered a slight economic recession, 1958-59; and both the Soviet Union and the U.S. orbited their first space satellites, 1957, 1958, respectively. Domestically, Eisenhower followed a course generally described as moderately conservative. Retiring to private life at the end of his two Presidential terms, Eisenhower settled on his farm at Gettysburg, Pa., and occasionally involved himself in Republican politics; he also worked on his memoirs. His wartime military rank, General of the Army, was restored to him by Congress in 1961. Eisenhower is of slightly more than medium height (5 feet 10½ inches) and of sturdy build. He is universally called "Ike." His wife was born in Boone, Iowa, Nov. 14, 1896.

★ **JOHN FITZGERALD KENNEDY (1917-63)** ★ *Thirty-fifth President (Jan. 20, 1961-Nov. 22, 1963)*

Born in Brookline, Mass., May 29, 1917. Irish in ancestry. Second child and second son (in a family of 4 boys and 5 girls) of Joseph Patrick Kennedy (1888-   ), a financier and former U.S. ambassador to England, and Rose Fitzgerald. Roman Catholic in religion. Attended Harvard University; graduated 1940. Lieutenant in U.S. Navy during Second World War; decorated for heroism while commanding PT boat in South Pacific, 1943. Studied law; worked as newspaper reporter. Entered Democratic politics; served in U.S. House of Representatives, 1947-53. On Sept. 12, 1953, married Jacqueline Lee Bouvier, 24, daughter of a banker. Had 2 sons and 1 daughter. Served in U.S. Senate, 1953-61. Wrote historical works: *Why England Slept* (1940); *Profiles in Courage* (1956), which won him Pulitzer Prize for biography, 1957. Campaigned unsuccessfully for Vice-Presidential nomination at Democratic national convention of 1956; at 1960 convention, received Democratic nomination for Presidency, with Lyndon Baines Johnson of Texas as running mate. In Presidential election, narrowly defeated Republican Richard Milhous Nixon. Inaugurated Jan. 20, 1961, at the age of 43, becoming youngest man ever elected to U.S. Presidency and also first Roman Catholic President in U.S. history. As President, Kennedy applied himself with great vigor·to his New Frontier programs. Domestically, these included the Peace Corps; civil-rights legislation; a tax cut; medical care for the aged; tariff reductions. In foreign affairs, he sponsored the Latin-American Alliance for Progress; took "sole responsibility" for the failure of the anti-Castro invasion of Cuba in 1961; increased U.S. aid to Southeast Asia; resisted Soviet efforts to force Allied troops out of Berlin, and reinforced the U.S. garrison there instead. In 1962 he took decisive action in the face of the suddenly discovered Soviet missile buildup in Cuba, and caused Soviet Premier Khrushchev to order withdrawal of the weapons. In 1963 he achieved agreement with the Soviet Union on a treaty providing for a limited ban on testing of nuclear weapons. While riding in a motorcade in Dallas, Texas, Nov. 22, 1963, he was shot (suppposedly by Lee Harvey Oswald) and died immediately. He was 46. Kennedy was tall (6 feet), red-haired, and of dynamically handsome appearance. "Jack" and "JFK" were among his nicknames. His wife, who survives him, was born in Southampton, N.Y., July 28, 1929.

★ **LYNDON BAINES JOHNSON (1908-   )** ★ *Thirty-sixth President (Nov. 22, 1963-   )*

Born near Stonewall, Texas, Aug. 27, 1908. Son of Sam Ealy Johnson, a farmer and legislator, and Rebekah Baines. Member of Christian Church. Attended Southwest State Teachers College; graduated 1930. Taught in Houston, Texas, public schools, 1930-32; served as secretary to U.S. Congressman Richard M. Kleberg of Texas, 1932-35. On Nov. 17, 1934, married Claudia Alta ("Lady Bird") Taylor, 21, daughter of a rancher, who bore him 2 daughters. Served as Texas state administrator, National Youth Admin., 1935-37; served as Democrat in U.S. House of Representatives, 1937-39, filling unexpired term of Congressman James P. Buchanan of Texas; elected to U.S. House of Representatives, 1938, and served 1939-49. In Second World War, was first member of Congress to enlist in armed forces after Pearl Harbor; served in Pacific as lieutenant commander, U.S. Navy, 1941-42; was awarded Silver Star; was recalled from active duty by order of President Franklin Roosevelt prohibiting members of Congress from serving in armed forces. Served in U.S. Senate, 1949-61; was Democratic whip, 1951-52; Senate Democratic leader, 1953-54; Senate majority leader, 1955-61. Sought Democratic Presidential nomination, 1960; when John F. Kennedy received nomination, accepted Vice-Presidential position on Democratic party ticket. Elected Vice-President, 1960; inaugurated Jan. 20, 1961. Performed one of most active roles of any Vice-President in U.S. history. Succeeded to Presidency on death of President Kennedy, Nov. 22, 1963. As President, Johnson used his official powers and his great experience to insure that most of President Kennedy's New Frontier programs would be enacted into law. He strove to demonstrate to the world that the policies of the assassinated President would be vigorously continued by his successor. In 1964 Johnson was nominated for the Presidency by the Democratic party, with Hubert Horatio Humphrey of Minnesota as his running mate; he defeated Republican Barry M. Goldwater of Arizona in the election. Aided by considerable Democratic majorities in Congress, Johnson moved forward with an ambitious legislative program, called the Great Society, involving education, civil rights, liberalized taxation, and many other aspects of life in the U.S. In foreign affairs, the military operations in Vietnam continued to pose the most difficult problems for the Johnson administration, as they had for the preceding administration. Lyndon Johnson is tall (6 feet 2 inches) and rangy, and is soft-spoken in manner. He is frequently referred to as LBJ. His wife was born in Marshall, Texas, Dec. 22, 1912.

PRESIDENTS

★ George Washington

1732	Born Westmoreland County, Va., Feb. 22
1748	Began surveying in the West
1749	Official surveyor of Culpeper County
1752	Adjutant General of Virginia Militia
1753	Sent to Pennsylvania to warn French out of Ohio Valley
1754	Surrendered Fort Necessity to French
1755	Aide to General Braddock; Commander-in-Chief of the Virginia Forces
1759	Married Martha Dandridge Custis
1759–74	Member House of Burgesses
1774–75	Member Continental Congress
1775–83	General and Commander-in-Chief of the Continental Forces
1787–88	Chairman Constitutional Convention
1789–97	President
1799	Died at Mount Vernon, Va., Dec. 14

★ John Adams

1735	Born Braintree (Quincy) Mass., Oct. 30
1755	Graduated from Harvard
1758	Admitted to the Bar
1764	Married Abigail Smith
1774	Elected to Continental Congress
1778	Commissioner to France
1785	Minister to England
1789–97	Vice-President
1797–1801	President
1826	Died Quincy, Mass., July 4

★ Thomas Jefferson

1743	Born Shadwell, Va., April 13
1762	Graduated College of William and Mary
1767	Admitted to the Bar
1772	Married Martha Wayles Skelton
1769–74	Member House of Burgesses
1775–76	Member Continental Congress
1776–79	Member Virginia House of Delegates
1779–81	Governor of Virginia
1783–85	Member Continental Congress
1785–89	Minister to France
1790–93	Secretary of State
1797–1801	Vice-President
1801–09	President
1826	Died Charlottesville, Va., July 4

★ James Madison

1751	Born Port Conway, Va., March 16
1771	Graduated from Princeton
1780–83	Member Continental Congress
1787	Member Constitutional Convention
1789–97	Member United States Congress
1794	Married Dolley Payne Todd
1801–09	Secretary of State
1809–17	President
1826–36	Rector, University of Virginia
1836	Died Montpelier, Va., June 28

★ James Monroe

1758	Born Westmoreland County, Va., April 28
1776	Graduated College of William and Mary
1776	Enlisted in Continental Army
1786	Married Eliza Kortright
1786–90	Practiced law, Fredericksburg, Va.
1790–94	United States Senator
1794–96	Minister to France
1799–1802	Governor of Virginia
1803–07	Minister to England
1811	Governor of Virginia
1811–17	Secretary of State (1814–15 Secretary of War)
1817–25	President
1823	Announced Monroe Doctrine
1831	Died Richmond, Va., July 4

★ John Quincy Adams

1767	Born Braintree (Quincy), Mass., July 11
1781	Secretary to United States Minister to Russia
1788	Graduated from Harvard
1791	Admitted to the Bar
1794	Minister to Holland
1797	Married Louisa Catherine Johnson
1797–1801	Minister to Prussia
1803–08	United States Senator
1809–11	Minister to Russia
1811	Refused appointment to U.S. Supreme Court
1814	Peace Commissioner at Ghent
1815–17	Minister to England
1817–25	Secretary of State
1825–29	President
1831–48	Member of Congress
1848	Died Washington, D.C., Feb. 23

★ Andrew Jackson

1767	Born Waxhaw, S.C., March 15
1780–81	Served as messenger in Revolution
1787	Admitted to the Bar
1788	Went to Nashville, Tenn., practiced law
1791	Married Rachael Donelson Robards (remarried in 1794)
1796–97	Member of Congress
1797–98	United States Senator
1798–1804	Justice of Tennessee Supreme Court
1802	Major General of Tennessee Militia
1812–15	Served in War of 1812
1817–18	Commanded troops, Seminole War
1821	Governor of Florida Territory
1823–25	United States Senator
1824	Unsuccessful Democratic candidate for President
1829–37	President
1845	Died Nashville, Tenn., June 8

★ Martin Van Buren

1782	Born Kinderhook, N.Y., Dec. 5
1803	Admitted to the Bar
1807	Married Hannah Hoes
1813–15	New York State Senator
1816	Settled in Albany, N.Y.
1816–19	Attorney General of New York
1821–29	United States Senator
1829	Governor of New York
1829–31	Secretary of State
1831–32	Minister to England
1833–37	Vice-President
1837–41	President
1840	Unsuccessful Democratic candidate for President
1848	Again defeated for President as Free-Soil candidate
1862	Died Kinderhook, N.Y., July 24

★ William Henry Harrison

1773	Born Berkeley, Va., Feb. 9
1791–96	Active in Indian fighting in the Northwest
1795	Married Anna Symmes
1798	Secretary, Northwest Territory
1799–1801	Territorial Delegate to Congress
1801–13	Governor of Indiana Territory
1811–12	Led United States troops against Indians in Northwest
1812–14	Major General in War of 1812
1816–19	Member of Congress from Ohio
1825–28	United States Senator
1828–29	Minister to Colombia
1836	Unsuccessful Whig candidate for President
1841	President
1841	Died Washington, D.C., April 4

★ John Tyler

1790	Born Greenway, Va., March 29
1807	Graduated College of William and Mary
1809	Admitted to the Bar
1813	Married Letitia Christian (died 1842)
1816–21	Member of Congress
1823–25	Member of Virginia Legislature
1825–26	Governor of Virginia
1827–36	United States Senator
1841	Vice-President, March 4–April 4
1841–45	President
1844	Married Julia Gardiner
1861–62	Member of Confederate Congress
1862	Died Richmond, Va., Jan. 18

★ James K. Polk

1795	Born Mecklenburg County, N.C., Nov. 2
1806	Moved to Tennessee
1818	Graduated from University of North Carolina
1820	Admitted to the Bar
1823–25	Member Tennessee Legislature
1824	Married Sarah Childress
1825–39	Member of Congress
1839–41	Governor of Tennessee
1841	Defeated for Governor
1843	Again defeated for Governor
1845–49	President
1849	Died Nashville, Tenn., June 15

★ Zachary Taylor

1784	Born Orange County, Va., Nov. 24
1785	Moved with family to Kentucky
1808	Commissioned Lieutenant, United States Army
1810	Married Margaret Smith
	Promoted to Captain
1812–15	Served in War of 1812
1816–32	Assigned to various Army posts
1832	Colonel in Black Hawk War
1836–37	Brigadier General in Seminole War
1845–47	Engaged in Mexican War
1849–50	President
1850	Died Washington, D.C., July 9

★ Millard Fillmore

1800	Born Locke, N.Y., Jan. 7
1823	Admitted to the Bar
1826	Married Abigail Powers (died 1853)
1828–31	Member of New York Assembly
1833–35	Member of Congress
1837–45	Member of Congress
1844	Defeated for Governor of New York
1846–47	Chancellor University of Buffalo
1847	Comptroller of New York State
1849–50	Vice-President
1850–53	President
1856	Defeated for President
1858	Married Caroline McIntosh

1862	President Buffalo Historical Society
1874	Died Buffalo, N.Y., March 8

★ Franklin Pierce

1804	Born Hillsboro, N.H., Nov. 23
1824	Graduated from Bowdoin College
1827	Admitted to the Bar
1829–33	Member New Hampshire Legislature
1833–37	Member of Congress
1834	Married Jane Means Appleton
1837–42	United States Senator
1846–48	Served in Mexican War
1853–57	President
1869	Died Concord, N.H., Oct. 8

★ James Buchanan

1791	Born near Mercersburg, Pa., April 23
1809	Graduated from Dickinson College
1812	Admitted to the Bar
1814	Served in War of 1812
1815–16	Member Pennsylvania Legislature
1821–31	Member of Congress
1832–34	Minister to Russia
1834–45	United States Senator
1845–49	Secretary of State
1853–56	Minister to Great Britain
1857–61	President
1868	Died Lancaster, Pa., June 1

★ Abraham Lincoln

1809	Born near Hodgenville, Ky., Feb. 12
1816	Moved with parents to Indiana
1828	Made first flatboat trip to New Orleans (second in 1831)
1831–37	Settled in New Salem, Ill.: Captain in Black Hawk War, store owner, surveyor, postmaster
1836	Admitted to the Bar
1834–42	Member Illinois Legislature
1837	Moved to Springfield, Ill., practiced law
1842	Married Mary Todd
1847–49	Member of Congress
1858	Defeated for United States Senate
1861–65	President
1865	Died Washington, D.C., April 15

★ Andrew Johnson

1808	Born Raleigh, N.C., Dec. 29
1826	Opened a tailor shop in Greenville, Tenn.
1827	Married Eliza McCardle
1830–33	Mayor of Greenville
1835–43	State Representative and Senator
1843–53	Member of Congress
1853–57	Governor of Tennessee
1857–62	United States Senator
1862–65	Military Governor of Tennessee
1865	Vice-President, March 4–April 15
1865–69	President
1875	United States Senator
	Died Carter's Station, Tenn., July 31

★ Ulysses S. Grant

1822	Born Point Pleasant, Ohio, April 27
1843	Graduated from West Point
1846–48	Served in Mexican War
1848	Married Julia Dent
1854	Resigned from the Army
1854–61	Farmer, real estate dealer, clerk in Missouri and Ohio
1861–65	Engaged in the Civil War
1866	Promoted to rank of General
1869–77	President
1880	Formed stock brokerage firm in New York
1884	Failed in business
1885	Wrote memoirs
	Died Mt. McGregor, N.Y., July 23

★ Rutherford B. Hayes

1822	Born Delaware, Ohio, Oct. 4
1842	Graduated from Kenyon College
1845	Graduated from Harvard Law School
	Admitted to the Bar
1852	Married Lucy Webb
1858–60	City Solicitor of Cincinnati
1861–65	Served in the Civil War
1865–67	Member of Congress
1868–72	Governor of Ohio
1872	Defeated for Congress
1876–77	Governor of Ohio
1877–81	President
1881	Retired to Fremont, Ohio
1893	Died Fremont, Ohio, Jan. 17

★ James A. Garfield

1831	Born Orange, Ohio, Nov. 19
1856	Graduated from Williams College
1857–61	Instructor at and President of Hiram Institute, Ohio
1858	Married Lucretia Rudolph
1859–61	State Senator
1860	Admitted to the Bar
1861–63	Served in the Civil War
1863–80	Member of Congress
1880	Elected United States Senator
1881	President
	Died Elberon, N.J., Sept. 19

★ Chester A. Arthur

1830	Born Fairfield, Vt., Oct. 5
1848	Graduated from Union College
1851–53	Taught school at Pownall, Vt.
1853	Admitted to the Bar, New York City
1859	Married Ellen Lewis Herndon
1861–62	Quartermaster General of New York State
1871–78	Collector of the Port of New York
1878–81	Practiced law in New York City
1881	Vice-President, March 4–Sept. 19
1881–85	President
1886	Died New York City, Nov. 18

★ Grover Cleveland

1837	Born Caldwell, N.J., March 18
1841	Moved with parents to New York State
1859	Admitted to the Bar at Buffalo
1863–65	Assistant District Attorney of Erie County, New York
1870–73	Sheriff of Erie County
1882	Mayor of Buffalo
1883–85	Governor of New York
1885–89	President
1886	Married Frances Folsom
1888	Defeated for re-election
1889–93	Practiced law in New York City
1893–97	President
1908	Died Princeton, N.J., June 24

★ Benjamin Harrison

1833	Born North Bend, Ohio, Aug. 20
1852	Graduated Miami University, Ohio
1853	Married Caroline Scott (died 1892)
	Admitted to the Bar
1854	Practiced law in Indianapolis
1857–61	City Attorney
1861–62	Reporter, Indiana Supreme Court
1862–65	Served in the Civil War
1876	Defeated for Governor of Indiana
1881–87	United States Senator
1889–93	President
1896	Married Mary Scott Lord Dimmick
1901	Died Indianapolis, Ind., March 13

★ William McKinley

1843	Born Niles, Ohio, Jan. 29
1860	Attended Allegheny College
1861–65	Served in Civil War
1867–77	Practiced law, Canton, Ohio
1871	Married Ida Saxton
1877–91	Member of Congress (except for 1883–85)
1892–96	Governor of Ohio
1897–1901	President
1901	Died Buffalo, N.Y., Sept. 14

★ Theodore Roosevelt

1858	Born in New York City, Oct. 27
1880	Graduated from Harvard
	Married Alice H. Lee (died 1884)
1882–84	Member of New York Assembly
1884–86	Operated ranches, North Dakota
1886	Married Edith Kermit Carow
1889–95	Member of U.S. Civil Service Commission
1895–97	President, New York City Police Board
1897–98	Assistant Secretary of Navy
1898	Colonel of Rough Riders
1898–1900	Governor of New York
1901	Vice-President, March 4–Sept. 14
1901–09	President
1909–10	Hunted big game in Africa
1912	Defeated for President
1913–14	Explored Brazilian jungles
1919	Died Oyster Bay, N.Y., Jan. 6

★ William Howard Taft

1857	Born Cincinnati, Ohio, Sept. 15
1878	Graduated from Yale
1880	Admitted to the Bar
1886	Married Helen Herron
1887–90	Judge, Ohio Superior Court
1890–92	United States Solicitor General
1892–1900	U.S. Circuit Court Judge
1900–04	Commissioner and Governor of the Philippines
1904–08	Secretary of War
1909–13	President
1913–21	Professor of law at Yale
1921–30	Chief Justice, U.S. Supreme Court
1930	Died Washington, D.C., March 8

★ Woodrow Wilson

1856	Born Staunton, Va., Dec. 28
1873–74	Attended Davidson College
1879	Graduated from Princeton
1882	Graduated from University of Virginia Law School
	Admitted to the Bar
1882–83	Practiced law at Atlanta, Georgia
1883–85	Graduate student at Johns Hopkins
1885	Married Ellen Axson (died 1914)
1885–88	Instructor in history, Bryn Mawr
1888–90	Professor at Wesleyan University
1890–1902	Professor at Princeton
1902–10	President of Princeton
1911–13	Governor of New Jersey
1913–21	President
1915	Married Edith Bolling Galt
1924	Died Washington, D.C., Feb. 3

★ Warren G. Harding

1865	Born Corsica, Ohio, Nov. 2
1879–82	Attended Ohio Central College
1884	Became editor of the Marion *Star*
1891	Married Florence De Wolfe Kling
1900–04	Member of Ohio State Senate
1904–06	Lieutenant Governor of Ohio
1910	Defeated for Governor
1915–21	United States Senator
1921–23	President
1923	Died San Francisco, Calif., Aug. 2

★ Calvin Coolidge

1872	Born Plymouth, Vt., July 4
1895	Graduated from Amherst College
1897	Admitted to the Massachusetts Bar
1899	City Councilman, Northampton, Mass.
1900–01	City Solicitor
1904	Clerk of the courts
1905	Married Grace Anne Goodhue
1907–08	Member of Massachusetts State Legislature
1910–11	Mayor of Northampton, Mass.
1912–15	Member of Massachusetts State Senate
1916–18	Lieutenant Governor
1919–20	Governor
1921–23	Vice-President
1923–29	President
1933	Died Northampton, Mass., Jan. 5

★ Herbert C. Hoover

1874	Born West Branch, Iowa, Aug. 10
1895	Graduated from Stanford University
1895–1914	Mining engineer
1899	Married Lou Henry
1914–15	Chairman of the American Relief Committee, London
1915–19	Commissioner for Belgian Relief
1917–19	United States Food Administrator
1919–21	Served on various government economic and food councils including the American Relief Administration
1921–28	Secretary of Commerce
1929–33	President
1947	Coordinator of European Food Program
1947–49; 1953–55	Chairman of Commission for Reorganization of the Executive Branch
1964	Died New York City, Oct. 20

★ Franklin Delano Roosevelt

1882	Born Hyde Park, N.Y., Jan. 30
1904	Graduated from Harvard
1905	Married Eleanor Roosevelt
1907	Graduated from Columbia Law School Admitted to New York Bar
1907–10	Practiced law in New York City
1911–13	Member, state senate
1913–20	Assistant Secretary of the Navy
1920	Defeated for Vice-President
1921	Stricken with infantile paralysis
1921–29	Practiced law in New York City
1929–33	Governor of New York
1933–45	President
1945	Died Warm Springs, Ga., April 12

★ Harry S. Truman

1884	Born Lamar, Mo., May 8
1901–06	In Kansas City employed as a reporter on the *Star,* railroad time keeper, bank clerk
1906–17	Operated family farm
1917–19	Served in World War I
1919	Married Elizabeth Virginia Wallace
1919–22	Operated a haberdashery store in Kansas City
1922–24	Judge, Jackson County Court
1925–26	Automobile salesman, manager of a building and loan company
1926–34	Presiding Judge, Jackson County
1935–45	United States Senator
1945	Vice-President, Jan. 20–April 12
1945–53	President
1955–56	Published his memoirs

★ Dwight D. Eisenhower

1890	Born Denison, Texas, Oct. 14
1891	Moved with family to Abilene, Kansas
1915	Graduated from West Point
1916	Married Mamie Geneva Doud
1916–41	Assigned to various military posts, advanced through grades from lieutenant to colonel
1941	Made Brigadier General
1942	Lieutenant General, Allied Commander in Chief of North Africa
1943	Commanding General of Allied Powers in European Theater
1944	Invaded Normandy, General of the Army
1945–48	Chief of Staff, United States Army
1948	Published "Crusade in Europe"
1948–52	President of Columbia University
1950–52	Supreme Commander of Allied Powers in Europe
1952	Resigned from the Army
1953–61	President
1962	Dedicated Eisenhower library at Abilene, Kansas

★ John Fitzgerald Kennedy

1917	Born Brookline, Mass., May 29
1940	Graduated from Harvard
1941–45	Served in U. S. Navy, World War II
1947–53	Member of Congress
1953	Married Jacqueline Lee Bouvier
1953–60	United States Senator
1954	Wrote *Profiles In Courage,* won Pulitzer Prize
1961	Inaugurated President
1962	Forced Soviet Union to dismantle its missile bases on Cuba
1963	Died Dallas, Texas, Nov. 22

★ Lyndon Baines Johnson

1908	Born near Stonewall, Texas, Aug. 27
1930	Graduated from Southwest Texas State Teachers College
1930–32	Teacher in Houston, Texas, public schools
1934	Married Claudia Alta (Lady Bird) Taylor
1935–37	State Director, National Youth Administration of Texas
1937–49	Member of Congress (during which he served seven months of active duty in U.S. Naval Reserve as Lt. Commander, beginning in December 1941)
1949–61	United States Senator
1961–63	Vice-President
1963–	President

☆ JOHN ADAMS
[*Under George Washington, first and second terms*]
   1789   April 21–March 3, 1797. Vice-President
1797–1801   2nd President (See Chronology of Presidents)

☆ THOMAS JEFFERSON
[*Under John Adams*]
   1797   March 4–March 3, 1801. Vice-President
1801–09   3rd President (See Chronology of Presidents)

☆ AARON BURR
[*Under Thomas Jefferson, first term*]
   1756   Born in Newark, N.J., Feb. 6
1791–97   Served in U.S. Senate (Democratic-Republican, N.Y.)
   1801   March 4–March 3, 1805. Vice-President
   1804   Killed Alexander Hamilton in duel
   1836   Died in Staten Island, N.Y., Sept. 14

☆ GEORGE CLINTON
[*Under Thomas Jefferson, second term; and under James Madison, first term*]
   1739   Born in Little Britain, N.Y., July 26
1775–76   Served in Continental Congress
1777–95; 1801–04   Governor of New York
   1805   March 4–March 3, 1809. Vice-President under Jefferson
   1809   March 4–April 20, 1812. Vice-President under Madison
   1812   Died in Washington, D.C., April 20

☆ ELBRIDGE GERRY
[*Under James Madison, second term*]
   1744   Born in Marblehead, Mass., July 17
1776–81; 1782–85   Served in Continental Congress
1789–93   Served in U.S. House of Representatives (Democratic-Republican, Mass.)
   1813   March 4–Nov. 23, 1814. Vice-President
   1814   Died in Washington, D.C., Nov. 23

☆ DANIEL D. TOMPKINS
[*Under James Monroe, first and second terms*]
   1774   Born in Fox Meadows (now Scarsdale), N.Y., June 21
1807–17   Governor of New York
   1817   March 4–March 3, 1825. Vice-President
   1825   Died in Tompkinsville, Staten Island, N.Y., June 11

☆ JOHN CALDWELL CALHOUN
[*Under John Quincy Adams; and under Andrew Jackson, first term*]
   1782   Born in Abbeville District, S.C., March 18
1811–17   Served in U.S. House of Representatives (Democratic-Republican, S.C.)
1817–25   Secretary of War
   1825   March 4–March 3, 1829. Vice-President under Adams
   1829   March 4–Dec. 28, 1832. Vice-President under Jackson
1832–43; 1845–50   Served in U.S. Senate
1844–45   Secretary of State
   1850   Died in Washington, D.C., March 31

☆ MARTIN VAN BUREN
[*Under Andrew Jackson, second term*]
   1833   March 4–March 3, 1837. Vice-President
1837–41   8th President (See Chronology of Presidents)

☆ RICHARD MENTOR JOHNSON
[*Under Martin Van Buren*]
   1780   Born in Floyd's Station, Ky., Oct. 17
1807–19; 1829–37   Served in U.S. House of Representatives (Democratic-Republican, Ky.)
1819–29   Served in U.S. Senate
   1837   March 4–March 3, 1841. Vice-President
   1850   Died in Frankfort, Ky., Nov. 19

☆ JOHN TYLER
[*Under William Henry Harrison*]
   1841   March 4–April 6, 1841. Vice-President
1841–45   10th President (See Chronology of Presidents)

☆ GEORGE MIFFLIN DALLAS
[*Under James K. Polk*]
   1792   Born in Philadelphia, Pa., July 10
1831–33   Served in U.S. Senate (Democratic, Pa.)
1833–35   Attorney General of Pennsylvania
1837–39   U.S. Minister to Russia
   1845   March 4–March 3, 1849. Vice-President
1856–61   U.S. Minister to Great Britain
   1864   Died in Philadelphia, Pa., Dec. 31

☆ MILLARD FILLMORE
[*Under Zachary Taylor*]
   1849   March 4–July 9, 1950. Vice-President
1850–53   13th President (See Chronology of Presidents)

☆ WILLIAM RUFUS DE VANE KING
[*Under Franklin Pierce*]
   1786   Born in Sampson County, N.C., April 7
1811–16   Served in U.S. House of Representatives (Democratic, N.C.)
1819–44; 1848–52   Served in U.S. Senate
   1853   March 4–April 18, 1853. Vice-President
   1853   Died in Cahawba, Ala., April 18

☆ JOHN CABELL BRECKINRIDGE
[*Under James Buchanan*]
   1821   Born in Lexington, Ky., Jan. 21
1851–55   Served in U.S. House of Representatives (Democratic, Ky.)
   1857   March 4–March 3, 1861. Vice-President
   1875   Died in Lexington, Ky., May 17

☆ HANNIBAL HAMLIN
[*Under Abraham Lincoln, first term*]
   1809   Born in Paris, Me., Aug. 27
1843–47   Served in U.S. House of Representatives (Republican, Me.)
1848–57; 1857–61; 1869–81   Served in U.S. Senate
   1861   March 4–March 3, 1865. Vice-President
   1891   Died in Bangor, Me., July 4

☆ ANDREW JOHNSON
[*Under Abraham Lincoln, second term*]
   1865   March 4–April 15, 1865. Vice-President
1865–69   17th President (See Chronology of Presidents)

☆ SCHUYLER COLFAX
[*Under Ulysses S. Grant, first term*]
   1823   Born in New York, N.Y., March 23
1855–69   Served in U.S. House of Representatives (Republican, Ind.)
1863–69   Speaker of House
   1869   March 4–March 3, 1873. Vice-President
   1885   Died in Mankato, Minn., Jan. 13

☆ HENRY WILSON
[*Under Ulysses S. Grant, second term*]
   1812   Born in Farmington, N.H., Feb. 16
1844–46; 1850–52   Served in Massachusetts senate
1855–73   Served in U.S. Senate (Republican, Mass.)
   1873   March 4–Nov. 22, 1875. Vice-President
   1875   Died in Washington, D.C., Nov. 22

☆ WILLIAM ALMON WHEELER
[*Under Rutherford B. Hayes*]
   1819   Born in Malone, N.Y., June 30

1850–51 Served in New York state assembly
1858–59 Served in New York state senate
1861–63; 1869–77 Served in U.S. House of Representatives
(Republican, N.Y.)
1877 March 4–March 3, 1881. Vice-President
1887 Died in Malone, N.Y., June 4

☆ CHESTER ALAN ARTHUR
[*Under James A. Garfield*]
1881 March 4–Sept. 19, 1881. Vice-President
1881–85 21st President (See Chronology of Presidents)

☆ THOMAS ANDREWS HENDRICKS
[*Under Grover Cleveland, first term*]
1819 Born in Muskingum County, Ohio, Sept. 7
1851–55 Served in U.S. House of Representatives (Democratic, Ind.)
1863–69 Served in U.S. Senate
1883–87 Governor of Indiana
1885 March 4–Nov. 25, 1885. Vice-President
1885 Died in Indianapolis, Ind., Nov. 25

☆ LEVI PARSONS MORTON
[*Under Benjamin Harrison*]
1824 Born in Shoreham, Vt., May 16
1879–81 Served in U.S. House of Representatives
(Republican, N.Y.)
1881–85 U.S. Minister to France
1889 March 4–March 3, 1893. Vice-President
1895–97 Governor of New York
1920 Died in Rhinebeck, N.Y., May 16

☆ ADLAI EWING STEVENSON
[*Under Grover Cleveland, second term*]
1835 Born in Christian County, Ky., Oct. 23
1875–77; 1879–81 Served in U.S. House of Representatives
(Democratic, Ill.)
1885–89 Assistant U.S. Postmaster General
1893 March 4–March 3, 1897. Vice-President
1914 Died in Chicago, Ill., June 14

☆ GARRET AUGUSTUS HOBART
[*Under William McKinley, first term*]
1844 Born in Long Branch, N.J., June 3
1872–76 Served in New Jersey state assembly (Republican)
1876–82 Served in New Jersey state senate
1897 March 4–Nov. 21, 1899. Vice-President
1899 Died in Paterson, N.J., Nov. 21

☆ THEODORE ROOSEVELT
[*Under William McKinley, second term*]
1901 March 4–Sept. 14, 1901. Vice-President
1901–09 26th President (See Chronology of Presidents)

☆ CHARLES WARREN FAIRBANKS
[*Under Theodore Roosevelt, second term*]
1852 Born in Unionville Center, Ohio, May 11
1897–1905 Served in U.S. Senate (Republican, Ind.)
1905 March 4–March 3, 1909. Vice-President
1918 Died in Indianapolis, Ind., June 4

☆ JAMES SCHOOLCRAFT SHERMAN
[*Under William H. Taft*]
1855 Born in Utica, N.Y., Oct. 24
1887–91; 1893–1909 Served in U.S. House of Representatives
(Republican, N.Y.)
1909 March 4–Oct. 30, 1912. Vice-President
1912 Died in Utica, N.Y., Oct. 30

☆ THOMAS RILEY MARSHALL
[*Under Woodrow Wilson, first and second terms*]
1854 Born in North Manchester, Ind., March 14
1909–13 Governor of Indiana
1913 March 4–March 3, 1921. Vice-President

1925 Died in Washington, D.C., June 1

☆ CALVIN COOLIDGE
[*Under Warren G. Harding*]
1921 March 4–Aug. 3, 1923. Vice-President
1923–29 30th President (See Chronology of Presidents)

☆ CHARLES GATES DAWES
[*Under Calvin Coolidge, second term*]
1865 Born in Marietta, Ohio, Aug. 27
1898–1901 U.S. Comptroller of the Currency
1925 March 4–March 3, 1929. Vice-President
1951 Died in Evanston, Ill., April 23

☆ CHARLES CURTIS
[*Under Herbert Hoover*]
1860 Born in Topeka, Kan., Jan. 25
1893–1907 Served in U.S. House of Representatives
(Republican, Kan.)
1907–13; 1915–29 Served in U.S. Senate
1929 March 4–March 3, 1933. Vice-President
1936 Died in Washington, D.C., Feb. 8

☆ JOHN NANCE GARNER
[*Under Franklin D. Roosevelt, first and second terms*]
1868 Born in Red River County, Tex., Nov. 22
1903–33 Served in U.S. House of Representatives
(Democratic, Tex.)
1933 March 4–Jan. 20, 1941. Vice-President

☆ HENRY AGARD WALLACE
[*Under Franklin D. Roosevelt, third term*]
1888 Born in Adair County, Iowa, Oct. 7
1933–40 U.S. Secretary of Agriculture
1941 Jan. 20–Jan. 20, 1945. Vice-President
1945–46 U.S. Secretary of Commerce
1948 Ran unsuccessfully for President as candidate of
Progressive Party
1965 Died in Danbury, Conn., Nov. 18

☆ HARRY S. TRUMAN
[*Under Franklin D. Roosevelt, fourth term*]
1945 Jan. 20–April 12, 1945. Vice-President
1945–53 33rd President (See Chronology of Presidents)

☆ ALBEN WILLIAM BARKLEY
[*Under Harry S. Truman, second term*]
1877 Born near Lowes, Graves County, Ky., Nov. 24
1913–27 Served in U.S. House of Representatives
(Democratic, Ky.)
1927–49; 1955–56 Served in U.S. Senate
1949 Jan. 20–Jan. 20, 1953. Vice-President
1956 Died in Lexington, Va., April 30

☆ RICHARD MILHOUS NIXON
[*Under Dwight D. Eisenhower, first and second terms*]
1913 Born in Yorba Linda, Calif., Jan. 9
1947–50 Served in U.S. House of Representatives (Republican,
Calif.)
1951–53 Served in U.S. Senate
1953 Jan. 20–Jan. 20, 1961. Vice-President

☆ LYNDON BAINES JOHNSON
[*Under John F. Kennedy*]
1961 Jan. 20–Nov. 22, 1963. Vice-President
1963 36th President (See Chronology of Presidents)

☆ HUBERT HORATIO HUMPHREY
[*Under Lyndon B. Johnson, second term*]
1911 Born in Wallace, S.D., May 27
1945–48 Mayor of Minneapolis, Minn.
1948–64 Served in U.S. Senate (Democratic, Minn.)
1965 Jan. 20–Vice-President

ELECTION OF 1789 [George Washington elected]
John Adams (See Chronology of Presidents)

ELECTION OF 1792 [George Washington elected]
John Adams (See Chronology of Presidents)
George Clinton (See Chronology of Vice-Presidents)

ELECTION OF 1796 [John Adams elected]
Thomas Jefferson (See Chronology of Presidents)
Thomas Pinckney (Federalist)
  Born in Charleston, S.C., Oct. 23, 1750
  Lawyer, diplomat
  Governor of South Carolina, 1787–89
  U.S. Minister to Great Britain, 1792–94
  Served in U.S. House of Representatives, 1797–1801
  Died in Charleston, S.C., Nov. 2, 1828
Aaron Burr (See Chronology of Vice-Presidents)

ELECTION OF 1800 [Thomas Jefferson elected]
Aaron Burr (See Chronology of Vice-Presidents)
John Adams (See Chronology of Presidents)
John Jay (Federalist)
  Born in New York, N.Y., Dec. 12, 1745
  Jurist, statesman
  President of Continental Congress, 1778–79
  U.S. Secretary of Foreign Affairs, 1784–89
  Chief Justice of U.S. Supreme Court, 1789–95
  Governor of New York, 1795–1801
  Died in Bedford, Westchester County, N.Y., May 17, 1829

ELECTION OF 1804 [Thomas Jefferson elected]
Charles Cotesworth Pinckney (Federalist)
  Born in Charleston, S.C., Feb. 25, 1746
  Statesman, diplomat
  Served in American Revolution
  Aided in framing the Constitution
  Died in Charleston, S.C., Aug. 16, 1825

ELECTION OF 1808 [James Madison elected]
Charles Cotesworth Pinckney (See Election of 1804)
George Clinton (See Chronology of Vice-Presidents)

ELECTION OF 1812 [James Madison elected]
De Witt Clinton (Democrat-Republican)
  Born in Little Britain, N.Y., March 2, 1769
  Lawyer, statesman
  U.S. Senator, 1802–03
  Mayor of New York City, 1803–07; 1810; 1811; 1813; 1814–15
  Governor of New York, 1817–21; 1825–28
  Died in Albany, N.Y., Feb. 11, 1828

ELECTION OF 1816 [James Monroe elected]
Rufus King (Federalist)
  Born in Scarboro, Maine, March 24, 1755
  Statesman
  Served in Continental Congress, 1784–87
  U.S. Senator, 1789–96; 1813–25
  U.S. Minister to Great Britain, 1796–1803; 1825–26
  Died in Jamaica, N.Y., April 29, 1827

ELECTION OF 1820 [James Monroe elected]
John Quincy Adams (See Chronology of Presidents)

ELECTION OF 1824 [John Quincy Adams elected]
Andrew Jackson (See Chronology of Presidents)
William Harris Crawford (faction of Democratic-Republican)
  Born in Amherst County, Va., Feb. 24, 1772
  Lawyer
  U.S. Senator, 1807–13
  U.S. Secretary of War, 1815–16
  U.S. Secretary of the Treasury, 1816–25
  Died in Ellerton, Ga., Sept. 15, 1834

Henry Clay (faction of Democratic-Republican)
  Born in Hanover County, Va., April 12, 1777
  Lawyer
  U.S. Senator, 1806–07; 1810–11; 1831–42; 1849–52
  Served in U.S. House of Representatives, 1811–14; 1815–21; 1823–25
  U.S. Secretary of State, 1825–29
  Died in Washington, D.C., June 29, 1852

ELECTION OF 1828 [Andrew Jackson elected]
John Quincy Adams (See Chronology of Presidents)

ELECTION OF 1832 [Andrew Jackson elected]
Henry Clay (See Election of 1824)

ELECTION OF 1836 [Martin Van Buren elected]
William Henry Harrison (See Chronology of Presidents)
Hugh Lawson White (Whig)
  Born in Iredell County, N.C., Oct. 30, 1773
  Lawyer
  U.S. Senator, 1825–40
  Died near Knoxville, Tenn., April 10, 1840
Daniel Webster (Whig)
  Born in Salisbury, N.H., Jan. 18, 1782
  Lawyer
  Served in U.S. House of Representatives, 1813–17; 1823–27
  U.S. Senator, 1827–41; 1845–50
  U.S. Secretary of State, 1841–43; 1850–52
  Died in Marshfield, Mass., Oct. 24, 1852

ELECTION OF 1840 [William Henry Harrison elected]
Martin Van Buren (See Chronology of Presidents)

ELECTION OF 1844 [James K. Polk elected]
Henry Clay (See Election of 1824)

ELECTION OF 1848 [Zachary Taylor elected]
Lewis Cass (Democratic)
  Born in Exeter, N.H., Oct. 9, 1782
  Lawyer
  U.S. Secretary of War, 1831–36
  U.S. Minister to France, 1836–42
  U.S. Senator, 1845–48; 1849–57
  U.S. Secretary of State, 1857–60
  Died in Detroit, Mich., June 17, 1866
Martin Van Buren (See Chronology of Presidents)

ELECTION OF 1852 [Franklin Pierce elected]
Winfield Scott (Whig)
  Born near Petersburg, Va., June 13, 1786
  Army officer
  Died in West Point, N.Y., May 29, 1866

ELECTION OF 1856 [James Buchanan elected]
John Charles Frémont (Republican)
  Born in Savannah, Ga., Jan. 21, 1813
  Explorer, Army officer
  U.S. Senator, 1850–51
  Governor of Territory of Arizona, 1878–83
  Died in New York, N.Y., July 13, 1890
Millard Fillmore (See Chronology of Presidents)

ELECTION OF 1860 [Abraham Lincoln elected]
Stephen Arnold Douglas (Democratic)
  Born in Brandon, Vt., April 23, 1813
  Lawyer, jurist
  Served in U.S. House of Representatives, 1843–47
  U.S. Senator, 1847–61
  Died in Chicago, Ill., June 3, 1861
John Cabell Breckinridge (See Chronology of Vice-Presidents)
John Bell (Constitutional Union)
  Born near Nashville, Tenn., Feb. 15, 1797
  Lawyer

Served in U.S. House of Representatives, 1827–41
U.S. Secretary of War, 1841
U.S. Senator, 1847–59
Died in Steward County, Tenn., Sept. 10, 1869

ELECTION OF 1864 [Abraham Lincoln elected]
George Brinton McClellan (Democratic)
 Born in Philadelphia, Pa., Dec. 3, 1826
 Army officer
 Governor of New Jersey, 1878–81
 Died in Orange, N.J., Oct. 29, 1885

ELECTION OF 1868 [Ulysses S. Grant elected]
Horatio Seymour (Democratic)
 Born in Onondaga County, N.Y., May 31, 1810
 Politician
 Governor of New York, 1853–55; 1863–65
 Died in Utica, N.Y., Feb. 12, 1886

ELECTION OF 1872 [Ulysses S. Grant elected]
Horace Greeley (Democratic, Liberal Republican)
 Born in Amherst, N.H., Feb. 3, 1811
 Journalist, newspaper publisher
 Founded New York Tribune, 1841
 Died in Pleasantville, N.Y., Nov. 29, 1872

ELECTION OF 1876 [Rutherford B. Hayes elected]
Samuel Jones Tilden (Democratic)
 Born in New Lebanon, N.Y., Feb. 9, 1814
 Lawyer
 Governor of New York, 1875–76
 Died in Yonkers, N.Y., Aug. 4, 1886

ELECTION OF 1880 [James A. Garfield elected]
Winfield Scott Hancock (Democratic)
 Born in Montgomery Square, Pa., Feb. 14, 1824
 Army officer
 Died on Governors Island, near New York, N.Y., Feb. 9, 1886
James Baird Weaver (Greenback-Labor)
 Born in Dayton, Ohio, June 12, 1833
 Lawyer
 Served in U.S. House of Representatives, 1879–81; 1885–89
 Died in Des Moines, Iowa, Feb. 6, 1912

ELECTION OF 1884 [Grover Cleveland elected]
James Gillespie Blaine (Republican)
 Born in West Brownsville, Pa., Jan. 31, 1830
 Statesman
 Served in U.S. House of Representatives, 1863–76
 Speaker of House, 1869–75
 U.S. Senator, 1876–81
 U.S. Secretary of State, 1881; 1889–92
 Died in Washington, D.C., Jan. 27, 1893

ELECTION OF 1888 [Benjamin Harrison elected]
Grover Cleveland (See Chronology of Presidents)

ELECTION OF 1892 [Grover Cleveland elected]
Benjamin Harrison (See Chronology of Presidents)
James Baird Weaver (See Election of 1880)

ELECTION OF 1896 [William McKinley elected]
William Jennings Bryan (Democratic, Populist)
 Born in Salem, Ill., March 19, 1860
 Lawyer
 Served in U.S. House of Representatives, 1891–95
 Renominated for President, 1900, 1908
 U.S. Secretary of State, 1913–15
 Died in Dayton, Tenn., July 26, 1925

ELECTION OF 1900 [William McKinley elected]
William Jennings Bryan (See Election of 1896)

ELECTION OF 1904 [Theodore Roosevelt elected]
Alton Brooks Parker (Democratic)
 Born in Cortland, N.Y., May 14, 1852
 Jurist
 Judge of New York Court of Appeals, 1889–96

Judge of Appellate Division of New York Supreme Court, 1896–97
 Chief Justice of New York Court of Appeals, 1898–1904
 Died in New York, N.Y., May 10, 1926
Eugene Victor Debs (Socialist)
 Born in Terre Haute, Ind., Nov. 5, 1855
 Political leader
 Organized Social Democratic Party of America, 1897
 Died in Elmhurst, Ill., Oct. 20, 1926

ELECTION OF 1908 [William H. Taft elected]
William Jennings Bryan (See Election of 1896)
Eugene Victor Debs (See Election of 1904)

ELECTION OF 1912 [Woodrow Wilson elected]
Theodore Roosevelt (See Chronology of Presidents)
William Howard Taft (See Chronology of Presidents)
Eugene Victor Debs (See Election of 1904)

ELECTION OF 1916 [Woodrow Wilson elected]
Charles Evans Hughes (Republican)
 Born in Glens Falls, N.Y., April 11, 1862
 Jurist
 Governor of New York, 1907–10
 Associate Justice of U.S. Supreme Court, 1910–16
 U.S. Secretary of State, 1921–25
 Chief Justice of U.S. Supreme Court, 1930–41
 Died in Osterville, Mass., Aug. 27, 1948

ELECTION OF 1920 [Warren G. Harding elected]
James Middleton Cox (Democratic)
 Born in Jacksonburg, Ohio, March 31, 1870
 Newspaper publisher
 Served in U.S. House of Representatives, 1909–13
 Governor of Ohio, 1913–15; 1917–21
 Died in Dayton, Ohio, July 15, 1957
Eugene Victor Debs (See Election of 1904)

ELECTION OF 1924 [Calvin Coolidge elected]
John William Davis (Democratic)
 Born in Clarksburg, W.Va., April 13, 1873
 Lawyer
 Served in U.S. House of Representatives, 1911–13
 U.S. Solicitor General, 1913–15
 U.S. Ambassador to Great Britain, 1918–21
 Died in Charleston, S.C., March 24, 1955
Robert Marion La Follette (Progressive)
 Born in Primrose, Wisc., June 14, 1855
 Political leader
 Served in U.S. House of Representatives, 1885–91
 U.S. Senator, 1906–25
 Died in Washington, D.C., June 18, 1925

ELECTION OF 1928 [Herbert C. Hoover elected]
Alfred Emanuel Smith (Democratic)
 Born in New York, N.Y., Dec. 30, 1873
 Political leader
 Member of New York state legislature, 1903–15
 Sheriff of New York County, 1915–17
 Governor of New York, 1919–20; 1923–25
 Died in New York, N.Y., Oct. 4, 1944

ELECTION OF 1932 [Franklin D. Roosevelt elected]
Herbert Clark Hoover (See Chronology of Presidents)
Norman Mattoon Thomas (Socialist)
 Born in Marion, Ohio, Nov. 20, 1884
 Political leader, writer

ELECTION OF 1936 [Franklin D. Roosevelt elected]
Alfred Mossman Landon (Republican)
 Born in West Middlesex, Pa., Sept. 9, 1887
 Businessman
 Governor of Kansas, 1933–37

ELECTION OF 1940 [Franklin D. Roosevelt elected]
Wendell Lewis Willkie (Republican)
 Born in Elwood, Ind., Feb. 18, 1892
 Lawyer, business executive
 Died in New York, N.Y., Oct. 8, 1944

ELECTION OF 1944 [Franklin D. Roosevelt elected]
Thomas Edmund Dewey (Republican)
　Born in Owosso, Mich., March 24, 1902
　Lawyer
　District Attorney of New York County, 1937–38
　Governor of New York, 1942–54

ELECTION OF 1948 [Harry S. Truman elected]
Thomas Edmund Dewey (See Election of 1944)
J. Strom Thurmond (States' Rights Democratic)
　Born in Edgefield, S.C., Dec. 5, 1902
　Governor of South Carolina, 1947–51
　U.S. Senator, 1955–
Henry Agard Wallace (See Chronology of Vice-Presidents)

ELECTION OF 1952 [Dwight D. Eisenhower elected]
Adlai Ewing Stevenson (Democratic)
　Born in Los Angeles, Calif., Feb. 5, 1900
　Lawyer
　Assistant to U.S. Secretary of the Navy, 1941–44
　Governor of Illinois, 1949–53
　Chief U.S. Delegate to the U.N., 1961–65
　Died in London, England, July 14, 1965

ELECTION OF 1956 [Dwight D. Eisenhower elected]
Adlai Ewing Stevenson (See Election of 1952)

ELECTION OF 1960 [John F. Kennedy elected]
Richard Milhous Nixon (See Chronology of Vice-Presidents)

ELECTION OF 1964 [Lyndon B. Johnson elected]
Barry Morris Goldwater (Republican)
　Born in Phoenix, Ariz., Jan. 1, 1909
　Businessman
　U.S. Senator, 1953–65

★　★　★

Presidential Election Returns from 1789 to the Present

(F) Federalist; (D) Democrat; (R) Republican; (DR) Democrat-Republican;
(NR) National Republican; (W) Whig; (P) People's; (Pr) Progressive;
(SR) States' Rights

YEAR	PRESIDENTS ELECTED	POPULAR VOTE	ELECTORAL VOTE	DEFEATED CANDIDATES	POPULAR VOTE	ELECTORAL VOTE
1789	George Washington (No party)	Unknown	69	No opponent		
1792	George Washington (F)	Unknown	132	No opponent		
1796	John Adams (F)	Unknown	71	Thomas Jefferson (DR)		68
1800	Thomas Jefferson (DR)	Unknown	73	Aaron Burr (DR)		73
1804	Thomas Jefferson (DR)	Unknown	162	Charles Pinckney (F)		14
1808	James Madison (DR)	Unknown	122	Charles Pinckney (F)		47
1812	James Madison (DR)	Unknown	128	De Witt Clinton (F)		89
1816	James Monroe (DR)	Unknown	183	Rufus King (F)		34
1820	James (Monroe (DR)	Unknown	231	John Quincy Adams (DR)		1
1824	John Quincy Adams (NR)	105,321	84	Andrew Jackson (D)	155,872	99
				Henry Clay (DR)	46,587	37
				William H. Crawford (DR)	44,282	41
1828	Andrew Jackson (D)	647,276	178	John Quincy Adams (NR)	508,064	83
1832	Andrew Jackson (D)	687,502	219	Henry Clay (DR)	530,189	49
1836	Martin Van Buren (D)	762,678	170	William H. Harrison (W)	548,007	73
1840	William H. Harrison (W)	1,275,017	234	Martin Van Buren (D)	1,128,702	60
1844	James K. Polk (D)	1,337,243	170	Henry Clay (W)	1,299,068	105
1848	Zachary Taylor (W)	1,360,101	163	Lewis Cass (D)	1,220,544	127
1852	Franklin Pierce (D)	1,601,474	254	Winfield Scott (W)	1,386,578	42
1856	James C. Buchanan (D)	1,927,995	174	John C. Frémont (R)	1,391,555	114
1860	Abraham Lincoln (R)	1,866,352	180	Stephen A. Douglas (D)	1,375,157	12
				John C. Breckinridge (D)	845,763	72
1864	Abraham Lincoln (R)	2,216,067	212	George B. McClellan (D)	1,808,725	21
1868	Ulysses S. Grant (R)	3,015,071	214	Horatio Seymour (D)	2,709,615	80
1872	Ulysses S. Grant (R)	3,597,070	286	Horace Greeley (D) [died Nov. 29, 1872]	2,834,079	
1876	Rutherford B. Hayes (R)	4,033,950	185	Samuel J. Tilden (D)	4,284,855	184
1880	James A. Garfield (R)	4,449,053	214	Winfield S. Hancock (D)	4,442,030	155

YEAR	PRESIDENTS ELECTED	POPULAR VOTE	ELECTORAL VOTE	DEFEATED CANDIDATES	POPULAR VOTE	ELECTORAL VOTE
1884	Grover Cleveland (D)	4,911,017	219	James G. Blaine (R)	4,848,334	182
1888	Benjamin Harrison (R)	5,440,216	233	Grover Cleveland (D)	5,538,233	168
1892	Grover Cleveland (D)	5,554,414	277	Benjamin Harrison (R)	5,190,802	145
				James Weaver (P)	1,027,329	22
1896	William McKinley (R)	7,035,638	271	William J. Bryan (D)	6,467,946	176
1900	William McKinley (R)	7,219,530	292	William J. Bryan (D)	6,358,071	155
1904	Theodore Roosevelt (R)	7,628,834	336	Alton B. Parker (D)	5,084,491	140
1908	William H. Taft (R)	7,679,006	321	William J. Bryan (D)	6,409,106	162
1912	Woodrow Wilson (D)	6,286,214	435	Theodore Roosevelt (Pr)	4,126,020	88
				William H. Taft (R)	3,483,922	8
1916	Woodrow Wilson (D)	9,129,606	277	Charles E. Hughes (R)	8,538,231	254
1920	Warren G. Harding (R)	16,152,200	404	James M. Cox (D)	9,147,553	127
1924	Calvin Coolidge (R)	15,725,016	382	John W. Davis (D)	8,386,503	136
				Robert M. LaFollette (Pr)	4,822,856	13
1928	Herbert Hoover (R)	21,429,109	444	Alfred E. Smith (D)	15,005,497	87
1932	Franklin D. Roosevelt (D)	22,851,857	472	Herbert Hoover (R)	15,761,841	59
1936	Franklin D. Roosevelt (D)	27,751,612	523	Alfred Landon (R)	16,679,583	8
1940	Franklin D. Roosevelt (D)	27,244,160	449	Wendell L. Willkie (R)	22,305,198	82
1944	Franklin D. Roosevelt (D)	25,602,504	432	Thomas E. Dewey (R)	22,014,201	99
1948	Harry S. Truman (D)	24,105,695	303	Thomas E. Dewey (R)	21,969,170	189
				J. Strom Thurmond (SR)	1,169,021	39
				Henry A. Wallace (Pr)	1,156,103	0
1952	Dwight D. Eisenhower (R)	33,936,252	442	Adlai E. Stevenson (D)	27,314,992	89
1956	Dwight D. Eisenhower (R)	35,582,236	457	Adlai E. Stevenson (D)	26,028,887	73*
1960	John F. Kennedy (D)	34,226,925	303	Richard Nixon (R)	34,114,124	219
1964	Lyndon B. Johnson (D)	43,126,506	486	Barry Goldwater (R)	27,176,799	52

Presidents not listed above are John Tyler (1841–45), Millard Fillmore (1850–53), Andrew Johnson (1865–69), and Chester Arthur (1881–85), who attained the Presidency through the accident of death of their predecessor and were never elected to the office. Theodore Roosevelt, Coolidge, Truman and Lyndon Johnson, who also inherited the Presidency, were elected following their first terms.

Stevenson polled 74 electoral votes but when the Electoral College met W. F. Turner of Montgomery, Ala., though pledged to vote for Stevenson, voted for Circuit Judge W. B. Jones of Alabama for President and Gov. Herman Talmadge of Georgia for Vice-President. (Turner was the 4th elector to vote independently.)

★ ★ ★

Members of the United States Cabinets from 1789 to the Present

Following is a list of the Cabinets of all Presidents of the United States. The first date given for each officer is the date on which he assumed his duties. When no concluding date or a successor's date are given, the officer retained his post throughout the administration.

GEORGE WASHINGTON: First Administration (1789-93)

VICE-PRESIDENT: John Adams, of Massachusetts.

SECY OF STATE: John Jay, of New York, was Secretary for Foreign Affairs under the Confederation and continued to act until Jefferson took office. Thomas Jefferson, of Virginia, March 22, 1790.

SECY OF THE TREASURY: Alexander Hamilton, of New York, Sept. 11, 1789.

SECY OF WAR: Henry Knox, of Massachusetts, Sept. 12, 1789.

ATTY GEN: Edmund Randolph, of Virginia, Feb. 2, 1790.

POSTMASTER GEN: Samuel Osgood, of Massachusetts, Sept. 26, 1789. Timothy Pickering, of Pennsylvania, Aug. 19, 1791.

GEORGE WASHINGTON: Second Administration (1793-97)

VICE-PRESIDENT: John Adams.

SECY OF STATE: Thomas Jefferson, continued from preceding administration. Edmund Randolph, of Virginia, Jan. 2, 1794. Timothy Pick-

ering, of Pennsylvania (Secretary of War), ad interim, Aug. 20, 1795; Timothy Pickering, Dec. 10, 1795.

SECY OF THE TREASURY: Alexander Hamilton, continued from preceding administration. Oliver Wolcott, Jr., of Connecticut, Feb. 2, 1795.

SECY OF WAR: Henry Knox, continued from preceding administration. Timothy Pickering, Jan. 2, 1795. Timothy Pickering (Secretary of State), ad interim, Dec. 10, 1795. James McHenry, of Maryland, Feb. 6, 1796.

ATTY GEN: Edmund Randolph, continued from preceding administration. William Bradford, of Pennsylvania, Jan. 29, 1794. Charles Lee, of Virginia, Dec. 10, 1795.

POSTMASTER GEN: Timothy Pickering, continued from preceding administration. Joseph Habersham, of Georgia, Feb. 25, 1795.

JOHN ADAMS (1797-1801)

VICE-PRESIDENT: Thomas Jefferson, of Virginia.

SECY OF STATE: Timothy Pickering, continued from preceding administration. Charles Lee, of Virginia (Attorney General), ad interim, May 13, 1800. John Marshall, of Virginia, June 6, 1800. John Marshall, of Virginia (Chief Justice of the U.S.), ad interim, Feb. 4, 1801.

SECY OF THE TREASURY: Oliver Wolcott, Jr., continued from preceding administration. Samuel Dexter, of Massachusetts, Jan. 1, 1801.

SECY OF WAR: James McHenry, continued from preceding administration. Benjamin Stoddert, of Maryland (Secretary of the Navy), ad interim, June 1, 1800. Samuel Dexter, June 12, 1800. Samuel Dexter (Secretary of the Treasury), ad interim, Jan. 1, 1801.

ATTY GEN: Charles Lee, continued from preceding administration.

POSTMASTER GEN: Joseph Habersham, continued from preceding administration.

SECY OF THE NAVY: Benjamin Stoddert, June 18, 1798.

THOMAS JEFFERSON: First Administration (1801-05)

VICE-PRESIDENT: Aaron Burr, of New York.

SECY OF STATE: John Marshall (Chief Justice of the U.S.). Levi Lincoln, of Massachusetts (Attorney General), ad interim, March 5, 1801. James Madison, of Virginia, May 2, 1801.

SECY OF THE TREASURY: Samuel Dexter, continued from preceding administration. Albert Gallatin, of Pennsylvania, May 14, 1801.

SECY OF WAR: Henry Dearborn, of Massachusetts, March 5, 1801.

ATTY GEN: Levi Lincoln, March 5, 1801.

POSTMASTER GEN: Joseph Habersham, continued from preceding administration. Gideon Granger, of Connecticut, Nov. 28, 1801.

SECY OF THE NAVY: Benjamin Stoddert, continued from preceding administration. Henry Dearborn (Secretary of War), ad interim, April 1, 1801. Robert Smith, of Maryland, July 27, 1801.

THOMAS JEFFERSON: Second Administration (1805-09)

VICE-PRESIDENT: George Clinton, of New York.

SECY OF STATE: James Madison, continued from preceding administration.

SECY OF THE TREASURY: Albert Gallatin, continued from preceding administration.

SECY OF WAR: Henry Dearborn, continued from preceding administration. John Smith, chief clerk, ad interim, Feb. 17, 1809.

ATTY GEN: John Breckenridge, of Kentucky, Aug. 7, 1805 (died Dec. 14, 1806). Caesar A. Rodney, of Delaware, Jan. 20, 1807.

POSTMASTER GEN: Gideon Granger, continued from preceding administration.

SECY OF THE NAVY: Robert Smith, continued from preceding administration.

JAMES MADISON: First Administration (1809-13)

VICE-PRESIDENT: George Clinton (died April 20, 1812).

PRESIDENT PRO TEMPORE OF THE SENATE: William H. Crawford, of Georgia.

SECY OF STATE: Robert Smith, March 6, 1809. James Monroe, of Virginia, April 6, 1811.

SECY OF THE TREASURY: Albert Gallatin, continued from preceding administration.

SECY OF WAR: John Smith, chief clerk, ad interim, continued from preceding administration. William Eustis, of Massachusetts, April 8, 1809. James Monroe (Secretary of State), ad interim, Jan. 1, 1813. John Armstrong, of New York, Feb. 5, 1813.

ATTY GEN: Cæsar A. Rodney, continued from preceding administration; resigned Dec. 5, 1811. William Pinkney, of Maryland, Jan. 6, 1812.

POSTMASTER GEN: Gideon Granger, continued from preceding administration.

SECY OF THE NAVY: Robert Smith, continued from preceding administration. Charles W. Goldsborough, chief clerk, ad interim, March 8, 1809. Paul Hamilton, of South Carolina, May 15, 1809-Dec. 31, 1812. Charles W. Goldsborough, ad interim, Jan. 7-18, 1813. William Jones, of Pennsylvania, Jan. 19, 1813.

JAMES MADISON: Second Administration (1813-17)

VICE-PRESIDENT: Elbridge Gerry, of Massachusetts (died Nov. 23, 1814).

PRESIDENT PRO TEMPORE OF THE SENATE: John Gaillard, of South Carolina.

SECY OF STATE: James Monroe, continued from preceding administration.

SECY OF THE TREASURY: Albert Gallatin, continued from preceding administration. William Jones (Secretary of the Navy), April 21,

1813. George W. Campbell, of Tennessee, Feb. 9, 1814. Alexander J. Dallas, of Pennsylvania, Oct. 14, 1814. William H. Crawford, of Georgia, Oct. 22, 1816.

SECY OF WAR: John Armstrong, continued from preceding administration. James Monroe (Secretary of State), ad interim, Aug. 30, 1814. James Monroe, Oct. 1, 1814. James Monroe (Secretary of State), ad interim, March 1, 1815. Alexander J. Dallas (Secretary of the Treasury), ad interim, March 14. William H. Crawford, Aug. 8, 1815. George Graham, chief clerk, ad interim, Oct. 22, 1816.

ATTY GEN: William Pinkney, continued from preceding administration. Richard Rush, of Pennsylvania, Feb. 11, 1814.

POSTMASTER GEN: Gideon Granger, continued from preceding administration. Return J. Meigs, Jr., of Ohio, April 11, 1814.

SECY OF THE NAVY: William Jones, continued from preceding administration. Benjamin Homans, chief clerk, ad interim, Dec. 2, 1814. Benjamin W. Crowninshield, of Massachusetts, Jan. 16, 1815.

JAMES MONROE: First Administration (1817-21)

VICE-PRESIDENT: Daniel D. Tompkins, of New York.

SECY OF STATE: John Graham, chief clerk, ad interim, March 4, 1817. Richard Rush (Attorney General), ad interim, March 10, 1817. John Quincy Adams, of Massachusetts, Sept. 22, 1817.

SECY OF THE TREASURY: William H. Crawford, continued from preceding administration.

SECY OF WAR: George Graham, ad interim, March 4, 1817. John C. Calhoun, of South Carolina, Dec. 10, 1817.

ATTY GEN: Richard Rush, continued from preceding administration. William Wirt, of Virginia, Nov. 15, 1817.

POSTMASTER GEN: Return J. Meigs, Jr., continued from preceding administration.

SECY OF THE NAVY: Benjamin W. Crowninshield, continued from preceding administration. John C. Calhoun (Secretary of War), ad interim, Oct. 1, 1818. Smith Thompson, of New York, Jan. 1, 1819.

JAMES MONROE: Second Administration (1821-25)

VICE-PRESIDENT: Daniel D. Tompkins.

SECY OF STATE: John Quincy Adams, continued from preceding administration.

SECY OF THE TREASURY: William H. Crawford, continued from preceding administration.

SECY OF WAR: John C. Calhoun, continued from preceding administration.

ATTY GEN: William Wirt, continued from preceding administration.

POSTMASTER GEN: Return J. Meigs, Jr., continued from preceding administration. John McLean, of Ohio, July 1, 1823.

SECY OF THE NAVY: Smith Thompson, continued from preceding administration. John Rodgers, ad interim, Sept. 1, 1823. Samuel L. Southard, of New Jersey, Sept. 16, 1823.

JOHN QUINCY ADAMS (1825-29)

VICE-PRESIDENT: John C. Calhoun, of South Carolina.

SECY OF STATE: Daniel Brent, chief clerk, ad interim, March 4, 1825. Henry Clay, of Kentucky, March 7, 1825.

SECY OF THE TREASURY: Samuel L. Southard (Secretary of the Navy), ad interim, March 7, 1825. Richard Rush, Aug. 1, 1825.

SECY OF WAR: James Barbour, of Virginia, March 7, 1825. Samuel L. Southard (Secretary of the Navy), ad interim, May 26, 1828. Peter B. Porter, of New York, June 21, 1828.

ATTY GEN: William Wirt, continued from preceding administration.

POSTMASTER GEN: John McLean, continued from preceding administration.

SECY OF THE NAVY: Samuel L. Southard, continued from preceding administration.

ANDREW JACKSON: First Administration (1829-33)

VICE-PRESIDENT: John C. Calhoun (resigned Dec. 28, 1832).

PRESIDENT PRO TEMPORE OF THE SENATE: Hugh Lawson White, of Tennessee.

SECY OF STATE: James A. Hamilton, of New York, ad interim, March 4, 1829. Martin Van Buren, of New York, March 28, 1829. Edward Livingston, of Louisiana, May 24, 1831.

SECY OF THE TREASURY: Samuel D. Ingham, of Pennsylvania, March 6, 1829. Asbury Dickins, chief clerk, ad interim, June 21, 1831. Louis McLane, of Delaware, Aug. 8, 1831.

SECY OF WAR: John H. Eaton, of Tennessee, March 9, 1829. Philip G. Randolph, chief clerk, ad interim, June 20, 1831. Roger B. Taney, of Maryland (Attorney General), ad interim, July 21, 1831. Lewis Cass, of Ohio, Aug. 8, 1831.

Atty Gen: John M. Berrien, of Georgia, March 9, 1829-June 22, 1831. Roger B. Taney, July 20, 1831.

Postmaster Gen: John McLean, continued from preceding administration. William T. Barry, of Kentucky, April 6, 1829.

Secy of the Navy: Charles Hay, chief clerk, ad interim, March 4, 1829. John Branch, of North Carolina, March 9, 1829. John Boyle, chief clerk, ad interim, May 12, 1831. Levi Woodbury, of New Hampshire, May 23, 1831.

ANDREW JACKSON: Second Administration (1833-37)

Vice-President: Martin Van Buren, of New York.

Secy of State: Edward Livingston, continued from preceding administration. Louis McLane, May 29, 1833. John Forsyth, of Georgia, July 1, 1834.

Secy of the Treasury: Louis McLane, continued from preceding administration. William J. Duane, of Pennsylvania, June 1, 1833. Roger B. Taney, Sept. 23, 1833. McClintock Young, chief clerk, ad interim, June 25, 1834. Levi Woodbury, July 1, 1834.

Secy of War: Lewis Cass, continued from preceding administration. Carey A. Harris, of Tennessee (Commissioner of Indian Affairs), ad interim, Oct. 5, 1836. Benjamin F. Butler, of New York (Attorney General), ad interim, Oct. 26, 1836. Benjamin F. Butler, commissioned March 3, 1837, ad interim.

Atty Gen: Roger B. Taney, continued from preceding administration. Benjamin F. Butler, Nov. 18, 1833.

Postmaster Gen: William T. Barry, continued from preceding administration. Amos Kendall, of Kentucky, May 1, 1835.

Secy of the Navy: Levi Woodbury, continued from preceding administration. Mahlon Dickerson, of New Jersey, June 30, 1834.

MARTIN VAN BUREN (1837-41)

Vice-President: Richard M. Johnson, of Kentucky.

Secy of State: John Forsyth, continued from preceding administration.

Secy of the Treasury: Levi Woodbury, continued from preceding administration.

Secy of War: Benjamin F. Butler, ad interim, continued from preceding administration. Joel R. Poinsett, of South Carolina, March 14, 1837.

Atty Gen: Benjamin F. Butler, continued from preceding administration. Felix Grundy, of Tennessee, Sept. 1, 1838. Henry D. Gilpin, of Pennsylvania, Jan. 11, 1840.

Postmaster Gen: Amos Kendall, continued from preceding administration. John M. Niles, of Connecticut, May 26, 1840.

Secy of the Navy: Mahlon Dickerson, continued from preceding administration. James K. Paulding, of New York, July 1, 1838.

WILLIAM HENRY HARRISON (1841)

Vice-President: John Tyler, of Virginia.

Secy of State: J. L. Martin, chief clerk, ad interim, March 4, 1841. Daniel Webster, of Massachusetts, March 5, 1841.

Secy of the Treasury: McClintock Young, ad interim, March 4, 1841. Thomas Ewing, of Ohio, March 5, 1841.

Secy of War: John Bell, of Tennessee, March 5, 1841.

Atty Gen: John J. Crittenden, of Kentucky, March 5, 1841.

Postmaster Gen: Selah R. Hobbie, of New York (First Assistant Postmaster General), ad interim, March 4, 1841. Francis Granger, of New York, March 8, 1841.

Secy of the Navy: John D. Simms, chief clerk, ad interim, March 4, 1841. George E. Badger, of North Carolina, March 5, 1841.

JOHN TYLER (1841-45)

President Pro Tempore of the Senate: Samuel L. Southard, of New Jersey; Willie P. Mangum, of North Carolina.

Secy of State: Daniel Webster, continued from preceding administration. Hugh S. Legaré, of South Carolina (Attorney General), ad interim, May 9, 1843. William S. Derrick, chief clerk, ad interim, June 21, 1843. Abel P. Upshur, of Virginia (Secretary of the Navy), ad interim, June 24, 1843. Abel P. Upshur, July 24, 1843. John Nelson, of Maryland (Attorney General), ad interim, Feb. 29, 1844. John C. Calhoun, April 1, 1844.

Secy of the Treasury: Thomas Ewing, continued from preceding administration. McClintock Young, ad interim, Sept. 13, 1841. Walter Forward, of Pennsylvania, Sept. 13, 1841. McClintock Young, ad interim, March 1, 1843. John C. Spencer, of New York, March 8, 1843. McClintock Young, ad interim, May 2, 1844. George M. Bibb, of Kentucky, July 4, 1844.

Secy of War: John Bell, continued from preceding administration.

Albert M. Lea, of Maryland, ad interim, Sept. 12, 1841. John C. Spencer, of New York, Oct. 12, 1841. James M. Porter, of Pennsylvania, March 8, 1843. William Wilkins, of Pennsylvania, Feb. 20, 1844.

Atty Gen: John J. Crittenden, continued from preceding administration. Hugh S. Legaré, Sept. 20, 1841 (died June 20, 1843). John Nelson, July 1, 1843.

Postmaster Gen: Francis Granger, continued from preceding administration. Selah R. Hobbie (First Assistant Postmaster General), ad interim, Sept. 14, 1841. Charles A. Wickliffe, of Kentucky, Oct. 13, 1841.

Secy of the Navy: George E. Badger, continued from preceding administration. John D. Simms, chief clerk, ad interim, Sept. 11, 1841. Abel P. Upshur, Oct. 11, 1841. David Henshaw, of Massachusetts, July 24, 1843. Thomas W. Gilmer, of Virginia, Feb. 19, 1844. Lewis Warrington (captain, U.S. Navy), ad interim, Feb. 29, 1844. John Y. Mason, of Virginia, March 26, 1844.

JAMES K. POLK (1845-49)

Vice-President: George M. Dallas, of Pennsylvania.

Secy of State: John C. Calhoun, continued from preceding administration. James Buchanan, of Pennsylvania, March 10, 1845.

Secy of the Treasury: George M. Bibb, continued from preceding administration. Robert J. Walker, of Mississippi, March 8, 1845.

Secy of War: William Wilkins, continued from preceding administration. William L. Marcy, of New York, March 8, 1845.

Atty Gen: John Nelson, continued from preceding administration. John Y. Mason, March 11, 1845. Nathan Clifford, of Maine, Oct. 17, 1846. Isaac Toucey, of Connecticut, June 29, 1848.

Postmaster Gen: Charles A. Wickliffe, continued from preceding administration. Cave Johnson, of Tennessee, March 6, 1845.

Secy of the Navy: John Y. Mason, continued from preceding administration. George Bancroft, of Massachusetts, March 10, 1845. John Y. Mason, Sept. 9, 1846.

ZACHARY TAYLOR (1849-50)

Vice-President: Millard Fillmore, of New York.

Secy of State: James Buchanan, continued from preceding administration. John M. Clayton, of Delaware, March 7, 1849.

Secy of the Treasury: Robert J. Walker, continued from preceding administration. McClintock Young, ad interim, March 6, 1849. William M. Meredith, of Pennsylvania, March 8, 1849.

Secy of War: William L. Marcy, continued from preceding administration. Reverdy Johnson, of Maryland (Attorney General), March 8, 1849. George W. Crawford, of Georgia, March 14, 1849.

Atty Gen: Isaac Toucey, continued from preceding administration. Reverdy Johnson, March 8, 1849.

Postmaster Gen: Cave Johnson, continued from preceding administration. Selah R. Hobbie, ad interim, March 6, 1849. Jacob Collamer, of Vermont, March 8, 1849.

Secy of the Navy: John Y. Mason, continued from preceding administration. William B. Preston, of Virginia, March 8, 1849.

Secy of the Interior: Thomas Ewing, of Ohio, March 8, 1849.

MILLARD FILLMORE (1850-53)

President Pro Tempore of the Senate: William R. King, of Alabama; David R. Atchison, of Missouri.

Secy of State: John M. Clayton, continued from preceding administration. Daniel Webster, July 22, 1850 (died Oct. 24, 1852). Charles M. Conrad, of Louisiana (Secretary of War), ad interim, Oct. 25, 1852. Edward Everett, of Massachusetts, Nov. 6, 1852.

Secy of the Treasury: William M. Meredith, continued from preceding administration. Thomas Corwin, of Ohio, July 23, 1850.

Secy of War: George W. Crawford, continued from preceding administration. Samuel J. Anderson, chief clerk, ad interim, July 23, 1850. Winfield Scott (major general, U.S. Army), ad interim, July 24, 1850. Charles M. Conrad, of Louisiana, Aug. 14, 1850.

Atty Gen: Reverdy Johnson, continued from preceding administration. John J. Crittenden, of Kentucky, Aug. 14, 1850.

Postmaster Gen: Jacob Collamer, continued from preceding administration. Nathan K. Hall, of New York, July 23, 1850. Samuel D. Hubbard, of Connecticut, Sept. 14, 1852.

Secy of the Navy: William B. Preston, continued from preceding administration. Lewis Warrington, ad interim, July 23, 1850. William A. Graham, of North Carolina, Aug. 2, 1850. John P. Kennedy, of Maryland, July 26, 1852.

Secy of the Interior: Thomas Ewing, continued from preceding administration. Daniel C. Goddard, chief clerk, ad interim, July 23,

1850. Thomas M. T. McKennan, of Pennsylvania, Aug. 15, 1850. Daniel C. Goddard, ad interim, Aug. 27, 1850. Alexander H. H. Stuart, of Virginia, Sept. 16, 1850.

FRANKLIN PIERCE (1853-57)

VICE-PRESIDENT: William R. King (died April 18, 1853).
PRESIDENT PRO TEMPORE OF THE SENATE: David R. Atchison; Lewis Cass; Jesse D. Bright, of Indiana; Charles E. Stuart; James M. Mason, of Virginia.
SECY OF STATE: William Hunter, chief clerk, ad interim, March 4, 1853. William L. Marcy, of New York, March 7, 1853.
SECY OF THE TREASURY: Thomas Corwin, continued from preceding administration. James Guthrie, of Kentucky, March 7, 1853.
SECY OF WAR: Charles M. Conrad, continued from preceding administration. Jefferson Davis, of Mississippi, March 7, 1853. Samuel Cooper (Adjutant General, U.S. Army), ad interim, March 3, 1857.
ATTY GEN: John J. Crittenden, continued from preceding administration. Caleb Cushing, of Massachusetts, March 7, 1853.
POSTMASTER GEN: Samuel D. Hubbard, continued from preceding administration. James Campbell, of Pennsylvania, March 7, 1853.
SECY OF THE NAVY: John P. Kennedy, continued from preceding administration. James C. Dobbin, of North Carolina, March 7, 1853.
SECY OF THE INTERIOR: Alexander H. H. Stuart, continued from preceding administration. Robert McClelland, of Michigan, March 7, 1853.

JAMES BUCHANAN (1857-61)

VICE-PRESIDENT: John C. Breckinridge, of Kentucky.
SECY OF STATE: William L. Marcy, continued from preceding administration. Lewis Cass, March 6, 1857. William Hunter, chief clerk, ad interim, Dec. 15, 1860. Jeremiah S. Black, of Pennsylvania, Dec. 17, 1860.
SECY OF THE TREASURY: James Guthrie, continued from preceding administration. Howell Cobb, of Georgia, March 6, 1857. Isaac Toucey (Secretary of the Navy), ad interim, Dec. 10, 1860. Philip R. Thomas, of Maryland, Dec. 12, 1860. John A. Dix, of New York, Jan. 15, 1861.
SECY OF WAR: Samuel Cooper, ad interim, March 4, 1857. John B. Floyd, of Virginia, March 6, 1857. Joseph Holt, of Kentucky (Postmaster General), Jan. 1, 1861.
ATTY GEN: Caleb Cushing, continued from preceding administration. Jeremiah S. Black, March 11, 1857. Edwin M. Stanton, of Pennsylvania, Dec. 22, 1860.
POSTMASTER GEN: James Campbell, continued from preceding administration. Aaron V. Brown, of Tennessee, March 6, 1857 (died March 8, 1859). Horatio King, of Maine (First Assistant Postmaster General), ad interim, March 9, 1859. Joseph Holt, March 14, 1859. Horatio King, Jan. 1, 1861.
SECY OF THE NAVY: James C. Dobbin, continued from preceding administration. Isaac Toucey, of Connecticut, March 6, 1857.
SECY OF THE INTERIOR: Robert McClelland, continued from preceding administration. Jacob Thompson, March 10, 1857. Moses Kelly, chief clerk, ad interim, Jan. 10, 1861.

ABRAHAM LINCOLN: First Administration (1861-65)

VICE-PRESIDENT: Hannibal Hamlin, of Maine.
SECY OF STATE: Jeremiah S. Black, continued from preceding administration. William H. Seward, of New York, March 5, 1861.
SECY OF THE TREASURY: John A. Dix, continued from preceding administration. Salmon P. Chase, of Ohio, March 7, 1861. George Harrington, of the District of Columbia (Assistant Secretary), ad interim, July 1, 1864. William P. Fessenden, of Maine, July 5, 1864.
SECY OF WAR: Joseph Holt, continued from preceding administration. Simon Cameron, of Pennsylvania, March 11, 1861. Edwin M. Stanton, Jan. 20, 1862.
ATTY GEN: Edwin M. Stanton, continued from preceding administration. Edward Bates, of Missouri, March 5, 1861. James Speed, of Kentucky, Dec. 5, 1864.
POSTMASTER GEN: Horatio King, continued from preceding administration. Montgomery Blair, of the District of Columbia, March 9, 1861. William Dennison, of Ohio, Oct. 1, 1864.
SECY OF THE NAVY: Isaac Toucey, continued from preceding administration. Gideon Welles, of Connecticut, March 7, 1861.
SECY OF THE INTERIOR: Moses Kelly, chief clerk, ad interim, March 4, 1861. Caleb B. Smith, of Indiana, March 5, 1861. John P. Usher, of Indiana, Jan. 1, 1863.

ABRAHAM LINCOLN: Second Administration (1865)

VICE-PRESIDENT: Andrew Johnson, of Tennessee.
SECY OF STATE: William H. Seward, continued from preceding administration.
SECY OF THE TREASURY: George Harrington, ad interim, March 4, 1865. Hugh McCulloch, of Indiana, March 9, 1865.
SECY OF WAR: Edwin M. Stanton, continued from preceding administration.
ATTY GEN: James Speed, continued from preceding administration.
POSTMASTER GEN: William Dennison, continued from preceding administration.
SECY OF THE NAVY: Gideon Welles, continued from preceding administration.
SECY OF THE INTERIOR: John P. Usher, continued from preceding administration.

ANDREW JOHNSON (1865-69)

PRESIDENT PRO TEMPORE OF THE SENATE: Lafayette S. Foster, of Connecticut; Benjamin F. Wade, of Ohio.
SECY OF STATE: William H. Seward, continued from preceding administration.
SECY OF THE TREASURY: Hugh McCullock, continued from preceding administration.
SECY OF WAR: Edwin M. Stanton, continued from preceding administration; suspended Aug. 12, 1867. Ulysses S. Grant, of Ohio, ad interim, Aug. 12, 1867. Edwin M. Stanton, reinstated Jan. 13, 1868. John M. Schofield, of Illinois, June 1, 1868.
ATTY GEN: James Speed, continued from preceding administration. J. Hubley Ashton, of Pennsylvania (Assistant Attorney General), acting, July 17, 1866. Henry Stanbery, of Ohio, July 23, 1866. Orville H. Browning, of Illinois (Secretary of the Interior), ad interim, March 13, 1868. William M. Evarts, of New York, July 20, 1868.
POSTMASTER GEN: William Dennison, continued from preceding administration. Alexander W. Randall, of Wisconsin (First Assistant Postmaster General), ad interim, July 17, 1866. Alexander W. Randall, July 25, 1866.
SECY OF THE NAVY: Gideon Welles, continued from preceding administration.
SECY OF THE INTERIOR: John P. Usher, continued from preceding administration. James Harlan, of Iowa, May 15, 1865. Orville H. Browning, of Illinois, Sept. 1, 1866.

ULYSSES S. GRANT: First Administration (1869-73)

VICE-PRESIDENT: Schuyler Colfax, of Indiana.
SECY OF STATE: William H. Seward, continued from preceding administration. Elihu B. Washburne, of Illinois, March 5, 1869. Hamilton Fish, of New York, March 17, 1869.
SECY OF TREASURY: Hugh McCulloch, continued from preceding administration. John F. Hartley, of Maine (Assistant Secretary), ad interim, March 5, 1869. George S. Boutwell, of Massachusetts, March 11, 1869.
SECY OF WAR: John M. Schofield, continued from preceding administration. John A. Rawlins, of Illinois, March 11, 1869. William T. Sherman, of Ohio, Sept. 11, 1869. William W. Belknap, of Iowa, Nov. 1, 1869.
ATTY GEN: William M. Evarts, continued from preceding administration. J. Hubley Ashton (Assistant Attorney General), acting, March 5, 1869. Ebenezer R. Hoar, of Massachusetts, March 11, 1869. Amos T. Akerman, of Georgia, July 8, 1870. George H. Williams, of Oregon, Jan. 10, 1872.
POSTMASTER GEN: St. John B. L. Skinner, of New York (First Assistant Secretary), ad interim, March 4, 1869. John A. J. Creswell, of Maryland, March 5, 1869.
SECY OF THE NAVY: William Faxon, of Connecticut (Assistant Secretary), ad interim, March 4, 1869. Adolph E. Borie, of Pennsylvania, March 9, 1869. George M. Robeson, of New Jersey, June 25, 1869.
SECY OF THE INTERIOR: William T. Otto, of Indiana (Assistant Secretary), ad interim, March 4, 1869. Jacob D. Cox, of Ohio, March 9, 1869. Columbus Delano, of Ohio, Nov. 1, 1870.

ULYSSES S. GRANT: Second Administration (1873-77)

VICE-PRESIDENT: Henry Wilson, of Massachusetts (died Nov. 22, 1875).
PRESIDENT PRO TEMPORE OF THE SENATE: Thomas W. Ferry, of Michigan.
SECY OF STATE: Hamilton Fish, continued from preceding administration.
SECY OF THE TREASURY: George S. Boutwell, continued from preced-

ing administration. William A. Richardson, of Massachusetts, March 17, 1873. Benjamin H. Bristow, of Kentucky, June 4, 1875. Charles F. Conant, of New Hampshire (Assistant Secretary), ad interim, June 21, 1876. Lot M. Morrill, of Maine, July 7, 1876.

SECY OF WAR: William W. Belknap, continued from preceding administration. George M. Robeson (Secretary of the Navy), ad interim, March 2, 1876. Alphonso Taft, of Ohio, March 11, 1876. James D. Cameron, of Pennsylvania, June 1, 1876.

ATTY GEN: George H. Williams, continued from preceding administration. Edwards Pierrepont, of New York, May 15, 1875. Alphonso Taft, June 1, 1876.

POSTMASTER GEN: John A. J. Creswell, continued from preceding administration. James W. Marshall, of Virginia, July 7, 1874. Marshall Jewell, of Connecticut, Sept. 1, 1874. James N. Tyner, of Indiana, July 12, 1876.

SECY OF THE NAVY: George M. Robeson, continued from preceding administration.

SECY OF THE INTERIOR: Columbus Delano, continued from preceding administration. Benjamin R. Cowen, of Ohio (Assistant Secretary), ad interim, Oct. 1, 1875. Zachariah Chandler, of Michigan, Oct. 19, 1875.

RUTHERFORD B. HAYES (1877-81)

VICE-PRESIDENT: William A. Wheeler, of New York.

SECY OF STATE: Hamilton Fish, continued from preceding administration. William M. Evarts, March 12, 1877.

SECY OF THE TREASURY: Lot M. Morrill, continued from preceding administration. John Sherman, of Ohio, March 10, 1877.

SECY OF WAR: James C. Cameron, continued from preceding administration. George W. McCrary, of Iowa, March 12, 1877. Alexander Ramsey, of Minnesota, Dec. 12, 1879.

ATTY GEN: Alphonso Taft, continued from preceding administration. Charles Devens, of Massachusetts, March 12, 1877.

POSTMASTER GEN: James N. Tyner, continued from preceding administration. David M. Key, of Tennessee, March 12, 1877-Aug. 24, 1880. Horace Maynard, of Tennessee, Aug. 25, 1880.

SECY OF THE NAVY: George M. Robeson, continued from preceding administration. Richard W. Thompson, of Indiana, March 12, 1877. Alexander Ramsey (Secretary of War), ad interim, Dec. 20, 1880. Nathan Goff, Jr., of West Virginia, Jan. 6, 1881.

SECY OF THE INTERIOR: Zachariah Chandler, continued from preceding administration. Carl Schurz, of Missouri, March 12, 1877.

JAMES A. GARFIELD (1881)

VICE-PRESIDENT: Chester A. Arthur, of New York.

SECY OF STATE: William M. Evarts, continued from preceding administration. James G. Blaine, of Maine, March 7, 1881.

SECY OF THE TREASURY: Henry F. French, of Massachusetts (Assistant Secretary), ad interim, March 4, 1881. William Windom, of Minnesota, March 8, 1881.

SECY OF WAR: Alexander Ramsey, continued from preceding administration. Robert T. Lincoln, of Illinois, March 11, 1881.

ATTY GEN: Charles Devens, continued from preceding administration. Wayne MacVeagh, of Pennsylvania, March 7, 1881.

POSTMASTER GEN: Horace Maynard, continued from preceding administration. Thomas L. James, of New York, March 8, 1881.

SECY OF THE NAVY: Nathan Goff, Jr., continued from preceding administration. William H. Hunt, of Louisiana, March 7, 1881.

SECY OF THE INTERIOR: Carl Schurz, continued from preceding administration. Samuel J. Kirkwood, of Iowa, March 8, 1881.

CHESTER A. ARTHUR (1881-85)

PRESIDENT PRO TEMPORE OF THE SENATE: Thomas F. Bayard, of Delaware; David Davis, of Illinois; George F. Edmunds, of Vermont.

SECY OF STATE: James G. Blaine, continued from preceding administration. Frederick T. Frelinghuysen, of New Jersey, Dec. 19, 1881.

SECY OF THE TREASURY: William Windom, continued from preceding administration. Charles J. Folger, of New York, Nov. 14, 1881 (died Sept. 4, 1884). Charles E. Coon, of New York (Assistant Secretary), ad interim, Sept. 4, 1884. Henry F. French, of Massachusetts (Assistant Secretary), ad interim, Sept. 8, 1884. Charles E. Coon (Assistant Secretary), ad interim, Sept. 15, 1884. Walter Q. Gresham, of Indiana, Sept. 24, 1884. Henry F. French (Assistant Secretary), ad interim, Oct. 29, 1884. Hugh McCulloch, of Indiana, Oct. 31, 1884.

SECY OF WAR: Robert T. Lincoln, continued from preceding administration.

ATTY GEN: Wayne MacVeagh, continued from preceding administration. Samuel F. Phillips, of North Carolina (Solicitor General), ad interim, Nov. 14, 1881. Benjamin H. Brewster, of Pennsylvania,

Jan. 3, 1882.

POSTMASTER GEN: Thomas L. James, continued from preceding administration. Timothy O. Howe, of Wisconsin, Jan. 5, 1882 (died March 25, 1883). Frank Hatton, of Iowa (First Assistant Postmaster General), ad interim, March 26, 1883. Walter Q. Gresham, of Indiana, April 11, 1883. Frank Hatton, Sept. 25, 1884.

SECY OF THE NAVY: William H. Hunt, continued from preceding administration. William E. Chandler, of New Hampshire, April 17, 1882.

SECY OF THE INTERIOR: Samuel J. Kirkwood, continued from preceding administration. Henry M. Teller, of Colorado, April 17, 1882.

GROVER CLEVELAND: First Administration (1885-89)

VICE-PRESIDENT: Thomas A. Hendricks, of Indiana (died Nov. 25, 1885).

PRESIDENT PRO TEMPORE OF THE SENATE: John Sherman, of Ohio; John J. Ingalls, of Kansas.

SECY OF STATE: Frederick T. Frelinghuysen, continued from preceding administration. Thomas F. Bayard, of Delaware, March 6, 1885.

SECY OF THE TREASURY: Hugh McCulloch, continued from preceding administration. Daniel Manning, of New York, March 8, 1885. Charles S. Fairchild, of New York, April 1, 1887.

SECY OF WAR: Robert T. Lincoln, continued from preceding administration. William C. Endicott, of Massachusetts, March 6, 1885.

ATTY GEN: Benjamin H. Brewster, continued from preceding administration. Augustus H. Garland, of Arkansas, March 9, 1885.

POSTMASTER GEN: Frank Hatton, continued from preceding administration. William F. Vilas, of Wisconsin, March 6, 1885. Don M. Dickinson, of Michigan, Jan. 16, 1888.

SECY OF THE NAVY: William E. Chandler, continued from preceding administration. William C. Whitney, of New York, March 6, 1885.

SECY OF THE INTERIOR: Merritt L. Joslyn, of Illinois (Assistant Secretary), ad interim, March 4, 1885. Lucius Q. C. Lamar, of Mississippi, March 6, 1885. Henry L. Muldrow, of Mississippi (First Assistant Secretary), ad interim, Jan. 11, 1888. William F. Vilas, Jan. 16, 1888.

SECY OF AGRICULTURE: Norman J. Colman, of Missouri, Feb. 13, 1889.

BENJAMIN HARRISON (1889-93)

VICE-PRESIDENT: Levi P. Morton, of New York.

SECY OF STATE: Thomas F. Bayard, continued from preceding administration. James G. Blaine, March 7, 1889. William F. Wharton, of Massachusetts (Assistant Secretary), ad interim, June 4, 1892. John W. Foster, of Indiana, June 29, 1892. William F. Wharton, ad interim, Feb. 23, 1893.

SECY OF THE TREASURY: Charles S. Fairchild, continued from preceding administration. William Windom, March 7, 1889 (died Jan. 29, 1891). Allured B. Nettleton, of Minnesota (Assistant Secretary), ad interim, Jan. 30, 1891. Charles Foster, of Ohio, Feb. 24, 1891.

SECY OF WAR: William C. Endicott, continued from preceding administration. Redfield Proctor, of Vermont, March 5, 1889. Lewis A. Grant, of Minnesota (Assistant Secretary), ad interim, Dec. 6, 1891. Stephen B. Elkins, of West Virginia, Dec. 24, 1891.

ATTY GEN: Augustus H. Garland, continued from preceding administration. William H. H. Miller, of Indiana, March 6, 1889.

POSTMASTER GEN: Don M. Dickinson, continued from preceding administration. John Wanamaker, of Pennsylvania, March 5, 1889.

SECY OF THE NAVY: William C. Whitney, continued from preceding administration. Benjamin F. Tracy, of New York, March 5, 1889.

SECY OF THE INTERIOR: William F. Vilas, continued from preceding administration. John W. Noble, of Missouri, March 7, 1889.

SECY OF AGRICULTURE: Norman J. Colman, continued from preceding administration. Jeremiah M. Rusk, of Wisconsin, March 7, 1889.

GROVER CLEVELAND Second Administration (1893-97)

VICE-PRESIDENT: Adlai E. Stevenson, of Illinois.

SECY OF STATE: William F. Wharton, continued from preceding administration. Walter Q. Gresham, March 6, 1893 (died May 28, 1895). Edwin F. Uhl, of Michigan (Assistant Secretary), ad interim, May 28, 1895. Alvey A. Adee, of the District of Columbia (Second Assistant Secretary), ad interim, May 31, 1895. Edwin F. Uhl, ad interim, June 1, 1895. Richard Olney, of Massachusetts, June 10, 1895.

SECY OF THE TREASURY: Charles Foster, continued from preceding administration. John G. Carlisle, of Kentucky, March 6, 1893.

SECY OF WAR: Stephen B. Elkins, continued from preceding administration. Daniel S. Lamont, of New York, March 6, 1893.

ATTY GEN: William H. H. Miller, of Indiana, continued from preceding administration. Richard Olney, March 6, 1893. Judson Harmon, of Ohio, June 11, 1895.

POSTMASTER GEN: John Wanamaker, continued from preceding administration. Wilson S. Bissell, of New York, March 6, 1893. William L. Wilson, of West Virginia, April 4, 1895.

SECY OF THE NAVY: Benjamin F. Tracy, continued from preceding administration. Hilary A. Herbert, of Alabama, March 6, 1893.

SECY OF THE INTERIOR: John W. Noble, continued from preceding administration. Hoke Smith, of Georgia, March 6, 1893. John M. Reynolds, of Pennsylvania (Assistant Secretary), ad interim, Sept. 1, 1896. David R. Francis, of Missouri, Sept. 4, 1896.

SECY OF AGRICULTURE: Jeremiah M. Rusk, continued from preceding administration. Julius Sterling Morton, of Nebraska, March 6, 1893.

WILLIAM McKINLEY: First Administration (1897-1901)

VICE-PRESIDENT: Garret A. Hobart, of New Jersey (died Nov. 21, 1899).

PRESIDENT PRO TEMPORE OF THE SENATE: William P. Frye, of Maine.

SECY OF STATE: Richard Olney, continued from preceding administration. John Sherman, of Ohio, March 5, 1897; William R. Day, of Ohio, April 28, 1898. Alvey A. Adee (Second Assistant Secretary), ad interim, Sept. 17, 1898. John Hay, of the District of Columbia, Sept. 30, 1898.

SECY OF THE TREASURY: John G. Carlisle, continued from preceding administration. Lyman J. Gage, of Illinois, March 5, 1897.

SECY OF WAR: Daniel S. Lamont, continued from preceding administration. Russell A. Alger, of Michigan, March 5, 1897. Elihu Root, of New York, Aug. 1, 1899.

ATTY GEN: Judson Harmon, continued from preceding administration. Joseph McKenna, of California, March 7, 1897. John K. Richards, of Ohio (Solicitor General), ad interim, Jan. 26, 1898; John W. Griggs, of New Jersey, Feb. 1, 1898.

POSTMASTER GEN: William L. Wilson, continued from preceding administration. James A. Gary, of Maryland, March 5, 1897. Charles Emory Smith, of Pennsylvania, April 21, 1898.

SECY OF THE NAVY: Hilary A. Herbert, continued from preceding administration. John D. Long, of Massachusetts, March 5, 1897.

SECY OF THE INTERIOR: David R. Francis, continued from preceding administration. Cornelius N. Bliss, of New York, March 5, 1897. Ethan A. Hitchcock, of Missouri, Feb. 20, 1899.

SECY OF AGRICULTURE: Julius Sterling Morton, continued from preceding administration. James Wilson, of Iowa, March 5, 1897.

WILLIAM McKINLEY: Second Administration (1901)

VICE-PRESIDENT: Theodore Roosevelt, of New York.

SECY OF STATE: John Hay, continued from preceding administration.

SECY OF THE TREASURY: Lyman J. Gage, continued from preceding administration.

SECY OF WAR: Elihu Root, continued from preceding administration.

ATTY GEN: John W. Griggs, continued from preceding administration. John K. Richards, of Ohio (Solicitor General), ad interim, April 1, 1901. Philander C. Knox, of Pennsylvania, April 10, 1901.

POSTMASTER GEN: Charles Emory Smith, continued from preceding administration.

SECY OF THE NAVY: John D. Long, continued from preceding administration.

SECY OF THE INTERIOR: Ethan A. Hitchcock, continued from preceding administration.

SECY OF AGRICULTURE: James Wilson, continued from preceding administration.

THEODORE ROOSEVELT: First Administration (1901-05)

PRESIDENT PRO TEMPORE OF THE SENATE: William P. Frye, of Maine.

SECY OF STATE: John Hay, continued from preceding administration.

SECY OF THE TREASURY: Lyman J. Gage, continued from preceding administration. Leslie M. Shaw, of Iowa, Feb. 1, 1902.

SECY OF WAR: Elihu Root, continued from preceding administration. William H. Taft, of Ohio, Feb. 1, 1904.

ATTY GEN: Philander C. Knox, continued from preceding administration. William H. Moody, of Massachusetts, July 1, 1904.

POSTMASTER GEN: Charles Emory Smith, continued from preceding administration. Henry C. Payne, of Wisconsin, Jan. 9, 1902. Robert J. Wynne, of Pennsylvania, Oct. 10, 1904.

SECY OF THE NAVY: John D. Long, continued from preceding administration. William H. Moody, May 1, 1902. Paul Morton, of Illinois, July 1, 1904.

SECY OF THE INTERIOR: Ethan A. Hitchcock, continued from preceding administration.

SECY OF AGRICULTURE: James Wilson, continued from preceding administration.

SECY OF COMMERCE AND LABOR: George B. Cortelyou, of New York, Feb. 16, 1903. Victor H. Metcalf, of California, July 1, 1904.

THEODORE ROOSEVELT: Second Administration (1905-09)

VICE-PRESIDENT: Charles Warren Fairbanks, of Indiana.

SECY OF STATE: John Hay, continued from preceding administration (died July 1, 1905). Francis B. Loomis, of Ohio (Assistant Secretary), ad interim, July 1-18, 1905. Elihu Root, July 19, 1905. Robert Bacon, of New York, Jan. 27, 1909.

SECY OF THE TREASURY: Leslie M. Shaw, continued from preceding administration. George B. Cortelyou, March 4, 1907.

SECY OF WAR: William H. Taft, continued from preceding administration. Luke E. Wright, of Tennessee, July 1, 1908.

ATTY GEN: William H. Moody, continued from preceding administration. Charles J. Bonaparte, of Maryland, Dec. 17, 1906.

POSTMASTER GEN: Robert J. Wynne, continued from preceding administration. George B. Cortelyou, March 6, 1905. George von L. Meyer, of Massachusetts, March 4, 1907.

SECY OF THE NAVY: Paul Morton, continued from preceding administration. Charles J. Bonaparte, July 1, 1905. Victor H. Metcalf, Dec. 17, 1906. Truman H. Newberry, of Michigan, Dec. 1, 1908.

SECY OF THE INTERIOR: Ethan A. Hitchcock, continued from preceding administration. James R. Garfield, of Ohio, March 4, 1907.

SECY OF AGRICULTURE: James Wilson, continued from preceding administration.

SECY OF COMMERCE AND LABOR: Victor H. Metcalf, continued from preceding administration. Oscar S. Straus, of New York, Dec. 17, 1906.

WILLIAM H. TAFT (1909-13)

VICE-PRESIDENT: James S. Sherman (died Oct. 30, 1912).

PRESIDENT PRO TEMPORE OF THE SENATE: William P. Frye, resigned April 27, 1911. Jacob H. Gallinger, of New Hampshire, and Augustus O. Bacon, of Georgia, alternating.

SECY OF STATE: Robert Bacon, continued from preceding administration. Philander C. Knox, March 5, 1909.

SECY OF THE TREASURY: George B. Cortelyou, continued from preceding administration. Franklin MacVeagh, of Illinois, March 8, 1909.

SECY OF WAR: Luke E. Wright, continued from preceding administration. Jacob M. Dickinson, March 12, 1909. Henry L. Stimson, of New York, May 22, 1911.

ATTY GEN: Charles J. Bonaparte, continued from preceding administration. George W. Wickersham, of New York, March 5, 1909.

POSTMASTER GEN: George von L. Meyer, continued from preceding administration. Frank H. Hitchcock, of Massachusetts, March 5, 1909.

SECY OF THE NAVY: Truman H. Newberry, continued from preceding administration. George von L. Meyer, March 5, 1909.

SECY OF THE INTERIOR: James R. Garfield, continued from preceding administration. Richard A. Ballinger, of Washington, March 5, 1909. Walter Lowrie Fisher, of Illinois, March 7, 1911.

SECY OF AGRICULTURE: James Wilson, continued from preceding administration.

SECY OF COMMERCE AND LABOR: Oscar S. Straus, continued from preceding administration. Charles Nagel, of Missouri, March 5, 1909.

WOODROW WILSON: First Administration (1913-17)

VICE-PRESIDENT: Thomas R. Marshall, of Indiana.

SECY OF STATE: Philander C. Knox, continued from preceding administration. William Jennings Bryan, of Nebraska, March 5, 1913. Robert Lansing, of New York, ad interim, June 9, 1915. Robert Lansing, June 23, 1915.

SECY OF THE TREASURY: Franklin MacVeagh, continued from preceding administration. William Gibbs McAdoo, of New York, March 6, 1913.

SECY OF WAR: Henry L. Stimson, continued from preceding administration. Lindley M. Garrison, of New Jersey, March 5, 1913. Hugh L. Scott (U.S. Army), ad interim, Feb. 12, 1916. Newton D. Baker, of Ohio, March 9, 1916.

ATTY GEN: George W. Wickersham, continued from preceding administration. James Clark McReynolds, of Tennessee, March 6, 1913. Thomas Watt Gregory, of Texas, Sept. 3, 1914.

POSTMASTER GEN: Frank H. Hitchcock, continued from preceding administration. Albert Sidney Burleson, of Texas, March 5, 1913.

SECY OF THE NAVY: George von L. Meyer, continued from preceding administration. Josephus Daniels, of North Carolina, March 5, 1913.

SECY OF THE INTERIOR: Walter Lowrie Fisher, continued from preceding administration. Franklin Knight Lane, of California, March 5, 1913.

SECY OF AGRICULTURE: James Wilson, continued from preceding administration. David Franklin Houston, of Missouri, March 6, 1913.

SECY OF COMMERCE: Charles Nagel, continued from preceding administration. William C. Redfield, of New York, March 5, 1913.

SECY OF LABOR: Charles Nagel, continued from preceding administration. William Bauchop Wilson, of Pennsylvania, March 5, 1913.

WOODROW WILSON: Second Administration (1917-21)

VICE-PRESIDENT: Thomas R. Marshall.

SECY OF STATE: Robert Lansing, continued from preceding administration. Frank L. Polk, of New York (Under-Secretary), ad interim, Feb. 14-March 13, 1920. Bainbridge Colby, of New York, March 23, 1920.

SECY OF THE TREASURY: William Gibbs McAdoo, continued from preceding administration. Carter Glass, of Virginia, Dec. 16, 1918. David F. Houston, Feb. 2, 1920.

SECY OF WAR: Newton D. Baker, continued from preceding administration.

ATTY GEN: Thomas Watt Gregory, continued from preceding administration. A. Mitchell Palmer, of Pennsylvania, March 5, 1919.

POSTMASTER GEN: Albert Sidney Burleson, continued from preceding administration.

SECY OF THE NAVY: Josephus Daniels, continued from preceding administration.

SECY OF THE INTERIOR: Franklin Knight Lane, continued from preceding administration. John Barton Payne, of Illinois, March 13, 1920.

SECY OF AGRICULTURE: David Franklin Houston, continued from preceding administration. Edwin T. Meredith, of Iowa, Feb. 2, 1920.

SECY OF COMMERCE: William C. Redfield, continued from preceding administration. Joshua Willis Alexander, of Missouri, Dec. 16, 1919.

SECY OF LABOR: William Bauchop Wilson, continued from preceding administration.

WARREN G. HARDING (1921-23)

VICE-PRESIDENT: Calvin Coolidge, of Massachusetts.

SECY OF STATE: Bainbridge Colby, continued from preceding administration. Charles Evans Hughes, of New York, March 5, 1921.

SECY OF THE TREASURY: David F. Houston, continued from preceding administration. Andrew W. Mellon, of Pennsylvania, March 5, 1921.

SECY OF WAR: Newton D. Baker, continued from preceding administration. John W. Weeks, of Massachusetts, March 5, 1921.

ATTY GEN: A. Mitchell Palmer, continued from preceding administration. Harry M. Daugherty, of Ohio, March 5, 1921.

POSTMASTER GEN: Albert Sidney Burleson, continued from preceding administration. Will H. Hays, of Indiana, March 5, 1921. Hubert Work, of Colorado, March 4, 1922. Harry S. New, of Indiana, March 5, 1923.

SECY OF THE NAVY: Josephus Daniels, continued from preceding administration. Edwin Denby, of Michigan, March 5, 1921.

SECY OF THE INTERIOR: John Barton Payne, continued from preceding administration. Albert B. Fall, of New Mexico, March 5, 1921. Hubert Work, March 5, 1923.

SECY OF AGRICULTURE: Edwin T. Meredith, continued from preceding administration. Henry C. Wallace, of Iowa, March 5, 1921.

SECY OF COMMERCE: Joshua Willis Alexander, continued from preceding administration. Herbert C. Hoover, of California, March 5, 1921.

SECY OF LABOR: William Bauchop Wilson, continued from preceding administration. James J. Davis, of Pennsylvania, March 5, 1921.

CALVIN COOLIDGE: First Administration (1923-25)

PRESIDENT PRO TEMPORE OF THE SENATE: Albert B. Cummins, of Iowa.

SECY OF THE STATE: Charles Evans Hughes, continued from preceding administration.

SECY OF THE TREASURY: Andrew W. Mellon, continued from preceding administration.

SECY OF WAR: John W. Weeks, continued from preceding administration.

ATTY GEN: Harry M. Daugherty, continued from preceding administration. Harlan F. Stone, of New York, April 9, 1924.

POSTMASTER GEN: Harry S. New, continued from preceding administration.

SECY OF THE NAVY: Edwin Denby, continued from preceding administration. Curtis D. Wilbur, of California, March 18, 1924.

SECY OF THE INTERIOR: Hubert Work, continued from preceding administration.

SECY OF AGRICULTURE: Henry C. Wallace, continued from preceding administration (died Oct. 25, 1924). Howard M. Gore, of West Vir-

ginia (Assistant Secretary), ad interim, Oct. 26, 1924. Howard M. Gore, Nov. 22, 1924.

SECY OF COMMERCE: Herbert C. Hoover, continued from preceding administration.

SECY OF LABOR: James J. Davis, continued from preceding administration.

CALVIN COOLIDGE: Second Administration (1925-29)

VICE-PRESIDENT: Charles G. Dawes, of Illinois.

SECY OF STATE: Charles Evans Hughes, continued from preceding administration. Frank B. Kellogg, of Minnesota, March 5, 1925.

SECY OF TREASURY: Andrew W. Mellon, continued from preceding administration.

SECY OF WAR: John W. Weeks, continued from preceding administration. Dwight F. Davis, of Missouri, Oct. 14, 1925.

ATTY GEN: James M. Beck, of Pennsylvania (Solicitor General), ad interim, March 4, 1925. John G. Sargent, of Vermont, March 18, 1925.

POSTMASTER GEN: Harry S. New, continued from preceding administration.

SECY OF THE NAVY: Curtis D. Wilbur, continued from preceding administration.

SECY OF THE INTERIOR: Hubert Work, continued from preceding administration. Roy O. West, of Illinois, July 25, 1928.

SECY OF AGRICULTURE: Howard M. Gore, continued from preceding administration. William M. Jardine, of Kansas, March 5, 1925.

SECY OF COMMERCE: Herbert C. Hoover, continued from preceding administration. William F. Whiting, of Massachusetts, Aug. 21, 1928.

SECY OF LABOR: James J. Davis, continued from preceding administration.

HERBERT C. HOOVER (1929-33)

VICE-PRESIDENT: Charles Curtis, of Kansas.

SECY OF STATE: Frank B. Kellogg, continued from preceding administration. Henry L. Stimson, of New York, March 29, 1929.

SECY OF THE TREASURY: Andrew W. Mellon, continued from preceding administration. Ogden L. Mills, of New York, Feb. 13, 1932.

SECY OF WAR: Dwight F. Davis, continued from preceding administration. James W. Good, of Illinois, March 6, 1929. Patrick J. Hurley, of Oklahoma, Dec. 9, 1929.

ATTY GEN: John G. Sargent, continued from preceding administration. James DeWitt Mitchell, of Minnesota, March 6, 1929.

POSTMASTER GEN: Harry S. New, continued from preceding administration. Walter F. Brown, of Ohio, March 6, 1929.

SECY OF THE NAVY: Curtis D. Wilbur, continued from preceding administration. Charles F. Adams, of Massachusetts, March 5, 1929.

SECY OF THE INTERIOR: Roy O. West, continued from preceding administration. Ray L. Wilbur, of California, March 5, 1929.

SECY OF AGRICULTURE: William M. Jardine, continued from preceding administration. Arthur M. Hyde, of Missouri, March 6, 1929.

SECY OF COMMERCE: William F. Whiting, continued from preceding administration. Robert P. Lamont, of Illinois, March 5, 1929. Roy D. Chapin, of Michigan, Aug. 8, 1932.

SECY OF LABOR: James J. Davis, continued from preceding administration. William N. Doak, of Virginia, Dec. 9, 1930.

FRANKLIN DELANO ROOSEVELT: First Administration (1933-37)

VICE-PRESIDENT: John N. Garner, of Texas.

SECY OF STATE: Cordell Hull, of Tennessee, March 4, 1933.

SECY OF THE TREASURY: William H. Woodin, of New York, March 4, 1933. Henry Morgenthau, Jr., of New York, Jan. 1, 1934.

SECY OF WAR: George H. Dern, of Utah, March 4, 1933 (died Aug. 27, 1936). Harry H. Woodring, of Kansas (Assistant Secretary), ad interim, Sept. 25, 1936-May 6, 1937.

ATTY GEN: Homer S. Cummings, of Connecticut, March 4, 1933.

POSTMASTER GEN: James A. Farley, of New York, March 4, 1933.

SECY OF THE NAVY: Claude A. Swanson, of Virginia, March 4, 1933.

SECY OF THE INTERIOR: Harold L. Ickes, of Illinois, March 4, 1933.

SECY OF AGRICULTURE: Henry A. Wallace, of Iowa, March 4, 1933.

SECY OF COMMERCE: Daniel C. Roper, of South Carolina, March 4, 1933.

SECY OF LABOR: Frances Perkins, of New York, March 4, 1933.

FRANKLIN DELANO ROOSEVELT Second Administration (1937-41)

VICE-PRESIDENT: John N. Garner.

SECY OF STATE: Cordell Hull, continued from preceding administration.

SECY OF THE TREASURY: Henry Morgenthau, Jr., continued from preceding administration.

SECY OF WAR: Harry H. Woodring, continued from preceding administration. Henry L. Stimson, July 10, 1940.

ATTY GEN: Homer S. Cummings, continued from preceding administration. Frank Murphy, of Michigan, Jan. 2, 1939. Robert H. Jackson, of New York, Jan. 18, 1940.

POSTMASTER GEN: James A. Farley, continued from preceding administration. Frank C. Walker, of Pennsylvania, Sept. 10, 1940.

SECY OF THE NAVY: Claude A. Swanson, continued from preceding administration (died July 7, 1939). Charles Edison, of New Jersey, Aug. 5, 1939. Frank Knox, of Illinois, July 10, 1940.

SECY OF THE INTERIOR: Harold L. Ickes, continued from preceding administration.

SECY OF AGRICULTURE: Henry A. Wallace, continued from preceding administration. Claude R. Wickard, of Indiana, Sept. 5, 1940.

SECY OF COMMERCE: Daniel C. Roper, continued from preceding administration. Harry L. Hopkins, of New York, Dec. 24, 1938. Jesse H. Jones, of Texas, Sept. 19, 1940.

SECY OF LABOR: Frances Perkins, continued from preceding administration.

FRANKLIN DELANO ROOSEVELT: Third Administration (1941-45)

VICE-PRESIDENT: Henry A. Wallace, of Iowa.

SECY OF STATE: Cordell Hull, continued from preceding administration. Edward R. Stettinius, of Virginia, Dec. 1, 1944.

SECY OF THE TREASURY: Henry Morgenthau, Jr., continued from preceding administration.

SECY OF WAR: Henry L. Stimson, continued from preceding administration.

ATTY GEN: Robert H. Jackson, continued from preceding administration. Francis Biddle, of Pennsylvania, Sept. 5, 1941.

POSTMASTER GEN: Frank C. Walker, continued from preceding administration.

SECY OF THE NAVY: Frank Knox, continued from preceding administration (died April 28, 1944). James V. Forrestal, of New York, May 18, 1944.

SECY OF THE INTERIOR: Harold L. Ickes, continued from preceding administration.

SECY OF AGRICULTURE: Claude R. Wickard, continued from preceding administration.

SECY OF COMMERCE: Jesse H. Jones, continued from preceding administration.

SECY OF LABOR: Frances Perkins, continued from preceding administration.

FRANKLIN DELANO ROOSEVELT: Fourth Administration (1945)

VICE-PRESIDENT: Harry S. Truman, of Missouri.

SECY OF STATE: Edward R. Stettinius, continued from preceding administration.

SECY OF THE TREASURY: Henry Morgenthau, Jr., continued from preceding administration.

SECY OF WAR: Henry L. Stimson, continued from preceding administration.

ATTY GEN: Francis Biddle, continued from preceding administration.

POSTMASTER GEN: Frank C. Walker, continued from preceding administration.

SECY OF THE NAVY: James V. Forrestal, continued from preceding administration.

SECY OF THE INTERIOR: Harold L. Ickes, continued from preceding administration.

SECY OF AGRICULTURE: Claude R. Wickard, continued from preceding administration.

SECY OF COMMERCE: Jesse H. Jones, continued from preceding administration. Henry A. Wallace, March 2, 1945.

SECY OF LABOR: Frances Perkins, continued from preceding administration.

HARRY S. TRUMAN: First Administration (1945-49)

PRESIDENT PRO TEMPORE OF THE SENATE: Kenneth McKellar, of Tennessee. Arthur S. Vandenberg, of Michigan, Jan. 4, 1947.

SECY OF STATE: Edward R. Stettinius, continued from preceding administration. James F. Byrnes, of South Carolina, July 3, 1945. George C. Marshall, Jan. 21, 1947.

SECY OF THE TREASURY: Henry Morgenthau, Jr., continued from preceding administration. Fred M. Vinson, of Kentucky, July 23, 1945. John W. Snyder, of Missouri, June 25, 1946.

SECY OF DEFENSE: James V. Forrestal, Sept. 17, 1947.

SECY OF WAR:[1] Henry L. Stimson, continued from preceding administration. Robert Porter Patterson, of New York, Sept. 27, 1945. Kenneth C. Royall, of North Carolina, July 25, 1947.

ATTY GEN: Francis Biddle, continued from preceding administration. Tom C. Clark, of Texas, July 1, 1945.

POSTMASTER GEN: Frank C. Walker, continued from preceding administration. Robert E. Hannegan, of Missouri, July 1, 1945. Jesse M. Donaldson, of Missouri, Dec. 16, 1947.

SECY OF THE NAVY:[1] James V. Forrestal, continued from preceding administration.

SECY OF THE INTERIOR: Harold L. Ickes, continued from preceding administration. Julius A. Krug, of Wisconsin, March 18, 1946.

SECY OF AGRICULTURE: Claude R. Wickard, continued from preceding administration. Clinton P. Anderson, of New Mexico, June 30, 1945. Charles F. Brannan, of Colorado, June 2, 1948.

SECY OF COMMERCE: Henry A. Wallace, continued from preceding administration. William Averell Harriman, of New York, Sept. 28, 1946. Charles Sawyer, of Ohio, May 6, 1948.

SECY OF LABOR: Frances Perkins, continued from preceding administration. Lewis B. Schwellenbach, of Washington, July 1, 1945 (died June 10, 1948). Maurice J. Tobin, of Massachusetts, ad interim, Aug. 13, 1948.

HARRY S. TRUMAN: Second Administration (1949-53)

VICE-PRESIDENT: Alben W. Barkley, of Kentucky.

SECY OF STATE: Dean G. Acheson, of Connecticut, Jan. 21, 1949.

SECY OF THE TREASURY: John W. Snyder, continued from preceding administration.

SECY OF DEFENSE: James V. Forrestal, continued from preceding administration. Louis A. Johnson, March 28, 1949.

ATTY GEN: Tom C. Clark, continued from preceding administration. J. Howard McGrath, of Rhode Island, Aug. 24, 1949.

POSTMASTER GEN: Jesse M. Donaldson, continued from preceding administration.

SECY OF THE INTERIOR: Julius A. Krug, continued from preceding administration. Oscar L. Chapman, of Colorado, Dec. 1, 1949.

SECY OF AGRICULTURE: Charles F. Brannan, continued from preceding administration.

SECY OF COMMERCE: Charles Sawyer, continued from preceding administration.

SECY OF LABOR: Maurice J. Tobin, continued from preceding administration (full Cabinet member, Feb. 1, 1949).

DWIGHT D. EISENHOWER: First Administration (1953-57)

VICE-PRESIDENT: Richard M. Nixon, of California.

SECY OF STATE: John Foster Dulles, of New York, Jan. 21, 1953.

SECY OF THE TREASURY: George M. Humphrey, of Ohio, Jan. 21, 1953.

SECY OF DEFENSE: Charles E. Wilson, of Michigan, Jan. 28, 1953.

ATTY GEN: Herbert Brownell, Jr., of New York, Jan. 21, 1953.

POSTMASTER GEN: Arthur E. Summerfield, of Michigan, Jan. 21, 1953.

SECY OF THE INTERIOR: Douglas McKay, of Oregon, Jan. 21, 1953. Frederick A. Seaton, of Nebraska, June 8, 1956.

SECY OF AGRICULTURE: Ezra Taft Benson, of Utah, Jan. 21, 1953.

SECY OF COMMERCE: Sinclair Weeks, of Massachusetts, Jan. 21, 1953.

SECY OF LABOR: Martin P. Durkin, of Maryland, Jan. 21, 1953. James P. Mitchell, of New Jersey, Oct. 9, 1953.

SECY OF HEALTH, EDUCATION, AND WELFARE: Oveta Culp Hobby, of Texas, April 11, 1953. Marion B. Folsom, of New York, Aug. 1, 1955.

DWIGHT D. EISENHOWER: Second Administration (1957-61)

VICE-PRESIDENT: Richard M. Nixon.

SECY OF STATE: John Foster Dulles, continued from preceding administration. Christian A. Herter, of Massachusetts, April 22, 1959.

SECY OF THE TREASURY: George M. Humphrey, continued from preceding administration. Robert Bernerd Anderson, of Connecticut, July 29, 1957.

SECY OF DEFENSE: Charles E. Wilson, continued from preceding administration. Neil H. McElroy, of Ohio, Oct. 9, 1957. Thomas S. Gates, Jr., of Pennsylvania, Dec. 1, 1959.

ATTY GEN: Herbert Brownell, Jr., continued from preceding administration. William P. Rogers, of Maryland, Nov. 8, 1957.

POSTMASTER GEN: Arthur E. Summerfield, continued from preceding administration.

SECY OF THE INTERIOR: Frederick A. Seaton, continued from preceding administration.

---

[1] With the enactment of the National Security Act of 1947, the Secretaries of the Army and Navy lost their seats in the Cabinet on Sept. 17, 1947, but retained their right of access to the President.

SECY OF AGRICULTURE: Ezra Taft Benson, continued from preceding administration.

SECY OF COMMERCE: Sinclair Weeks, continued from preceding administration. Lewis L. Strauss, of New York, ad interim, Nov. 13, 1958. Frederick H. Mueller, of Michigan (Under Secretary), July 21, 1959.

SECY OF LABOR: James P. Mitchell, continued from preceding administration.

SECY OF HEALTH, EDUCATION, AND WELFARE: Marion B. Folsom, continued from preceding administration. Arthur S. Flemming, of Ohio, Aug. 1, 1958.

JOHN F. KENNEDY (1961-63)

VICE-PRESIDENT: Lyndon Baines Johnson, of Texas.

SECY OF STATE: Dean Rusk, of Georgia, Jan. 21, 1961.

SECY OF THE TREASURY: C. Douglas Dillon, of New York, Jan. 21, 1961.

SECY OF DEFENSE: Robert S. McNamara, of California, Jan. 21, 1961.

ATTY GEN: Robert F. Kennedy, of Massachusetts, Jan. 21, 1961.

POSTMASTER GEN: J. Edward Day, of Illinois, Jan. 21, 1961. John A. Gronouski, of Wisconsin, Sept. 30, 1963.

SECY OF THE INTERIOR: Stewart L. Udall, of Arizona, Jan. 21, 1961.

SECY OF AGRICULTURE: Orville L. Freeman, of Minnesota, Jan. 21, 1961.

SECY OF COMMERCE: Luther H. Hodges, of Virginia, Jan. 21, 1961.

SECY OF LABOR: Arthur J. Goldberg, of Illinois, Jan. 21, 1961. W. Willard Wirtz, of Illinois, Sept. 25, 1961.

SECY OF HEALTH, EDUCATION, AND WELFARE: Abraham A. Ribicoff, of Connecticut, Jan. 21, 1961. Anthony J. Celebrezze, of Ohio, July 20, 1962.

LYNDON BAINES JOHNSON: First Administration (1963-65)

SPEAKER OF THE HOUSE OF REPRESENTATIVES: John W. McCormack, of Massachusetts.

PRESIDENT PRO TEMPORE OF THE SENATE: Carl Hayden, of Arizona.

SECY OF STATE: Dean Rusk, continued from preceding administration.

SECY OF THE TREASURY: C. Douglas Dillon, continued from preceding administration.

SECY OF DEFENSE: Robert S. McNamara, continued from preceding administration.

ATTY GEN: Robert F. Kennedy, continued from preceding administration. Nicholas deB. Katzenbach, of Pennsylvania (Deputy Attorney General), ad interim, Sept. 3, 1964-Jan. 28, 1965.

POSTMASTER GEN: John A. Gronouski, continued from preceding administration.

SECY OF THE INTERIOR: Stewart L. Udall, continued from preceding administration.

SECY OF AGRICULTURE: Orville L. Freeman, continued from preceding administration.

SECY OF COMMERCE: Luther H. Hodges, continued from preceding administration. John T. Connor, of New York, Jan. 18, 1965.

SECY OF LABOR: W. Willard Wirtz, continued from preceding administration.

SECY OF HEALTH, EDUCATION, AND WELFARE: Anthony J. Celebrezze, continued from preceding administration.

LYNDON BAINES JOHNSON: Second Administration (1965-   )

VICE-PRESIDENT: Hubert H. Humphrey, of Minnesota.

SECY OF STATE: Dean Rusk, continued from preceding administration.

SECY OF THE TREASURY: C. Douglas Dillon, continued from preceding administration. Henry H. Fowler, of Virginia, April 1, 1965.

SECY OF DEFENSE: Robert S. McNamara, continued from preceding administration.

ATTY GEN: Nicholas deB. Katzenbach, continued from preceding administration.

POSTMASTER GEN: John A. Gronouski, continued from preceding administration. Lawrence F. O'Brien, of Massachusetts, Nov. 4, 1965.

SECY OF THE INTERIOR: Stewart L. Udall, continued from preceding administration.

SECY OF AGRICULTURE: Orville L. Freeman, continued from preceding administration.

SECY OF COMMERCE: John T. Connor, continued from preceding administration.

SECY OF LABOR: W. Willard Wirtz, continued from preceding administration.

SECY OF HEALTH, EDUCATION, AND WELFARE: Anthony J. Celebrezze, continued from preceding administration. John W. Gardner, of California, Aug. 18, 1965.

SECY OF HOUSING AND URBAN DEVELOPMENT: Robert Clifton Weaver, of Washington, D.C.

Acknowledgments

Credits and References

Index

★   ★   ★

★ Acknowledgments

The authors wish to express their particular gratitude to Miss Mary Cunningham of the New York State Historical Association for her valued assistance in the preparation of this book.

For their co-operation in supplying pictures and information we are greatly indebted to:
Clarence S. Brigham, American Antiquarian Society
Harry Collins, Brown Brothers
Alice Pickup, Buffalo Historical Society
Mrs. David Claire, The Corcoran Gallery of Art
Florence Osborne and staff, Essex Institute
Herman Kahn and Grace Suckley, Franklin D. Roosevelt Library
Mrs. Henry W. Howell, Jr., and Helen Sanger, Frick Art Reference Library
Thomas Little, Harvard College Library
Rosanna Bagg and Mrs. Millicent Maybe, Huntington Memorial Library, Oneonta, New York
Carleton Thorpe, Peter A. Juley and Son
Virginia Daiker and Milton Kaplan, Library of Congress
Vera Andrus, Metropolitan Museum of Art
Mrs. Richard Kimball, American Museum of Natural History
Josephine Cobb, National Archives
Arthur Carlson, Caroline Scoon and Sylvester Vigilanti, New-York Historical Society
Louis C. Jones, New York State Historical Association
Wilson G. Duprez, William Mortenson, Saro J. Riccardi and Elizabeth E. Roth, New York Public Library
Sidney Solomon, Pageant Book Store
Margaret W. Brown and Mendel L. Petersen, Smithsonian Institution
Raymond B. Seymour, Sons of the Revolution
Mae Manning, Theodore Roosevelt Association
Edward August and Harold Feder, United Press Newspictures

★ Credits and References

PAGE	POSITION	
2		Facsimile of the Declaration of Independence. Painting by John Trumbull, Yale University, courtesy The Bettmann Archive.
3	top	Picture Department, New York Public Library.
3	bottom	*Historical Collections of Virginia* by Henry Howe.
4		Painting by Grant Wood, Associated American Artists, courtesy Mrs. John Marquand.
5	top	*Life of Washington* by J. T. Headley.
5	bottom	Painting by W. S. Mount, collection of Miss Kate Strong, courtesy Frick Art Reference Library.
6	top	Painting by Edward Willard Deming, courtesy State Historical Society of Wisconsin.
6	bottom	American Museum of Natural History.
7	top, left	Library of Congress.
7	top, right	American Museum of Natural History.
7	bottom	Library of Congress.
8	top	Detail of painting by John Ward Dunsmore, courtesy of the Sons of the Revolution, headquarters Fraunces Tavern, New York City.
8	bottom	Painting by John Ward Dunsmore, courtesy Sons of the Revolution.
9	top	*Harper's Weekly,* July 10, 1875.
9	bottom	Painting by John Ward Dunsmore, courtesy Sons of the Revolution.
10	top	Painting by John Ward Dunsmore, courtesy Sons of the Revolution.
10	bottom	*The Home of Washington* by Benson J. Lossing.
11		Portrait by Charles Wilson Peale, courtesy Metropolitan Museum of Art.
12		*Frank Leslie's Illustrated Newspaper,* October 22, 1881.
13	top	Detail of painting by John Ward Dunsmore, courtesy Sons of the Revolution.
13	bottom	Library of Congress.
14		The Pierpont Morgan Library.
15		Portrait by Adolf Ulric Wertmüller, courtesy Metropolitan Museum of Art.
16	top	Painting by John Ward Dunsmore, courtesy Sons of the Revolution.
16	bottom	American Museum of Natural History.
17		The Seamans Bank for Savings, New York.
18		*Harper's Bazaar,* May 11, 1889.
19	top	New-York Historical Society.
19	bottom	*The Home of Washington* by Benson J. Lossing.
20	top	American Museum of Natural History.
20	bottom	Painting by Daniel Huntington, collection of the Brooklyn Museum.
21		New-York Historical Society.
22	top	Smithsonian Institution, courtesy Penn Mutual Life Insurance Co.
22	bottom	Courtesy Mr. Joseph A. Heckel.
23	top	*Harper's Weekly,* December 18, 1869.
23	bottom, left	The Bank of Manhattan, courtesy New York Stock Exchange.
23	bottom, right	New-York Historical Society.
24	top	American Scenic and Historical Preservation Society.
24	bottom	Metropolitan Museum of Art.
25	top	New-York Historical Society.
25	bottom	American Museum of Natural History.
26		Portrait by Asher B. Durand after the original by Gilbert Stuart, courtesy New-York Historical Society.
27		*Gleason's Pictorial Drawing Room Companion.*
28		Painting by Benjamin West, Henry F. du Pont Collection, courtesy Frick Art Reference Library.
29		Portrait by L. S. Russell, courtesy Society for the Preservation of New England Antiquities.
30	top	Maryland Historical Society.

Index

All references to pages 188-368 are in Volume 2.